In Search of Captain Cook

In Search of Captain Cook

Exploring the Man Through His Own Words

Dan O'Sullivan

I.B. TAURIS
LONDON · NEW YORK

Published in 2008 by I.B. Tauris & Co Ltd
6 Salem Road, London W2 4BU
175 Fifth Avenue, New York NY 10010
www.ibtauris.com

In the United States and Canada distributed by Palgrave Macmillan
a division of St Martin's Press
175 Fifth Avenue, New York NY 10010

ISBN 13: 978 1 84511 483 1

A full CIP record for this book is available from the British Library
A full CIP record for this book is available from the Library of Congress

Library of Congress Catalog Card: available

Typeset by Swales & Willis, Exeter, Devon
Printed and bound in the Czech Republic by FINIDR, s.r.o.

Contents

10 How to Study Natives   123

11 How to Treat Natives   136

12 Natives Cook Knew   147

13 Sex in the South Seas   161

Part IV Assumptions, Ambitions, Achievements   **175**

14 Cook and Divine Providence   177

15 Nation and Empire   187

16 Trade and Improvement   196

17 Science and Navigation   206

    Timeline of the Third Voyage   215

18 The Death of Cook   223

    Conclusion   230

    Abbreviations used in References   234
    References   236
    Suggested Reading   255
    Index   257

Illustrations

Figures

Maps

(Cartographer: Ian Wilson)

Preface

Some years ago I was co-opted onto the Board of Trustees of the Captain Cook Schoolroom Museum in Great Ayton, the Yorkshire village where I live, and also where James Cook went to school. This was my very first introduction to Cook, and there followed a steep learning curve when the museum received a grant towards a complete re-vamp, and as the 'historian' on the Board I was expected to make a significant contribution to the new displays. Since then I have enjoyed getting to know Cook better, although in a fairly sedentary way. I must admit to having no desire at all to serve as a deckhand on the *Endeavour* replica, or even to sail a yacht to all the Pacific islands that Cook visited.

One of the perks of being connected with the museum was access to its library, and in particular to the four massive volumes of Cook's journals, edited by John Beaglehole for the Hakluyt Society between 1955 and 1967. When I started reading the journals I was overwhelmed by Beaglehole's scholarship, and his apparent omniscience in all matters pertaining to Cook. It may or may not be true, as Alfred North Whitehead is supposed to have once remarked, that all Western philosophy is nothing but a footnote to Plato, but it is certainly the case that modern students of Cook are in danger, if they are not careful, of merely providing footnotes to Beaglehole. Nevertheless, one does not necessarily have to agree with all the opinions of that eminent and prolific historian just because one enjoys the fruits of his editorship. Anyone who sets out to write history starts off from their own vantage point, with their own personal and political views, and obviously I am no exception. If one looks back over the centuries since the death of Cook, it is remarkable how many different voices, how many vested interests, have interpreted his story in the particular way that suits them. Here is one more to add to the list.

Introduction

Captain James Cook was certainly the most renowned explorer of his day, and, it might be claimed, one of the greatest of all time. He was a leader of men, a master voyager who journeyed to unknown places, a seeker of knowledge who commanded three intensely scientific expeditions. He and his crews had encounters with Pacific peoples which were intense and fleeting, violent and peaceful, sexual and commercial. Even before he died his exploits were widely admired, but his death at the hands of Hawaiians turned him into a legendary figure, a hero of the Enlightenment, who was said to have brought civilization to the Pacific, while yielding up his own life in the process.

To write on this topic is to enter into an already existing discourse engaged in by large numbers of reputable scholars and authors, past and present. Many books have been written about Cook, and a variety of different approaches are possible. In this one I take his journals as my starting point and, having investigated their nature, attempt to use them as evidence for what he himself was really like. Naturally this entails some awareness of what his contemporaries said about him, and I have also tried to keep up with the flood of books and articles written about Cook over the last 40 years or so, since John Beaglehole completed his editorship of the journals.

On first acquaintance with the journals, one of the things that intrigued me most was how Cook managed to write so much about his own actions, and yet give away so little about himself. In spite of this first impression, I now think he does give away a certain amount, and it is this certain amount on which I have tried to focus in the following chapters. 'A man may discover himself even in a ship's journal or a log-book', wrote Walter Besant, a nineteenth-century biographer of Cook.[1] So this book is really a meditation on two inter-related topics. One is James Cook, the man, and the other is the nature of the journals that he composed during or after each of his three great voyages of discovery.

The vast majority of books about Cook follow a similar pattern, in presenting a narrative of his life and voyages, and there are good reasons for this. In the first place everyone likes an exciting story, and Cook's story is as exciting as any. Secondly, it is no easy matter to turn the spotlight on Cook himself rather than on where he went and what he achieved. Beaglehole was once asked to write an article specifically about Cook's character for a journal. He stuck to his brief for about three pages, but then reverted to a narrative of Cook's life and achievements, arguing that 'as he was a man of action, we have to be clear both about what he did, and how he did it'.[2] Here, I attempt to organize information and ideas from the journals into topics, each relating to an aspect of Cook, his attitudes, ambitions and personal relationships. I do think that this topic method can produce unexpected insights which a straightforward narrative might obscure. The traditional chronological approach assimilates random facts into one type of order and the topical approach into another. When dealing topic by topic one might lose the page-turning quality of a narrative but on the other hand it becomes easier to back up particular points with a range of evidence taken from different times and places. Narrative also seems less appropriate when it comes to trying to describe the various facets of someone's character and outlook. The two approaches – narrative and topical – can of course be complementary, as Cook himself demonstrates. When he first makes contact with a hitherto unknown Pacific community he records day-to-day events in his journal, but on leaving he invariably attempts to summarize by topic what has been learnt about the new society.

My approach means that at the very least I am presenting some of the known facts about Cook in a different, and original, sequence, but I hope I am doing more than this, and that the various subjects will combine in the mind of the reader to give a more rounded assessment of Cook's personality than is customarily the case. I also hope that those who know little of Cook will find this book a readable introduction, and that even those who are Cook experts will come across some ideas worth debating.

The narrative element is preserved to the extent that I have inserted 'timelines' for the three voyages, based mainly on brief excerpts from Cook's journals. The idea here is not only to remind the reader when and where he went, but also to give an additional taste of Cook's journal-writing, which is, of course, one of my two main themes.

It might be argued that this focus on Cook himself through the medium of his journals is rather unfair. After all, he was a brilliant explorer, navigator and map-maker, but he was not primarily an author. As a man of action, his journals are intended to be about what he did, not about himself, and he was in no sense the composer of a personal diary like Samuel Pepys before him, or

James Woodforde, his near contemporary. Cook's journals were merely reports required of him by the Admiralty – they form part of his job-description. According to Hammond Innes, one of the numerous band of modern authors fascinated by Cook's career, the journals tell us nothing at all about the man himself. Innes tried to remedy this deficiency by inventing a more personal Cook journal of the third voyage, the manuscript of which 'only recently came to light in the cellars of the Old St James Club'.[3] And the opinion of Beaglehole, who spent most of his career researching Cook, is not so very different. He writes, 'Everybody knows Cook's name; yet, I have always felt, extraordinarily little is known about him. He is an exceptionally difficult man to get inside.'[4]

In spite of all this, when it comes to saying something meaningful about one of the outstanding figures of his generation and of his country, the journals – these cautious, objective-seeming texts, full of the minutiae of daily events – are practically the only sources available. Unfortunately, Cook's widow burnt all his personal letters to her, so there mostly remains for us only his business correspondence, which involves itself with topics such as whether the *Resolution* should be supplied with currants and almonds, or how many tons of iron ballast were required for the *Endeavour*.

Apart from the timelines and a preliminary chapter on some of Cook's more obvious characteristics, the book is divided into four sections. The first section is focused on the nature of the journals; while the other three all relate, in one way or another, to Cook himself.

Chapter 1

Cook the Unknown

Who was Captain Cook? Perhaps no famous figure of modern times has documented his own life so comprehensively, recording his day-to-day activities over many years, in the shape of his journals and their successive drafts. Yet we know precious little about him as a human being – his likes and dislikes, his attitudes and prejudices. All this mass of documentation is practical and impersonal. We know a lot about how he performed his duties, and about the 'Remarkable Occurrences on board the Bark *Endeavour*' (as he titled his journal of the first voyage), but rarely about his inner thoughts, and never about his private life.

There is a new term current among critics, 'life writing', which includes biographies, autobiographies, memoirs and diaries. Such documents are among the most fascinating materials available to the historian because they tend to illuminate not merely the outward facts of a given situation but also the motives, prejudices and emotions of their authors. Any lengthy text which is narrated from the point of view of the main protagonist is likely to give the reader a strong impression of the personality of that person, the 'I' of the story, and this goes for fictional, as well as purportedly factual, accounts, and applies to the Ancient Mariner and Robinson Crusoe as well as to Samuel Pepys. In fact much of the interest of such accounts often consists primarily in this insight into the character of the narrator and his relationships with other characters in the narrative. This may still be the case even when the author or narrator makes no obvious attempt to describe his own feelings, but apparently confines himself to a narrative of particulars.

Just because they are journals, Cook's three journals of discovery seem to fall into this category of 'life writing', and as such may be presumed to share, to some degree at least, the characteristics of this genre. We might therefore set out to investigate them with a view to finding out something about their author – the characteristics of his personality, his beliefs and prejudices, and the way he interacts with other people. This is what I have tried to do here, though it has not been a particularly easy task. Partly because of the official nature of his journals, and partly because he was the kind of man he was, Cook made heroic attempts to leave his 'real' self out of the story wherever possible. The result is that we, the readers, hardly get to know the real James Cook at all, even though 'Cook' is present on practically every page as the 'I' who made the decisions and initiated the action. Cook may be the author, and 'Cook', the protagonist, but this author is not in the business of exposing his hero's human qualities, as opposed to his professional virtues, if he can help it. We easily form a strong impression that 'Cook' possesses all the attributes necessary for his role as commander and explorer, but we remain slightly hazy about him as a rounded human being. Michael Hoare, the editor of J.R.Forster's *Resolution Journal*, writes that journals of exploration are often 'among men's most revealing documents of self',[1] and this is certainly true of Forster's writing, as well as of other journals such as Joseph Banks' from the first voyage, and Charles Clerke's and David Samwell's from the third. Unfortunately, with Cook it is far from being the case, even when, as on the second and third voyages, he was clearly writing with a view to general publication.

We do know something about what Cook looked like, thanks to a couple of brief verbal descriptions plus the various portraits of him by Dance, Hodges and Webber, which were done after the second voyage, or during the third in the case of Webber. The descriptions tell us that he was over six feet tall, handsome, yet 'plain both in address and appearance', with a small head, and dark brown hair which he wore tied up. His eyes, also brown, were said to be small but piercing, his nose well-shaped and his eyebrows prominent 'which gave his countenance altogether an air of austerity'.[2] One distinguishing mark he possessed was a scar on one hand, caused by an accident with a powder horn in 1764. Fifteen years later it was this scar that helped to identify parts of his mutilated body after his death in Hawaii.

As for the portraits, they all show him in naval uniform, and tend on the whole to emphasise the professional, rather than the private, man. The most famous, the society painting by Nathaniel Dance, reveals a strong, somewhat stern, face – too stern according to Mrs Cook, who disliked it, while admitting it was a reasonable likeness. Dance has him sitting at a desk, bewigged, and studying a chart of the Pacific. He looks studious, even meditative, as opposed to one of John Webber's portrayals, which concentrates on the man of action. Here, he is standing beside a rocky seashore, looking commandingly at the viewer, with telescope in hand. The portrait by William Hodges, which was known to have existed through engravings, was only rediscovered in 1986, at a country house sale in Ireland. The estimate at the auction was £350–£450, but

The best known portrait of Captain James Cook, painted by Nathaniel Dance, a fashionable
society artist, in 1776, shortly before Cook set off on his final voyage. This portrait was
said by David Samwell to be 'the only one I have ever seen that bears any resemblance
to him'.

it was eventually bought by the National Maritime Museum, Greenwich, for
£700,000, after they had identified it and traced its provenance back to Cook's
friend and patron, Sir Hugh Palliser. The uniform worn by Cook in this portrait
proves that it was painted after he was promoted to captain, in August 1775,
as was Dance's portrait, whereas Webber's several portraits were painted rather
later, during the third voyage.[3]

Captain Cook by John Webber, the artist who accompanied Cook on his last voyage. Webber painted at least four portraits of Cook. This one was probably painted at Capetown in late 1776.

The Hodges painting is perhaps the most interesting of the three. Certainly the most modern in treatment, it plays down the uniform and other trappings of professional life. It concentrates on Cook's face, a face undoubtedly rugged and powerful, yet with a certain hint of introspection, even sadness, about it that is quite absent from the other portraits. Nevertheless, the real problem

Captain Cook, painted by William Hodges sometime between August 1775, when Cook was promoted to captain, and July 1776, when he set off on his final voyage. This portrait was spotted at an auction in Ireland in 1986, having long been thought lost.

with all the portraits is that, unless one was told, one would hardly know they were all three of the same individual. 'I have gazed long, and with some intensity, at Cook's portraits', wrote Beaglehole, 'and I cannot say I have learnt much'.[4]

'Where is your *marai*?' This was the question directed at Cook by Orio, a chief from Raiatea in the Society Islands, after Cook had told him he was leaving the island, and therefore would probably never see him again. *Marais* were elaborate and sacred funeral sites where the bodies of dead islanders were exposed to the air until they decomposed, so Cook took this question to mean, where will you be buried? He replied, 'the parish of Stepney', because this was where he owned a house, and where his wife and family were waiting for his return. However, Orea was perhaps really asking, 'what place in the world are you particularly identified with?' – an awkward question to put to a professional seaman, especially a rootless, secular man like Cook, and it may be there was no real answer.[5]

Cook was born in North Yorkshire in 1728, the son of an agricultural labourer, and was brought up in the village of Marton until he was eight. Subsequently the family moved to the larger village of Great Ayton, where his father had obtained a post as foreman in a farm owned by Thomas Skottowe, the lord of the manor. He received a basic education at the village school, and then left to help his father on the farm, before becoming a shop assistant at Staithes on the North Yorkshire coast. When he was eighteen he moved to Whitby in order to be apprenticed to the Quaker ship-owner, John Walker. After nine years experience at sea, mainly involved in the coastal trade in coal, he made the rather surprising decision to transfer to the Royal Navy, where he saw some action at the start of the Seven Years War (1756–63), serving for two years in *HMS Eagle*, which on one occasion captured a French East Indiaman at the mouth of the Channel. Due to his previous experience at sea, and his ability, he won rapid promotion, first to master's mate, and after two years, to master, and he was one of a group of ships' masters involved in the vital task of surveying the St. Lawrence River during the campaign to capture Quebec in 1759.

His most remarkable achievement during these early years in the navy was to teach himself mathematics and marine surveying in his spare time. By the end of the war he had a considerable reputation as a surveyor, and for the next four years was given an independent command as master of a small schooner, the *Grenville*, and the task of surveying the coasts of Newfoundland, recently gained from the French. At this time, too, he may have studied astronomy, because in 1766 he conducted an important piece of scientific work outside his normal duties. He made careful measurements of an eclipse of the sun, from which he was able to calculate the longitude of his observational position in Newfoundland. This result was communicated to a member of the Royal Society and published in their *Philosophical Transactions* for 1767. It was probably the dual reputation Cook established from this paper coupled with his charts of Newfoundland that led him to be chosen to command the *Endeavour* the following year. It may also have been the case, as Glyndwr Williams suggests, that naval officers from a less lowly background might have demurred at being offered the command of a converted merchant vessel newly seconded from the coaling trade.[6] However, it is likely that Cook's astronomical expertise was the conclusive factor behind his selection, since at the time this voyage was first being considered by the authorities it was seen as primarily a scientific project, to record the Transit of Venus from a base in the South Seas. It became in addition a voyage of discovery almost by chance, due to the reported sighting by

Wallis of a continental landmass south of Tahiti, news of which reached England just before Cook was due to sail.[7]

Earlier, in 1762, Cook married Elizabeth Batts, the daughter of a Wapping publican, who was 13 years younger than him, and with whom he was to live intermittently, never for more than a year at a time. They set up home in Shadwell near the Thames, later moving north, to Mile End, Stepney, and of his six children, all born in Stepney, three died in infancy. By the time of his second voyage of exploration he had two sons, James and Nathaniel, both of whom he evidently hoped would follow him into the navy, as he entered their names onto the roll of the *Endeavour* in order to give them some seniority when the time came for them to apply for commissions. Yet there are no references whatever to his home or family in the journals, unless one counts the somewhat tasteless joke he made at the expense of the Tahitian 'Queen', Oborea, when he gave her a doll 'which I made her understand was the Picter of my wife'.[8] One does not, of course, normally look to naval journals for information about the home life of captains, and Cook by now had long left his Yorkshire roots behind him, socially as well as geographically. Among the numerous people he honoured on his voyages by naming capes, bays and islands after them, not one was related to himself or came from the places where he had been brought up.[9]

A fair amount was written about Cook's character by those who knew him. There were the stately but bland phrases by his patron, Sir Hugh Palliser, on what was probably the very first of all the memorials dedicated to Cook: 'He possessed, in an eminent degree, all the qualifications requisite for his profession and great undertakings; together with the amiable and worthy qualities of the best men.'[10] There are remarks from various colleagues, including Anders Sparrman from the second voyage, and Trevenen and Samwell from the third. There is an important character sketch by the German, Heinrich Zimmerman, the only ordinary seaman to have written about his captain. There is, too, the adulatory piece entitled 'Cook the Discoverer' by George Forster, composed in German long after Cook's death, and there are numerous remarks about Cook, mostly uncomplimentary, by George's father, the irascible Johann Reinhold Forster, in his journal of the second voyage, recently published for the first time.[11] However, even taken together, all these witnesses hardly present us with a rounded picture of a human being, especially as they occasionally contradict one another. Zimmerman, for instance, says Cook was a quiet man who never swore, but Trevenen said he was passionate and irritable, and that when he 'pitched a *heiva*' (stamped and shouted in Maori style) everyone knew they had to stay clear. And the prissy Swede, Sparrman, declares, when describing what happened when the *Resolution* struck a reef near Tahiti,

'I should have preferred to hear fewer "Goddams" from the officers and particularly the Captain, who, while the danger lasted, stamped about the deck and grew hoarse with shouting.'[12] It does seem that in this instance, Zimmerman, who after all did not have access to the quarterdeck, may have got his facts wrong.

What do emerge clearly from the journals – both his own and others – are Cook's sterling qualities – his sense of duty and determination, his methodical approach and obsession with accuracy, his desire for continuous activity, his ambition, and his personal courage. 'I flatter myself', he writes towards the end of the second voyage, 'that the intention of the voyage has in every respect been fully Answered',[13] and this is clearly true of his voyages as a whole. Cook seems always to have followed his instructions to the letter, and shows in this respect a different attitude to that of his predecessors in the Pacific, Captains Byron and Wallis, who had a more cavalier way with their orders. Wallis of the *Dolphin*, having come across Tahiti almost by accident, decided that he had explored enough, and took the shortest way home.[14] Perhaps this was because, unlike the others, Cook came from a class accustomed to taking orders, and his whole training had been in conscientious obedience to his superiors. According to Beaglehole, 'his serious Scottish-Yorkshire blood reinforced this literalness'.[15] But of course the whole point of Cook's achievement was that he often went even further than his orders required. The most obvious example of this is on the first voyage, when he decided to traverse the entire East coast of Australia on his way home from New Zealand, although there was no mention of this in his instructions from the Admiralty, and, having charted the coasts of New Zealand, he could have proceeded homewards directly, either via the Cape of Good Hope, or round Cape Horn. Later he wrote, in a letter to a young French would-be explorer, 'Je soutiens que celui qui ne fait qu'exécuter des orders ne fera jamais grandes figures dans les découvertes [I maintain that someone who only obeys orders will never make a name for himself as a discoverer.']'[16]

'Indefatigability' or 'perseverance' are attributes frequently applied to Cook. His first biographer, Andrew Kippis, thought that these qualities were the most distinguishing feature of his character, and the midshipman, John Trevenen, writes,

This indefatigability was a leading feature of his character. If he failed in, or could no longer pursue, his first great object, he immediately began to consider how he might be most useful in prosecuting some inferior one, procrastination and irresolution he was a stranger to. Action was life to him and repose a sort of death.[17]

Johann Reinhold Forster agreed, but there were occasions when he wished Cook possessed this quality to a somewhat lesser degree. At Christmas, 1773, with the *Resolution* drifting among the icebergs of the Antarctic, and after it had been made plain they would not be returning to England for at least another year, he rails in his journal:

> There are people, who are hardened to all feelings, & will give no ear to the dictates of humanity & reason; false ideas of *virtue & good conduct* are to them, to leave nothing to *chance*, and future discoverers, by their *perseverance*, which costs the lives of the poor Sailors or at least their healths.[18]

The need for continuous activity is seen as the key to Cook's personality by J. R. Forster's son, George, who argued that this need was strong enough to become a substitute for the sensual pleasures sought by most other men: 'The fundamental strength of his personality was his successful striving for action and for performing deeds. This urge was never at rest, it needed no stimulation by the senses, and enjoyment of sensuality meant nothing to him.'[19] So far as we can tell, Cook's abstemiousness seems to have been an innate quality, not the result of a persistent struggle. In view of all this one can quite see why he did not want to remain in his sinecure at Greenwich after the second voyage, and took little persuading to embark on his third and last. As he wrote to John Walker: 'now I am going to be confined within the limits of Greenwich Hospital, which are far too small for an active mind like mine. I must confess it a fine retreat and a pretty income, but whether I can bring myself to like ease and retirement time will show.'[20]

As for ambition, there are two well known, and often quoted, passages of introspection in the journals, one from the first voyage, after the *Endeavour* narrowly escaped shipwreck on the Great Barrier Reef. Having described the emergency, Cook writes: 'was it not for the pleasure which naturally results to a Man from being the first discoverer, even was it nothing more than sands and shoals, this service would be insuportable especialy in far distant parts, like this, short of Provisions and almost every other necessary'.[21] And on the second voyage, having penetrated below the Antarctic Circle until a solid sheet of ice threatened to surround the two vessels, he discusses the inevitability of turning back towards the north: 'I whose ambition leads me not only farther than any other man has been before me, but as far as I think it possible for man to go, was not sorry at meeting with this interruption, as it in some measure relieved us from the dangers and hardships, inseparable with the Navigation of the Southern polar regions.'[22] According to Nicholas Thomas, this may have been a riposte to a statement made by Alexander Dalrymple in a book which Cook is known to have had with him on the voyage.[23] Dalrymple wrote that 'true heroism' can be determined by the simple question, 'What has he done which no one else ever did before, or can do after him?' Cook may have been motivated by scientific curiosity, and he was certainly also carrying out his duty as a naval officer, but passages like these seem to show that his innermost motivation was always personal ambition.

Cook was, both according to his own accounts and those of others, a man of great physical courage. John Elliott, a midshipman on the second voyage, wrote that:

> . . . certainly no man could be better calculated to gain the confidence of Savages than Capt[n] Cook. He was Brave, uncommonly Cool, Humane, and Patient. He would land alone unarm'd – or lay aside his Arms, and sit down, when they threaten'd him with theirs, throwing them Beads, Knives, and other little presents then by degrees advancing nearer, till by Patience, and forbearance, he gain'd their friendship, and an intercourse with them; which to people in our situation, was of the utmost consequence.[24]

Cook himself describes several examples of this technique, one of which occurred on the third voyage when the *Resolution* had entered a bay on the Asian side of the Bering Strait, where a native settlement had been spotted, and it was decided to anchor and attempt a landing. He had no way of knowing what these particular people were like, or what they would do:

> To this place I went with three Armed boats, accompanied by some of the Officers, and found 40 or 50 Men each armed with a Spontoon Bow and Arrows drawn up on a rising ground on which the village stood. As we drew near three of them came down towards the shore and were so polite as to take of their Caps and make us a low bow: we returned the Compliment but this did not inspire them with sufficient confidence to wait our landing, for the Moment we put the boats a shore they retired. I followed them alone without any thing in my hand, and by signs and actions got them to stop and receive some trifles I presented them with . . . They seemed very fearfull and causious, making signs for no more of our people to come up, and on my laying my hand on one mans Shoulder he started back several paces. In proportion as I advanced they retreated backwards always in the attitude of being ready to make use of their Spears, while those

on the hill behind them stood ready to support them with their arrows. Insensibly my self and two or three more got in amongst them, a few beads distributed to those about us brought on a kind of confidence so that two or three more of our people joining us did not Alarm them, and by degrees a sort of traffick between us commenced.[25]

This meeting ended happily, with gifts being exchanged, and even some singing and dancing, but it easily might not have done. Cook was risking his own life here, as he had done many times before.

This is perhaps an appropriate moment to bring up the question of whether Cook's behaviour, and in particular his attitude towards Pacific islanders, differed markedly during the third voyage from earlier. Beaglehole's answer is that it was considerably different, and that Cook should never have allowed himself to be persuaded by his superiors to embark on a further expedition. He quotes Cook's first biographer, Kippis, who describes the fateful dinner party held at the house of Lord Sandwich, First Lord of the Admiralty, in February 1776 at which Cook agreed to take charge of the planned voyage. By this date, according to Beaglehole:

> His faculties had simply been stretched to the uttermost for a long period, and whatever he thought of himself, whatever conception he had of his own duty, however much he sheered off the idea of idleness, some sort of idleness was his fundamental need, not the activity that was his constant desire. Sandwich and his colleagues did not look deep enough. The dinner-party was a great success, a triumph of management. It was a disaster.[26]

Beaglehole did not argue that Cook was actually a sick man at this point, but his thesis was reinforced subsequently by others who did, and who suggested that it was his medical condition that largely accounts for the irrational aspects of his behaviour on the third voyage. Sir James Watt, who has produced an impressive theory about the nature of Cook's illness on the second voyage, goes so far as to say that 'the father-figure of the second voyage became the feared despot of the third'.[27] However, the anthropologist Gananath Obeyesekere derides what he describes as 'this bizarre thesis', especially Watt's reference to a change of personality, which he sees as 'a pathetic attempt to exonerate Cook from responsibility for his actions'.

A subsidiary thesis, but one which leaves out the medical issue, is maintained by Anne Salmond and others, who argue that by the third voyage Cook had become deeply disillusioned and even cynical about his role in the

Pacific, losing confidence in himself and in the possibility of achieving his goals, especially that of bringing civilized values to backward peoples.[28]

Quite a different explanation, no doubt subjective and self-serving, but perhaps worth taking into consideration, comes from J. R. Forster, Cook's civilian companion on the second voyage. Forster argues that the absence of civilians on board the *Resolution* on the third voyage removed from Cook the restraint which their presence on the earlier voyages had provided:

> On his first voyage Cook was accompanied by Banks and Solander, who were the representatives of science and art . . . and on the second voyage I and my son accompanied him and were his daily companions at table and elsewhere. He therefore of necessity acquired through our presence a greater respect and reverence for his own character and good name. Our mode of thought, our principles, and our habits had their effect on him in the course of time through having them con- stantly before his notice, and these restrained him from practicing cruelties upon the harmless South-Sea-Islanders.[29]

Nicholas Thomas has recently argued that Cook's behaviour on the third voyage was not significantly different from that of earlier voyages.[30] He points out that during the months of exploration of the North American and Alaskan coasts in 1778 his relations with the various tribes encountered were generally excellent, and that there is little evidence that he was getting increasingly irritable or impatient (except possibly with his own midshipmen, whom, according to James Trevenen, he was inclined to bully). Thomas also argues that if harsh treatment of natives is seen as a criterion for Cook's behaviour, then he was actually responsible for more deaths on the first voyage than on the third. Personally, I tend to agree that, on the evidence of his own journals at least, the Cook of the third voyage does not appear diametrically altered from the earlier Cook, which is one reason why I think it legitimate to attempt to present his views and personality as a whole, in topic format, rather than as the narrative of the voyages unfolds.

So much for a quick sketch of Cook's early career, and some of the more obvious features of his physical nature and personality. There now follows a timeline of Cook's first voyage of exploration using mainly extracts from his own journal. Subsequently, the nature of his journals is examined, before turning the spotlight back on Cook himself. And having weighed some of the evidence from the journals it may be that we can penetrate a little further into the enigma that Cook presents.

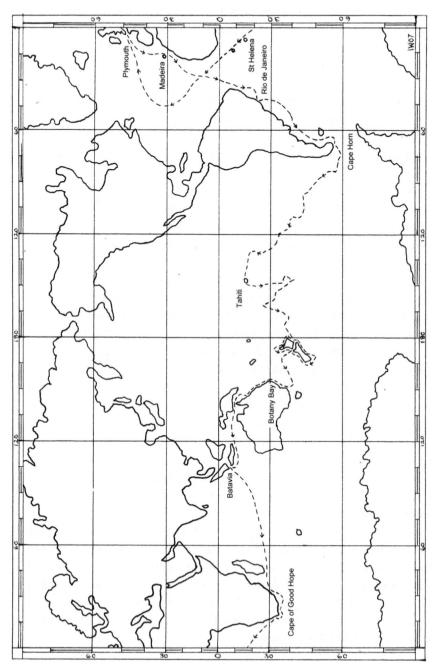

Map 1 *James Cook's first voyage in the* Endeavour *(1768–1771)*

Timeline of the
First Voyage

The Voyage of the *Endeavour* 1768–1771

1767 From a pamphlet by Alexander Dalrymple on the yet-to-be-discovered Southern Continent

The number of inhabitants in the Southern Continent is probably more than 50 millions, considering the extent, from the eastern part discovered by JUAN FERNANDEZ to the western coast seen by TASMAN, is about 100 deg. of longitude, which in the latitude of 40 deg. amounts to 4569 geographic, or 5323 statue miles. This is a greater extent than the whole civilized part of ASIA, from TURKEY to the eastern extremity of CHINA. There is at present no trade from EUROPE thither, though the scraps from this table would be sufficient to maintain the power, dominion, and sovereignty of BRITAIN, by employing all its manufacturing and ships.

15 Feb 1768 A Memorial of the Royal Society to George III

Humbly sheweth – That the passage of the Planet Venus over the Disc of the Sun, which will happen on the 3rd of June in the year 1769, is a Phaenomenon that must, if the same be accurately observed in proper places, contribute greatly to the improvement of astronomy on which navigation so much depends . . . That the like appearance after the 3rd of June will not happen for more than 100 years . . . That the British Nation have been justly celebrated in the learned world for their knowledge of Astronomy in which they are inferior to no Nation upon Earth, ancient or modern; and it would cast dishonour upon them should they neglect to have correct Observations made of this important Phaenomenon.

5 April 1768   Admiralty Minutes

Letter from Navy Board read; in accordance with order of 21st past they have purchased a cat-built vessel for conveying to the Southward the persons intended to be sent thither to observe the Transit of Venus over the Sun's Disc; resolved that they be directed to cause her to be sheathed, filled and fitted for that service, to be registered on the List of the navy as a Bark by the name of the Endeavour.

25 May 1768   Admiralty to Lieut. James Cook

Whereas we have appointed you first Lieutenant of His Majesty's Bark the Endeavour now at Deptford, and intend that you shall command her during her present intended voyage . . . You are hereby required and directed to use the utmost dispatch in getting her ready for the sea.

9 June 1768   Royal Society to Admiralty

Joseph Banks Esqr Fellow of this Society, a Gentleman of large fortune, who is well versed in natural history, being Desirous of undertaking the same voyage the Council very earnestly request their Lordships, that in regard to Mr Banks's great personal merit, and for the Advancement of useful knowledge, He also, together with his Suite, being seven persons more, that is, eight persons in all, together with their baggage, be received on board of the Ship, under the Command of Captain Cook.

26 August 1768   Journal of Captain James Cook

At 2pm got under sail and put to sea having on board 94 persons including Officers Seamen Gentlemen and their servants, near 18 months provision, 10 Carriage guns 12 Swivels with good store of Ammunition and stores of all kinds.

30 November 1768   Cook to the Secretary of the Royal Society from Rio de Janeiro

Neither Mr Green nor myself hath as yet been able to make any Observations worthy the Attention of the Royal Society, no one gentleman in this Ship have been permitted to go ashore at this place, this unheard of treatment has not only prevented Mr Green and myself from making any Astronomical observations here, but, Mr Banks & Doctor Solander from Collecting any of the productions of this country; I am at a loss to Assign the true reasons the Vice Roy had for treating us in the manner he hath . . . the account we gave of our Selves, of being bound to the Southward to observe the Transit of Venus (a phenomena they had not the least Idea of) appeared so very Strange to these narrow minded Portuguese that they thought it only an invented Story to cover some other design we must be upon.

12 April 1769   Journal

At 5PM King Georges Island [Tahiti] extending from NWbW to SW Distant 6 or 7 Leagues, and at 6AM it bore from SSW to WbN. Being little wind and calm several of the natives came off to us in their Canoes, but more to look at us than anything else we could not prevail with any of them to come on board and some would not come near the Ship, they brought with them Cocoa Nuts & a Fruit very much like a large Aple, but did not Eat half so good, for these we gave them Beads etc.

3 June 1769   Journal

This day prov'd as favourable to our purpose as we could wish, not a Clowd was to be seen the whole day and the Air was perfectly clear, so that we had every advantage we could desire in Observing the whole of the passage of the Planet Venus over the Suns disk; we very distinctly saw an Atmosphere or dusky shade round the body of the Planet which very much disturbed the times of the Contacts particularly the two internal ones.

8 October 1769 Journal

At 5PM seeing the opening of a Bay [Poverty Bay, their first landfall in New Zealand] that appear'd to run pretty far inland, hauled our wind and stood in for it . . . We saw in the Bay several Canoes, People upon the shore and some houses in the Country. The land on the Sea-Coast is high with white steep clifts and back inland are very high mountains.

17 January 1770 Journal

Soon after we landed [at Queen Charlotte's Sound, on the South Island of New Zealand] we met with two or three of the natives who not long before must have been regailing themselves upon human flesh, for I got from one of them the bone of the fore arm of a Man or a Woman which was quite fresh and the flesh had been but lately pick'd off which they told us they had eat, they gave us to understand that but a few days ago they had taken Kill'd and eat a Boats crew of their enemies or strangers, for I believe that they look upon all strangers as enemies.

31 March 1770 Journal

This country [New Zealand], which before now was thought to be a part of the imaginary southern continent, consists of Two large Islands divided from each other by a strait or passage of 4 or 5 Leagues broad . . . being now resolved to quit this country altogether and to bend my thoughts towards returning home by such a rout as might conduce most to the advantage of the service I am upon, I consulted with the officers upon the most eligible way of putting this in execution . . . It was therefore resolved to return by way of the East Indies by the following rout: upon leaving this coast to steer to the westward untill we fall in with the East Coast of New Holland and than to follow the deriction of that Coast to the northward or what other direction it may take.

29 April 1770   Journal

Saw as we came in on both points of the bay [Botany Bay] Several of the natives and a few hutts, Men, women and children on the south shore abreast of the Ship, to which place I went in hopes of speaking with them accompanied by Mr Banks Dr Solander and Tupia; as we approached the shore they all made off except two Men who seemd resolved to oppose our landing . . . I thout that they beckon'd to us to come a shore; but in this we were mistaken, for as soon as we put the boat in they again came to oppose us upon which I fired a musket between the two which had no other effect than to make them retire back where bundles of thier darts lay, and one of them took up a stone and threw at us which caused my fireing a second Musquet load with small shott, and altho some of the shott struck the man yet it had no other effect than to make him lay hold of a Shield or target to defend himself. Emmidiatly after this we landed which we had no sooner done than they throw'd two darts at us, this obliged me to fire a third shott soon after which they both made off, but not in such haste but what we might have taken one, but Mr Banks being of opinion that the darts were poisoned, made me cautious how I advanced into the woods. We found here a few Small hutts made of the bark of trees in one of which were four or five small children with whome we left some strings of beeds etc.

---

11 June 1770 Journal

Before 10 oClock we had 20 and 21 fathom and continued in that depth untill a few Minutes before a 11 when we had 17 and before the Man at the lead could heave another cast the Ship Struck and stuck fast. Emmediatly upon this we took in all our sails hoisted out the boats and sounded round the Ship, and found that we had got upon the SE edge of a reef of Coral rocks.

---

22 June 1770   Journal

At 4 in the PM having got out most of the Coals, cast loose the moorings and warped the Ship a little higher up the harbour to a place I had pitched upon to lay a Shore for stoping the leak [at the mouth of what is today the Endeavour River] . . . At 2 oClock in the AM the tide left her which gave us an opportunity to examine the leak which we found to be at her floor heads a little before the Starboard fore chains. Here the rocks had made their way thro' four Planks quite to and even into the timbers and wound'd three more. The manner these planks were damaged or cut out as I may say is hardly credible, scarce a splinter was to be seen but the whole was cut away as if it had been done by the hands of Man with a blunt edged tool.

Fortunatly for us the timbers in this place were very close, other ways it would have been impossible to have saved the ship and even as it was it appear'd very extraordinary that she made no more water than what she did. A large piece of Coral rock was sticking in one hole and several pieces of the fothereing, small stones, sand etc had made its way in and lodged between the timbers which had stoped the water from forceing its way in in great quantities.

14 July 1770 Journal

Mr Gore being out in the Country shott one of the Animals before spoke of, it was a small one of the sort weighing only 28 pound clear of the entrails. The head neck and shoulders of this Animal was very small in proportion to the other parts; the tail was nearly as long as the body, thick next the rump and tapering towards the end; the fore legs were 8 Inch long and the hind 22, its progression is by hoping or jumping 7 or 8 feet at each hop upon its hind legs only, for in this it makes no use of the fore, which seem to be only design'd for scratching in the ground etc. The Skin is covered with a short hairy fur of a dark Mouse or Grey Colour. Excepting the head and ears which I thought was something like a Hare's, it bears no sort of resemblance to any European Animal I ever saw.

16 August 1770   Journal [at the Great Barrier Reef]

We were not above 80 or 100 Yards from the breakers, the same Sea that washed the sides of the Ship rose in a breaker prodigiously high the very next time it did rise so that between us and distruction was only a dismal Vally the breadth of one wave and even now no ground could be felt with 120 fathoms . . . A Reef such as is here spoke of is scarcely known in Europe, it is a wall of Coral Rock rising all most perpendicular out of the unfathomable Ocean, always overflown at high-water generally 7 or 8 feet and dry in places at low-water . . . At this critical juncture when all our endeavours seem'd too little a small air of wind sprung up, but so small that at any other time in a Calm we should not have observed it, with this and the assistance of our boats we could observe the Ship to move off from the Reef.

22 *August 1770 Journal*

Having satisfied my self of the great Probability of a Passage, thro' which I intend going with the Ship, and therefore may land no more upon this Eastern coast of *New Holland*, and on the Western side I can make no new discovery the honour of which belongs to the Dutch Navigators; but the Eastern Coast from the Latitude of 38° South down to this place I am confident was never seen or viseted by any European before us, and Notwithstanding I had in the Name of His Majesty taken possession of several places upon this coast, I now once more hoisted English Coulers and in the Name of His Majesty King George the Third took possession of the whole Eastern Coast from the above Latitude down to this place by the name of *New South Wales.*

11 *October 1770 Journal*

At 4 oClock in the PM Anchor'd in Batavia Road . . . I had consulted with the Carpenter and all the other officers concearning the Leake, and they were all unanimously of opinion that it was not safe to proceed to Europe without first seeing her bottom. Accordingly I resolved to apply for leave to heave her down at this place, and as I understood that this was to be done in writeing I drew up a Request and in the Morning had it translated into dutch in order to be laid before the Governor.

25 *December 1770 Journal*

Having now completely refited the Ship & taken in a sufficient quantity of Provisions of all kinds, I this afternoon tooke leave of the General and such others of the principal Gentlemen as I had any connections with . . . Batavia is certainly a place that Europeans need not covet to go to, but if necessity obliges them they will do well to make their stay as short as possible otherwise they will soon feel the effects of the unwholsome air of Batavia which I firmly believe is the death of more Europeans than in any other place upon the Globe of the same extent, such at least is my opinion of it which is founded on facts. We came in here with as healthy a ships company as need go to Sea and after a stay of not quite 3 Months lift it in the condition of an Hospital ship besides the loss of 7 Men and yet all the Dutch Captains I had an opportunity to convers with said that we had been very lucky and wondered that we had not lost half our people in that time.

13 July 1771 Journal

At 3 oClock in the PM Anchor'd in the Downs, & soon after I landed in order to repair to London.

16 August 1771 London Evening Post

Thursday Lieutenant Cook, of the Royal Navy, who sailed round the Globe with Messrs. Solander, Banks, etc., was presented to his Majesty by Lord Sandwich, and had the Honour of presenting to his Majesty a compleat Journal of the said Voyage, together with some curious Maps and Charts that he had made of different Places during the said Voyage, which were graciously received, and at the same time he was presented with a Captain's Commission.

Part I

The Journals

Chapter 2

Entertaining the Reader

This is a book about books or, to be more precise, it is about Cook's three journals of exploration, and also about what they can tell us of Cook himself. 'Journalist' is a word that has changed its meaning since the eighteenth century, and Cook was a journalist in the older sense because he was the author of his famous journals. However, when he started out on his career as an explorer, he was a man who knew about maps rather than literary composition. He had spent the better part of his thirties in measurement and applied geometry. In the words of Nicholas Thomas, he had been, 'working magic on rugged and intricate coastlines, reducing a shoreline as torn as an awful wound to points and lines on paper'.[1] He had developed a new kind of accurate knowledge that showed up his predecessors' efforts for their amateurishness, and so long as he had to write about his specialisms – surveying, weather, bearings and courses – he was very much in his element. However, the instructions for his voyages of discovery demanded that he record matters quite outside this range, and outside the experience of the average naval commander. He was supposed to describe in detail his encounters with the various natives he met, as well as all kinds of facts about them and the places in which they lived. Matters involving ethnology, psychology, biology and so on were to be noted down for the perusal of his superiors at the Admiralty. This task weighed heavily on Cook who had enormous difficulty composing his journals, as the evidence of much painful redrafting suggests, and this is hardly surprising given that he was a self-educated man, a man of action, a surveyor and an astronomer amongst other things, and less at home with words than with figures. Cook himself seems to have had no illusions about his literary powers. In his introduction to the journal of the second voyage he declares that the journal was written:

> . . . by a man, who has not the advantage of Education, acquired, nor
> Natural abilities for writing; but by one who has been constantly

at sea from his youth, and who, with the Assistance of a few good friends gone through all the Stations belonging to a Seaman, from a prentice boy in the Coal Trade to a Commander in the Navy. After such a Candid confession he hopes the Public will not consider him as an author, but a man Zealously employed in the Service of his Country and obliged to give the best account he is able of his proceedings.[2]

This apparently modest apology for lack of polish may, however, also be read as an indirect boast and an assertion that in fact his style was more suitable to his subject matter than if it had been more literary and artificial. The more elaborate version of his disclaimer which was eventually published, having been modified by his editor, John Douglas, makes this interpretation rather more evident:

> And now it may be necessary to say that, as I am on the point of sailing on a third expedition, I leave this account of my last voyage in the hands of some friends, who, in my absence, have kindly accepted the office of correcting the press for me; who are pleased to think that what I have here to relate is better to be given in my own words, than in the words of another person, especially as it is a work designed for information, and not merely for amusement; in which it is their opinion, that candour and fidelity will counterbalance the want of ornament . . . After this account of myself, the public must not expect from me the elegance of a fine writer, or plausibility of a professed book maker; but will, I hope, consider me as a plain man, zealously exerting himself in the service of his country, and determined to give the best account he is able of his proceedings.[3]

In this version Cook – or possibly Douglas on his behalf – is perhaps mainly attempting to distance himself from the editor of his first journal, John Hawkesworth, but his statement was picked up by at least one reviewer and used as a stick to beat him with:

> He grounds his claim to indulgence on his ignorance of letters; but how can the consciousness of inability become the motive for undertaking a work of such length and importance?[4]

The problem was not that Cook was illiterate. In fact he was far from it, and other reviewers agreed with his own assessment, one of them writing that he could express himself 'with a plain natural strength and clearness, and an unaffected modesty which schools cannot teach'.[5] In other words, his style was felt to be perfectly appropriate for his subject matter. The difficulty he faced was, rather, the prejudices and expectations of the cultured reading public of the day. Horace Walpole's comment on the three volumes of Hawkesworth's *Voyages* (containing the official account of Cook's first voyage) was that 'the entertaining matter would not fill half a volume', and later he refused even to read the published narrative of the third voyage, writing to Lady Ossory that he was not interested in 'rows of savages', 'nor do I desire to know how unpolished the north or south poles have remained ever since Adam and Eve were just such mortals'.[6] A few years earlier Dr. Johnson had delivered a typically forthright opinion on the topic of voyages of discovery: 'It may, I think, be justly observed that few books disappoint their readers more than the narrations of travellers.'[7] Johnson was sceptical about the benefits gained from such voyages, and he once warned James Boswell, who had dined with Cook the previous evening, not to be 'carried away' by his enthusiasm.[8] On a later occasion, referring specifically to the massive volumes of Cook's third voyage, published in 1784, he gave it as his opinion that 'There can be little entertainment in such books; one set of savages is like another.'[9] Nevertheless, Johnson himself made more than one excursion into the realms of the travel narrative, his first published work being a translation from the French of the account of a voyage to Abyssinia by a Portuguese priest. It is true, however, that in the preface to this he explains that he has removed all potentially tedious material, being more concerned with the entertainment and edification of the British reader than with fidelity to the original account.[10]

Walpole and Johnson were literary lions, leaders of cultural fashion in mid-eighteenth-century London, and when people of their sort spoke of 'entertaining matter' they did not mean quite what we might mean today. They held that the task of literature, as well as being one of entertainment in our sense, was also to edify and instruct the reader. By this date, descriptions of voyages, whether factual or fictional, were an established and popular – if minor – branch of literature. Best-sellers of the day included *Gulliver's Travels* and *Robinson Crusoe*, as well as the largely factual account of the voyages of William Dampier, a reformed pirate who had crossed the Pacific and even visited the West Coast of Australia. If narratives such as these were going to receive the stamp of approval from Walpole, Johnson and their peers, who wrote in the literary reviews and pontificated on matters of taste, then these were expected to be educational, as well as urbane and witty. Such travellers' tales had to avoid boring their readers with too much factual detail – especially nautical detail – and instead organise their narratives effectively, perhaps employing literary techniques such as irony and metaphor to adorn them. They should make free with comparisons and generalisations in order to draw attention to certain moral positions. Their authors were expected to be persons of literary taste, not artisans or horny-handed seamen, whose style might 'disgust' the reader. A quotation from the *Monthly Review*, one of the leading literary magazines of the day, gives some idea of the forces of opposition that faced potential authors such as Cook. This example is from a review of a certain Dr. Hasselquist's *Travels in Africa*, published in 1766:

> With respect to Dr Hasselquist himself, he appears to be a very honest man, and a sensible observer, both of men and things. He is not, however, an elaborate writer; at least, there are in this work, no extra-ordinary proofs of his talent for literary compositions. His remarks are cursorily set down, without any great regard to order or system; and have the appearance of a mere journal, published in the same negligent undress in which it was originally written, in the very course of the travels to which they relate.[11]

After Cook's second voyage, two journals were published: Cook's own, and that of George Forster who had accompanied his father as a naturalist on the *Resolution*. A reviewer in the *London Magazine*, making a comparison between the two, wrote: 'The former [Forster's] is the most entertaining for the general part of readers; the latter the more instructive to the seaman and navigator.'[12] And some years later, the anonymous reviewer of yet another volume of travels wrote in a similar vein about 'mere journals of occurences, loaded with tedious minuteness of detail, and seldom enlivened by ingenious remarks, or embellished with the graces of style'.[13]

The point made by all these authors was that a 'mere journal' was unlikely to please the public. This was partly because a journal, being by definition a record of (often trivial) day-to-day affairs, would hardly be exciting enough to hold the reader's interest, and also because its style and vocabulary were likely to be crude and pedestrian. One thing the *literati* despised more than anything was nautical jargon. Sailors tended to be seen as simple and impulsive beings, rather like children, and the specialised terms they used – the vocabulary of the sea – was often a suitable object of mirth, and hardly fit for the eye of a sophisticated reader. A manual on how to write correct English, published in 1797 by the influential grammarian, John Murray, gives an example of how sailors' talk should be translated into intelligible English. The original paragraph is as follows:

> Most of our hands were asleep in their berths, when the vessel shipped
> a sea, that carried away our pinnace and binnacle. Our dead-lights were

in, or we should have filled. The main mast was so sprung, that we were obliged to fish it, and bear away for Lisbon.

Murray suggests instead the following version:

> Most of our sailors were asleep in their apartments, when a heavy wave broke over the ship, and swept away one of our boats, and the box which contained our compasses, etc. Our cabin windows were secured, or the vessel would have been filled. The mainmast was so damaged, that we were obliged to strengthen it, and proceed for Lisbon.[14]

Leaving aside the question of whether sailors actually slept in apartments, the message here is clear. If an author wanted to describe a voyage – fictional or otherwise – he would be well advised to steer clear of the technical terms of his trade. In Part II of *Gulliver's Travels* Swift gives us a satirically exaggerated account of a storm in nautical terminology, but in his introduction to the book he makes the same point as Murray, through the mouth of his hero, Lemuel Gulliver:

> This volume would have been at least twice as large, if I had not made bold to strike out innumerable passages relating to the wind and tides, as well as to the variations and bearings in the several voyages; together with the minute descriptions of the management of the ship in storms, in the style of sailors: likewise the account of the longitudes and latitudes.[15]

George Forster, in the introduction to his journal of the second voyage makes a similar claim: 'I have studiously avoided nautical details both at sea and in the Harbour, Nor ventured to determine how often we reefed, or split a sail in a storm, how many times we tacked to weather a point, and how often our refractory bark disobeyed her palinurus, and missed stays.'[16] This was precisely the reason why *The London Magazine* reviewer quoted above is led to compare Cook's account unfavourably with Forster's. 'We naturally expected', he writes, 'that all nautical matters, so generally tedious and uninteresting, would be struck out of [Cook's] narrative.'[17] In fact, Hawkesworth, the editor of Cook's first journal, alleges that he was instructed by the Admiralty to insert more of such details than he had intended:

> It will probably be thought by many readers, that I have related the nautical events too minutely . . . I was not indeed myself sufficiently

apprised of the minuteness that was necessary in this part of the work, so that I was obliged to make many additions to it, after I had prepared my manuscript.[18]

The following extract from a best-seller of the day – the account of Commodore Anson's expedition to the Pacific in 1740–4 to attack Spanish ports and shipping – demonstrates the kind of elevated writing that an educated readership appreciated. The author is Richard Walter, a Cambridge graduate who had been chaplain on Anson's flagship, the *Centurion*. In the quotation below he explains the unsuitable arrangements made for providing Anson's fleet with soldiers. The recruits sent down to Portsmouth were mainly Chelsea out-pensioners, and quite unprepared for the rigours of such a voyage:

> All those who had limbs and strength to walk out of Portsmouth deserted, leaving behind them only such as were literally invalids, most of them being sixty years of age, and some of them upwards of seventy. Indeed it is difficult to convey a more moving scene than the embarkation of these unhappy veterans: They were themselves extremely averse to the service they were engaged in, and fully apprized of all the disasters they were afterwards exposed to; the apprehensions of which were strongly mark'd by the concern that appeared in their countenances, which was mixed with no small degree of indignation, to be thus hurried from their repose into a fatiguing employ, to which neither the strength of their bodies, nor the vigour of their minds, were any ways proportioned, and where, without seeing the face of an enemy, or in the least promoting the success of the enterprize, they would in all probability uselessly perish by lingring and painful diseases; and this too, after they had spent the activity and strength of their youth in their Country's service.[19]

Note the elaborate sentence construction and latinate vocabulary of this extract. Incidentally, these recruits were quite right to be apprehensive – the vast majority of them did die during the voyage, mostly from scurvy, and Anson returned to England with only one ship out of the eight that set off.[20]

But the pundits of the literary world did not have it all their own way. The outlook of those such as Galileo and Newton, who had initiated the scientific revolution of the previous century, was at this time rapidly becoming assimilated into enlightened discourse.[21] As such, journals of exploration, with all their technical detail, were valued by many as the unique records of men who had actually been on the spot and experienced the dangers and hardships. In the case of a sea journal there were also the needs of future voyagers to take into consideration. The next explorer would expect an accurate, unadulterated account of where his predecessor had been and what he had experienced. In other words, a journal needed to be scientific and 'authentic', its authenticity validated by the language of Baconian empiricism, and some readers – perhaps a growing number – held that this was far more important than its literary merit or sophistication. From this angle the whole point of a journal is that it is written by the explorer himself at the time concerned, and not rewritten later by a ghost writer. Its vocabulary should be similar to any kind of treatise, or description of natural phenomena – plain, simple and direct, avoiding ornaments of any kind, such as classical allusions, flowery metaphors, or moral digressions. This was exactly the kind of style recommended by the group of scientists and laymen who had founded the *Royal Society* in the reign of Charles II, a century earlier. These innovators sought to eliminate all mental or verbal imprecision and obscurity. They intended their texts to convey information to the reader as simply and directly as possible. In the words of Thomas Sprat, historian of the *Society*, there must be 'a constant Resolution, to reject all the Amplifications, Digressions, and swellings of Style; to return back to the primitive Purity and Shortness, when Men deliver'd so many Things, almost in an equal Number of Words'. Consequently, according to Sprat, the language of 'Artizans, Countrymen, and Merchants' was greatly to be preferred to that of wits or scholars.[22]

The implicit assumption behind this point of view was that words are, or should be, a direct representation of things, or, to put it differently (perhaps in the kind of trope that Sprat would have scorned), a magnifying glass through which the reader could perceive the real world. It was therefore vital to make this glass as clear as possible. Any unnecessary elaboration of style or vocabulary would merely dirty the glass and obscure the view. This particular style was also alleged to be democratic in that it could easily be grasped by every reader, and not merely the highly educated. In the view of its proponents, it was essentially a moral style, one suitable for a straightforward Englishman, who would have no truck with foreign linguistic importations and fripperies. It was, as one writer put it when approvingly describing the translated account of a voyage by the Russian explorer Otto von Kotzebue, 'a natural and manly language, as it would become an English naval officer to write'.[23] Here, in Jonathan Lamb's striking phrase, was being deployed the 'rhetoric of anti-rhetoric'.[24]

The term 'manly' points to another alleged feature of the unvarnished style. Many commentators held that this style – down-to-earth, robust, logical – was essentially *masculine*, as opposed to its alternative – poetic, showy, digressive – hence, *feminine*. It is surprising how often Cook's writing – and indeed

Cook himself – is described by his contemporaries as manly. 'His personal appearance', wrote an early biographer, George Young, was 'plain, but manly; a remark which applies to his manners, and his style of writing.'[25] Andrew Kippis, Cook's first biographer, makes the same point. He says that Cook learnt 'to express himself with a manly clearness and propriety', and when discussing the nature of Cook's genius he contrasts *vigour* (clearly supposed to be a masculine quality), with the more impractical and feminine forms of genius. Kippis writes:

> It cannot, I think, be denied that genius belonged to Captain Cook in an eminent degree. By genius I do not here understand imagination merely, or that power of culling the flowers of fancy which poetry delights in; but an inventive mind; a mind full of resources; and which, by its own native vigour, can suggest noble objects of pursuit, and the most effectual methods of attaining them.[26]

A reviewer of the published journals of the third voyage contrasts Cook's writing with that of the Oxford-educated Lieutenant James King who took over the account of the voyage after Cook's death. King, says this reviewer, is 'inferior in that expressive energy and manly force which particularly distinguish Captain Cook's style'.[27] Adjectives such as robust and vigorous may have ostensibly been used to categorise particular texts, but by implication they also applied to the authors of the texts. King, as we know, was 'small-bodied', 'well-bred' and 'genteel'.[28]

According to the feminist historian Michèle Cohen, this emphasis on a robust and masculine style of writing and speaking was typical of the final decades of the eighteenth century, and it represented an important cultural shift from previous years.[29] Earlier in the century commentators such as Addison, much influenced by French manners and civilization, had stressed the importance of politeness, the art of conversation, and the society of women in the self-fashioning of a gentleman. But the new emphasis demoted politeness, together with female influence and continental subtleties, and instead looked favourably on a certain roughness and lack of polish as integral to English manliness. While French was a 'language naturally made for graceful trifling', argued Captain Alexander Jardine in 1788, English was a 'plain rational and monosyllabic tongue', suited to its 'manly and laconic speakers'.[30] If this thesis is true, Cook would certainly have been seen as exemplifying the new style, both in his writing and in his person.

Nevertheless, for reasons already mentioned, the authorities, and publishers, continued to have their doubts as to whether 'manly and laconic' authors should be allowed to communicate directly with the book-buying public. A decade after Cook's death this problem was aired again by an anonymous reviewer when discussing the memoirs of Colonel Collins of the Royal Marines, who had been in charge of the convicts at Botany Bay. He writes:

> Such are the most important contents of Mr Collins' book, the style of which we very much approve, because it appears to be written by himself, and we must repeat again, that nothing can be more injurious to the opinion the public will form of the authenticity of a book of this kind, than the suspicion that it has been trick'd out, and embellished by other hands. These memoirs . . . are written in the style of a journal, which, though not the most agreeable mode of conveying information, is certainly the most authentic, and contrives to banish the suspicion (and most probably the reality) of the interference of a Book-maker – a species of gentleman who are now almost become necessary to deliver naval and military authors in their literary labours, though they do not always atone, by orthography and grammar, for the sacrifice of truth and simplicity.[31]

The 'Bookmaker' referred to here was what we might call a ghost writer – the sort of literary technician whose services are perhaps even more in demand today than they were in the eighteenth century. This reviewer claims to admire the spontaneity of memoirs and journals which were penned exclusively by their protagonists, but he also admits that in most cases naval and military authors did require a bookmaker's assistance. Such was the prevailing contemporary view amongst the critics, and it was also held to be what the public expected. Cook himself, it may be recalled, later wrote, by implication slightingly, about the 'plausibility of a professed book maker'. However, in his particular case, and given his lack of formal education, the need for a bookmaker seemed obvious to the authorities. Therefore, when Cook returned from his first voyage, in July 1771, the Admiralty, in the person of John Montagu, fourth Earl of Sandwich, set about finding a suitable candidate for the task.

Chapter 3

Bookmakers

At the return of the *Endeavour* in July 1771, all journals written during the voyage having been handed in to the authorities, the search was on for a suitable person to write the narrative of 'the late voyages to the South Seas', which would include not only Cook's but also the previous voyages of Byron, Carteret and Wallis. The idea was for this authorized edition to provide the official account as opposed to the various spurious and inaccurate texts already appearing in print. It would give positive proof of British domination of the Pacific, showing, for instance, that Tahiti had been first discovered by Wallis and not by the French under Bougainville. Two friends of Lord Sandwich, Charles Burney, the musical scholar, and David Garrick, the actor-impresario, recommended Hawkesworth as the right man for the task, and he it was who was chosen.

One might say that John Hawkesworth was really an inferior edition of Dr Johnson.[1] Described in the *Dictionary of National Biography* as 'a miscellaneous writer of humble origin', he was born in about 1715, and lived his entire life in or near London, ending up in Bromley, Kent. He started life as an attorney's clerk but soon showed his real talent when he turned to journalism, mostly of a literary kind. He became a prolific writer, producing dozens of essays and articles for the periodic press, especially *The Gentleman's Magazine*, for which he became for many years a major contributor. Although not classically educated in the conventional middle class way he was a gifted writer who could turn his hand to anything, from librettos, to inspiring moral tales, to translations from the French. He edited the works of Jonathan Swift in twelve volumes, followed by his letters in a further three, he collaborated with Samuel Johnson in a best-selling monthly series of collected essays entitled *The Adventurer*, and he also seems to have successfully imitated Johnson's ponderous and idiosyncratic style, so that contemporaries very often failed to tell their productions apart. It was the elevated and religious tone of

Hawkesworth's contributions to *The Adventurer* which led the Archbishop of Canterbury to confer on him in 1756 the degree of LL.D, so that he became from henceforth Dr. Hawkesworth. By this time he had acquired an influential circle of friends including Reynolds, Burney, Garrick and, of course, Johnson himself – although this friendship cooled in later years, Johnson describing him as 'one of the many whom success in the world has spoiled'. Hawkesworth was a regular visitor to the Burney household, and features in the diary of Burney's young daughter, Fanny, who at first found him affected but later changed her mind, writing 'I like the Doctor more and more every time I have the pleasure of seeing him; that stiffness and something resembling pedantry, which formerly struck me in him, upon further acquaintance and more intimacy either wear off or disappear. He was extremely natural and agreeable.'[2]

When Sandwich appointed him and handed over to him all the naval journals, Hawkesworth was naturally elated, but he was even more pleased when the civilian, Joseph Banks, also lent him his journal. As he explains in his introduction he used Banks's lively journal a great deal in order to spice up the narrative and supplement Cook's much more cautious and sober account.[3] Hawkesworth was now free to make his own arrangements with a publisher and he managed to negotiate a contract with the well-known firm of Strahan & Cadell for £6,000. This was an unheard of advance for any book at that time, considering that Johnson himself had recently received an advance of only £1575 for his *Dictionary*. Hawkesworth's good fortune was much talked about and resented, and lost him the friendship of Garrick who had expected him to sign up with a rival publisher.

Because he hoped to get Cook to check through the manuscript before setting out on his second voyage, Hawkesworth started on the narrative of the *Endeavour* voyage first, and at great speed. He finished it in four months, an impressive achievement considering his task involved collating the journals of Cook and Banks (as well as adding numerous comments of his own). He then wrote up the other three voyages and, after a delay for engraving the illustrations and printing, the book came out in June 1773. Although pricey, the three volumes sold well, going into a second edition within months, and the book was at first well received. However, soon a storm of criticism burst from various quarters, criticism which so surprised and depressed Hawkesworth who was expecting nothing but congratulation, that it probably contributed to his rapid decline and death in November the same year.

There is some doubt as to how much of the manuscript Cook did actually see before he left for the South Seas. Hawkesworth claimed that Cook's part of the book was read to him at the Admiralty, and the manuscript then left in his hands 'for a considerable time after the reading', but in his journal of the

John Hawkesworth (1720–1773), a prolific author of miscellaneous works who was picked by Lord Sandwich to edit the journal of Cook's first voyage, and who suffered bitter criticism for his editorship. An engraving by Warren.

second voyage Cook denies this.[4] The answer may be that Hawkesworth gave the manuscript to Sandwich under the impression that Cook and the other commanders were to see it, but that Sandwich only showed it to other naval experts and not Cook. This is the implication of a contemporary letter in *The Public Advertiser* in which the anonymous author states, 'Dr. H. submitted his Papers to the Examination and Correction (not of Scribblers, Witlings and Women) of a select Number of the most able and intelligent Seamen of long Experience, great Service and high Rank in their Profession. [These men] saw it, considered it, and greatly approved of the Stile, Manner, and Contents.'[5]

In any case, when Cook finally got to see the published version, which was when he called in at the Cape towards the end of the second voyage, he disliked it intensely. No doubt he disapproved of the way Hawkesworth had combined into one narrative the three components – his own comments and moralising, Banks's lively account, and Cook's journal itself. The result of this merging was that the 'I' of the narrative, whom most readers would have taken to be Cook himself – seemed to do things that the real Cook never did, and express sentiments that the real Cook never expressed. To take one small example, Cook and Banks once met a Tahitian woman who was in paroxysms of grief over the death of a relative. She expressed her sorrow by repeatedly cutting herself with a sharp stone, but then all at once her mood changed, and the next minute she was laughing cheerfully. Hawkesworth's 'Cook' reflects on this incident, but his sentiments and style are a long way from anything the real Cook would have produced:

> It is not indeed strange that the sorrows of these artless people should be transient, any more than that their passions should be suddenly and strongly expressed: what they feel they have never been taught either to disguise or suppress, and having no habits of thinking which perpetually recall the past, and anticipate the future, they are affected by all the changes of the passing hour, and reflect the colour of the time, however frequently it may vary: they have no project which is to be pursued from day to day, the subject of unremitted anxiety and solicitude, that first rushes into the mind when they awake in the morning, and is last dismissed when they sleep at night. Yet if we admit that they are upon the whole happier than we, we must admit that the child is happier than the man, and that we are losers by the perfection of our nature, the increase of our knowledge, and the enlargement of our views.[6]

Cook may have resented the fact that a passage like this was put in his name, but it was precisely digressions like these – and there were many of them – that might have led the average eighteenth-century reader to see Cook as not just an intrepid explorer but also as a humanist capable of expressing a degree of introspection and moral insight – in other words, a rounded personality and a fitting hero for the times. As W.H. Pearson, a modern commentator on

Hawkesworth, puts it, he 'is creating the prototype of that hero of Victorian boys' sea fiction, the magnanimous British commander and for all that Cook was embarrassed by his editor's intrusions and inaccuracies, the edition of his first voyage was the first contribution to his ennoblement as a national figure'.[7] But right up until today Hawkesworth has had a bad press as the man who distorted Cook. Modern readers, especially, look for authenticity from the editors of journals, and prefer any generalised moral disquisitions to be kept in a separate place. Yet all this is a little unjust to Hawkesworth who was only doing what he thought he had been paid for, which was to create a meaningful narrative out of the various journals. Hawkesworth had a theory of literature, which he saw as always having a moral purpose. The function of any narrative, whether fiction or factual, was to engage the reader, so that he might gain from it something which would benefit him personally, perhaps even spiritually. In the case of a voyage of discovery this should be done by pointing up the universal significance of particular events rather than just narrating the events themselves. For instance, if a native was shot for trying to steal a musket (as happened soon after Cook arrived in Tahiti) this ought to furnish the occasion for a debate about the rights and wrongs of killing natives who stole. Was not the airing of this moral issue more important than the dull details of navigation? Hawkesworth certainly thought so.

Another example of words having been put into Cook's mouth by Hawkesworth led to Cook's considerable embarrassment when the *Resolution* put in at St. Helena in May, 1775, on the way home. Banks – and Hawkesworth copying Banks – had made certain dubious and derogatory statements about the inhabitants of the island, such as that they treated their slaves abominably. Another such statement was that there were no wheeled vehicles on the island, so every morning of Cook's stay numerous wheelbarrows and carts were 'studiously placed before captain Cook's lodgings'. Furthermore, he was mercilessly teased for the mistakes in Hawkesworth by Mary Skottowe, wife of John Skottowe, the governor of the island (whom Cook had probably known when they were little boys back in Great Ayton).[8] The 'satirical sallies' of this lively lady, according to Anders Sparrman who was with Cook on the *Resolution*, 'probably troubled the naval officers more than many an ocean storm'.[9]

Hawkesworth was abused not only for deserting the original material with which he had been supplied, but also for 'damaging the narrative codes' which readers relied on to help them understand and enjoy a sea-voyage narrative.[10] Jonathan Lamb suggests that such codes included the providential, which Hawkesworth in his introduction expressly repudiates (see Chapter 14), as well as the sentimental, or pathetic, and the taxonomic, or Linnaean. All such codes or categories were employed by other narrators such as the Forsters, and were easily recognised and understood by contemporary readers as signposts to reassure the reader that he was on familiar territory, culturally if not geographically. An example of Hawkesworth's deliberate violation of the expectations of his readership comes in his account of the shootings at Poverty Bay, New Zealand, when his circumstantial account implicated Cook and his colleagues, thus failing 'to locate savagery always on the side of the exotic other', the result being 'the loss of the alibi that masks the oppression and violence of exploration'.[11]

Hawkesworth gave himself the task of interpreting to his readership a novel culture – that of the South Sea islanders – whose values often contradicted those of eighteenth-century England. He tried to be neutral when discussing the Tahitians and what they got up to, but his suspension of judgement was seen by his readers as complicity. To go by the torrent of abuse he received in letters to the press one might think he had personally been to Tahiti and participated in the inhabitants' outrageous sexual behaviour – yet for the most part he was only quoting Banks.[12] A further, underlying problem was the nature of his book. He was trying to do too many things at once, and satisfy too many different types of reader. On the one hand, this official account of British discoveries in the South Pacific was expected to contain enough data – about currents and winds, coastlines and bearings – to be of use to future explorers and navigators. Apparently, a copy was found helpful by the Bounty mutineers when they made their way to Pitcairn Island. Then there were the geographers, with their desire for ever more charts and maps, and among them that leading cartographer of the Pacific region, Alexander Dalrymple, who published a personal attack on Hawkesworth for his alleged inaccuracies. On the other hand, the book had to be entertaining enough to become a best-seller and justify its £6,000 advance from the publisher. As it was, there was far too much boring nautical detail for those such as Horace Walpole who complained unceasingly about its deficiencies in letters to his friends,[13] or Johnson, who said to Boswell that he thought it a mere 'subject of commerce' rather than a book which would increase human knowledge.[14]

Poor Hawkesworth lived only six months after the publication of his *Voyages*. Exactly how he died is uncertain but Fanny Burney described him on his last visit to the Burney home in October as 'thin, livid, harassed'.[15] One story is that he committed suicide by taking an overdose of opium, but it seems more likely death was brought on by the effect of months of overwork on a frail constitution coupled with the shame and depression that the attacks in the press caused him. A letter from his wife to Mrs Garrick tells of 'that Mind whose powers have for a long time been exerted almost to agony, but manifestly so as to have really destroyed Ye Fragile Fabric of the Body'.[16] Such was the sad end of the first of Cook's 'bookmakers'.

Apart from his dislike of Hawkesworth's narrative, there was a further reason why Cook may have been put out by the public treatment of himself and his journal. In the public reception of the voyage generally, much more prominence had been given to Banks than to Cook himself. The newspapers talked about 'Mr Banks's voyage', and Lieutenant Cook hardly featured in the reports at all. For instance, the *Public Advertiser*'s final verdict on the voyage was: 'Very great Expectations are formed from the Discoveries of Dr. Solander and Mr. Banks, and it is expected that the Territories of Great Britain will be widely extended in Consequence of those Discoveries'.[17]

All this must have been galling to the commander of the *Endeavour*, and so, in all probability, Cook then and there decided that when it came to his next voyage he would himself try as far as possible to prepare his journal for publication. The prospect of financial gain was no doubt an additional motive, given the large fee received by Hawkesworth. However, to produce an acceptable book was a bold undertaking for someone who, by his own admission, possessed practically no formal education or literary experience, and it certainly was to cost him much pain and effort. During the entire course of the second voyage he spent long hours writing and revising his journal, greatly expanding those parts that he thought the readers would find most interesting. And on the return to England the re-writing did not stop until Cook was finally satisfied enough to hand over his manuscript to the authorities. By this time – the summer of 1776 – there was yet another reason for his wanting to keep control of the publication of his own journal. As soon as he returned to England he would have become painfully aware of the press and public's often ribald and disrespectful reaction to Hawkesworth's account of events. The *Endeavour* voyage was still, in the public's estimation, Mr Banks's voyage, but readers now seemed to be more interested in Mr Banks's sexual adventures in Tahiti than in his territorial discoveries. The serious-minded Cook would certainly have been much offended by the various lampoons and satires about the voyage appearing in the press.[18] Ironically, however, Cook probably used Hawkesworth as a model when preparing his own account of the second voyage, borrowing from him the technique of writing in the past tense, as well as that of transferring his daily entries into 'chapters' and 'books'.[19]

Cook's reward for all his efforts was that the journal as published at the time was very much more his own work than the published version of the *Endeavour* journal had been. It was still not entirely his own, however, because there was again to be a bookmaker. Thus in the summer of 1776 Lord Sandwich looked round once more for a safe pair of hands to edit the journal of Cook's second voyage after the Hawkesworth fiasco. His choice fell on John Douglas, canon of Windsor, another man of letters who could, like Hawkesworth, apparently turn his pen to anything, but a better educated, and better connected, figure.[20] Douglas's career followed a conventional pattern for an ambitious clergyman of the day. He was born in a fairly remote part of the kingdom, at Pittenweem on the Firth of Forth, today a still unspoilt little fishing port, and where his father was a merchant and ship-owner. When he died, 86 years later, as bishop of Salisbury, his obituary stated: 'the most extraordinary feature in the career of this reverend prelate is his uniform good fortune, which makes the history of his life little more than the chronicle of the honours and preferments which were heaped upon him'.

This career, after Oxford and a spell abroad to learn French, really took off when the young Douglas was picked by the Earl of Bath to tutor his son, Lord Pulteney, and to accompany him on the Grand Tour. The son died soon afterwards, but by then Douglas had become the earl's favourite, and virtually his private chaplain. He received a string of preferments and livings, in none of which he ever resided, instead taking a house close to his patron's mansion in Bath, and accompanying him round fashionable watering places at home and abroad. But his real talent was for authorship – he could produce an effective pamphlet on any topic required of him, from a defence of the Gospel miracles against Hume, to exonerating Lord George Sackville from the charge of cowardice at the battle of Minden, to attacking the government for using mercenary troops against the rebel Americans. By the time he was approached by Sandwich, Douglas had acquired some reputation in London intellectual circles and he had, for instance, achieved the ultimate accolade of being invited to dine with Dr. Johnson at the Crown and Anchor Tavern in the Strand, although according to Boswell he was so frightened of Johnson's cutting wit that he hardly opened his mouth the whole evening.[21]

In view of what had happened to Hawkesworth, Douglas was extremely wary of publicity as editor of Cook's journals (he was to edit the third journal as well as the second). This time no notorious financial deal with a publisher was announced, and Douglas did his best to keep his own name out of the papers. Aware of the storm raised against Hawkesworth's interpolations, he claimed in his introduction to the second journal that it had hardly needed editing at all, and that he had merely altered 'a few inaccuracies in style'. He was very angry when the *Morning Chronicle* later identified him as the man who had 'digested and corrected' the second journal, and who is 'finishing grammatically the last'. However, when he came, towards the end of his life, to write some autobiographical notes for his children, Douglas admitted he had done rather more to the third journal. He wrote, 'the Journal if printed as the

Captain left it behind him would have been thought too incorrect, and have disgusted the reader . . . the Public never knew, how much they owe to me in this work'.[22]

Douglas hardly stood in need of fame or money as had Hawkesworth, since he possessed other sources of income. His feet were already firmly on the clerical career ladder and his literary services were in demand generally. For instance, at the time he edited the second journal he was also helping Lord Hardwicke, the Lord Chancellor, publish various volumes of state papers, and while editing the third he was simultaneously employed in upgrading the catalogues of the royal libraries at Windsor and Kew. His intention on taking on the journals was probably not so much financial as to gain royal favour. George III was known to be interested in Cook, and he it was who decided which clergymen were worthy of promotion to a bishopric. As Hardwicke wrote to Douglas, 'I hope your Great Friend at Windsor will take yr laudable labours into his Serious Consideration before the reward may have lost its Flavour and Merit.'[23] Presumably, the king did eventually take them into consideration, since Douglas did become a bishop, first of Carlisle, and then of Salisbury.

'As for the Journal, it must speak for itself. I can only say that it is my own narrative, and as it was written during the voyage.'[24] The first part of this statement by Cook about his second journal is correct, in that Douglas as editor generally made only minor changes regarding style, spelling and punctuation. The second part is not quite so truthful owing to the many hours Cook had spent in revision, both at sea and after he came home, so that the end result is a long way from a day-to-day record of events. There was also at least one passage which Douglas decided to excise completely, a passage in which Cook accuses Europeans, with their insatiable sexual demands, of having corrupted the morals of the New Zealand natives, as well as passing on venereal disease. Cook writes:

> we debauch their Morals already too prone to vice and we interduce among them wants and perhaps diseases which they never before knew and which serves only to disturb that happy tranquillity they and their fore Fathers has injoy'd. If any one denies the truth of this assertion let him tell me what the Natives of the whole extent of America have gained by the commerce they have had with Europeans.

Douglas may have decided this was a little too radical for his potential readership.[25]

This passage apart, the journal of the second voyage reached the public in a state very close to how Cook had written it – the only one of the three journals

*John Douglas (1721–1807), bishop of Carlisle, in his episcopal robes. Douglas was the editor
of the journals of Cook's second and third voyages, an undertaking which may have
influenced George III to make him a bishop. An engraving by Bartolozzi.*

to do so. But when it came to editing the third journal, with Cook himself no
longer there to keep an eye on things, it was a different story. Douglas trans-
formed the text in a fashion almost – though not quite – reminiscent of
Hawkesworth. In the first place, he used the journal of William Anderson,
surgeon on the *Resolution*, to supplement Cook, rather as Hawkesworth had
used Banks. Anderson was young, energetic, observant and articulate, and
interested especially in ethnology and natural history – in other words, a second

Banks. Beaglehole lists 16 topics, most of them several pages long, in which Douglas took Anderson's words and put them into Cook's mouth, sometimes with acknowledgement, more often without.[26] Then there were also Douglas's own reflections – admittedly much less numerous than Hawkesworth's, but nevertheless obtrusive. For example, at the start of the voyage Cook noted that several ships containing a division of Hessian troops bound for America were with them in Plymouth Sound waiting for a favourable wind. Douglas draws a sententious moral:

> It could not but occur to us as a singular and affecting circumstance, that at the very instant of our departure upon a voyage, the object of which was to benefit Europe by making fresh discoveries in North America, there should be the unhappy necessity of employing others of his Majesty's ships, and of conveying numerous bodies of land forces, to secure the obedience of those parts of that continent which had been discovered and settled by our countrymen in the last century.[27]

Another example when we have Douglas instead of Cook is when he makes Cook as author quote a long and totally fictitious farewell speech by Omai when he was about to be returned to Huahine. Douglas seems to realize he had gone rather too far on this occasion as he has Cook then write, 'Perhaps I have here made a better speech for my friend than he actually delivered.' And a few pages later, here is Douglas on why revolution is always unlikely in a civilized country – a very Hawkesworthian topic, and hardly the sort of thing Cook would ever have written:

> A man who is richer than his neighbours is sure to be envied by numbers who would see him brought down to their own level. But in countries where civilization, law, and religion, impose their restraints, the rich have a reasonable ground of security. And, besides, there being, in all such communities, a diffusion of property, no single individual need fear, that the efforts of all the poorer sort can ever be united to injure him, exclusively of others who are equally the object of envy . . .[28]

Throughout this journal Douglas radically 'improves' Cook's vocabulary, making it more long-winded and ornate, and frequently he extends Cook's words with phrases or sentences of his own. It would be tedious to spend much time giving examples; nevertheless, here are a couple of short ones, both relating to the extra sentence which adds nothing to the sense. When Cook writes: 'From the time of our putting into this place [Nootka Sound] till now we have had exceedingly fine weather without either Wind or rain; but in the Morning of the 8th the Wind freshened at SE', Douglas makes this: 'From the time of our putting into the Sound till now, the weather had been exceedingly fine, without either wind or rain. That comfort, at the very moment when the continuance of it would have been of most service, was withdrawn. In the morning of the 8th, the wind freshened at South East.'[29] Secondly, on saying goodbye to a chief at Nootka, Cook writes: 'He as also many others importuned us much to return to them again and by way of incouragement promised to lay in a good stock of skins for us, and I have not the least doubt but they will.' Douglas expands this to: 'He and also many others of his countrymen, importuned us much to pay them another visit; and by way of encouragement, promised to lay in a good stock of skins. I make no doubt, that whoever comes after me to this place, will find the natives prepared accordingly, with no inconsiderable supply of an article of trade, which, they could observe, we were eager to possess; and which we found could be purchased to great advantage.'[30] The result of all this is to make Cook sound like a rather pompous literary gentleman, and also to make the journal much longer than it would have been, which presumably fitted in with the publisher's wish to bring out a three-volume work on the voyage.

In an implied attack on Douglas's editorship, the *Morning Chronicle* of 18 January, 1783 wrote: 'Surely these Marine Gentlemen's [Anson's and Cook's] narratives must have been better told by themselves than by those uninterested in their scenes of pleasure and distress.'[31] It was not until 1893 that Cook's *Endeavour* journal was published more or less intact, and not until Beaglehole in 1967 that the third journal was similarly published.

Chapter 4

Journals as History

In his introduction to the twentieth-century edition of Cook's voyages, Malcolm Letts, president of the Hakluyt Society, writes, 'as a basis of scholarship neither Hawkesworth the *litérateur* nor Douglas the bishop can now be regarded as satisfactory'.[1] A new, scholarly edition for all the voyages was required, based as closely as possible on what Cook actually wrote in his journals. This would be an enormously demanding project, as manuscripts of Cook's journals as well as other journals and logs and much further relevant material were widely scattered among various archives, or in private hands, in England and abroad. Wide-ranging research and long and patient scholarship over many years would evidently be needed. The historian who chose to undertake this massive task was John Cawte Beaglehole, a New Zealander who had already spent much of his career investigating Cook. This chapter is about Beaglehole's work, and about the nature of the journals which he edited.

As a young graduate Beaglehole had obtained a scholarship in 1926 to study at the London School of Economics (LSE), and he had spent three years in London, being much influenced at the time by left-wing teachers such as Harold Laski and R. H. Tawney. After returning to his own country he worked as a Workers' Educational Association (WEA) lecturer before starting to establish an academic reputation with his first major book, *The Exploration of the Pacific*, in 1934, after which he tended to concentrate more and more on Cook. He became something of a polymath, with interests ranging from poetry and music to typography and book production. He also involved himself in issues of civil liberties, and for some time found it difficult to find an academic post, owing to his reputation as a radical. Eventually he became lecturer – later professor – at the Victoria University of Wellington.

Beaglehole became well-known internationally with his work on Cook's journals, which brought out his great gifts as historian and editor. It was not all desk work among the archives – he also travelled in Cook's wake, from

Whitby to Tahiti, to Tonga and to the New Hebrides. The four volumes that emerged between 1955 and 1967, which were subsidised by the New Zealand government, contained not only Cook's journals but also a mass of other contemporary material. The sheer size of the volumes, each of them approaching 1000 pages, seems disconcerting at first sight, but Beaglehole's long introductions intended to put the journals in context are very readable because written in a lucid, often witty or ironic style, a style which is, to make a very obvious point, a world apart from Cook's own.

For his edition of the journals, Beaglehole sought out the various surviving holograph journals of Cook in preference to copies by his clerks and others. For the first voyage he used the manuscript journal written by Cook now in the National Library of Australia at Canberra, and which only came to light when it was put up for sale in London in 1923.[2] Before this, it had been generally assumed that no journal of the voyage in Cook's handwriting had survived. When Admiral Wharton published a version of the journal in 1893, he used the copy made by Richard Orton, Cook's clerk, which had been shipped back to the Admiralty from Batavia, and even Arthur Kitson, who wrote a biography of Cook in 1912, believed that only copies of Cook's work existed. The story of the emergence of the holograph *Endeavour* journal in 1923 concerns Henry Bolckow, a nineteenth-century industrial magnate from Middlesbrough. Bolckow was a self-made tycoon who started life in a remote village in Prussia and emigrated to Newcastle when he was twenty years old. He later became wealthy through being one of the first to exploit the iron ore deposits near Middlesbrough, but according to his biographer he was confronted throughout his life with the problem of how best to assimilate himself into English culture. One of the ways he attempted to do this was by purchasing an estate in Marton, near Middlesbrough, which included the hamlet where Cook was born, and then seeking to collect documents and memorabilia associated with this English hero.[3] In 1868 Bolckow bought Cook's holograph *Endeavour* journal at a London auction, probably from relatives of Elizabeth Cook, his widow, but it seems that he did not broadcast his ownership of it. It was long after Bolckow's death, when his trustees again put the journal up for sale, that it finally came into public ownership.

For the second voyage Beaglehole used two other partial journals in Cook's hand, both of which had the same early history as the *Endeavour* journal.[4] All three were probably once owned by his widow, and sold by one of her relations at the same auction, in 1868. The difference was that these two manuscripts were not purchased by Bolckow but by the British Museum, and hence have been available for public consultation ever since their purchase. And for the third voyage Beaglehole's main source was a journal written and much revised

*John Cawte Beaglehole, OM (1901–71), the New Zealand scholar who edited Cook's
journals in four massive volumes between 1955 and 1967. His biography of Cook,
almost completed when he died, was published posthumously by his son. Portrait by
Bill Sutton.*

by Cook up to early January 1779, a month before he died. No one knows what
happened to the final month's entries, which he must certainly have made.[5]
This manuscript, too, is now held at the British Library although its history is
different. It was apparently retained by John Douglas, who had been lent it

by the Admiralty in order to edit it for the press, and so it passed on to his heirs, who sold it to the British Museum in 1872. As Beaglehole points out, it was bought back by the nation from those to whom it did not belong.

Before his death, in 1971, Beaglehole was in the process of revising the typescript of his biography of Cook, which was then seen through the press by his son, and which immediately became the acknowledged definitive biography. He died loaded with many honours, from his own country and abroad, among which was the Order of Merit. He was only the second New Zealander ever to be awarded this, the first being the nuclear physicist, Ernest Rutherford. Today it is quite impossible to write about Cook without an enormous debt to Beaglehole. In fact one might go further and say that there is some difficulty in visualising Cook at all except through Beaglehole's spectacles. Precisely because his work was so thorough and all-embracing, it is awkward for post-Beaglehole students of Cook to break away from his influence and come up with fresh insights. After Cook's death, there were available to the public only Hawkesworth-Cook and Douglas-Cook, and in contrast, during the last half century, the only feasible option open to serious enquirers has been Beaglehole-Cook, that is to say, Cook as mediated by the third and greatest of his editors. It is with trepidation, therefore, that one has the temerity to attempt any criticisms of this formidable authority. Nevertheless, it is also true that Beaglehole's work is, by and large, a continuation of the long tradition of Cook idealisation, a tradition from which recent research has started to disassociate itself.[6]

Beaglehole's Cook is a heroic figure who surmounted every kind of difficulty to achieve remarkable ends, a genius equal to every challenge, and who seldom puts a foot wrong. He presents a view of Cook, as a supremely practical, no-nonsense genius, and on the rare occasions when his hero apparently seems to fall short of this image, he is censorious. For instance, in the well known passage in which Cook expresses admiration for the lifestyle of the Australian aborigines, Beaglehole describes this as 'the conventional attitudinising of the day when considering extremely naked and dirty savages', and suggests ironically that Cook must have spent the voyage reading Rousseau.[7] He also takes a jaundiced view of those who had the effrontery to ever criticise his hero. These included Alexander Dalrymple, who allegedly suffered a life-long grudge against Cook for having been passed over as commander of the *Endeavour*, and who 'could be very foolish', and suffered from a 'lack of balance'.[8] Another such was John Reinhold Forster the naturalist, who accompanied Cook on the second voyage and sometimes argued with him, and about whom Beaglehole has little good, and much derogatory to say. Post-Beaglehole scholarship has now to some extent rehabilitated both Dalrymple and Forster from these verdicts.[9]

Beaglehole's editions of Cook's journals also contain lengthy extracts from the journals of Cook's colleagues, as well as a mass of further documentation including letters written to Cook, and by him, and extracts from contemporary newspapers. Nevertheless, his selection of which journals and documents to publish was inevitably influenced by his views as to their significance, which was tied up with their attitude to Cook. To take one obvious example, in July 1776, after his second voyage, Cook wrote a letter to Sir John Pringle, president of the Royal Society, explaining what had been done during the voyage to reduce the risk of scurvy. However, Beaglehole does not give us the text of this important document, although he prints many other letters connected with the voyages written during that particular month, some of them quite trivial. Is this because Cook clearly but mistakenly states that citrus fruits were less important as a remedy against scurvy than other remedies, especially malt? As regards extracts from other journals, Beaglehole chose not to print any substantial part of the anonymous journal attributed to James Magra from the first voyage, a journal which, as he points out, is the only one from that voyage frequently to display Cook in a disadvantageous light.[10] Nor does he print extracts from the two journalists of the third voyage who were perhaps the strongest critics of their captain, George Gilbert, a midshipman, and the Corporal of Marines, John Ledyard.[11]

In the voluminous introductions and footnotes to his editions of the journals, as well as in his biography of Cook, Beaglehole used a vast range of sources, including works on the history and sociology of Pacific islands, modern charts and aids to navigation, reference books on botany, zoology, and much else. Clearly his main sources, however, were the surviving logs and journals of the voyages themselves. At this point it might be appropriate to make clear the distinction between a naval log and a journal, with a view to moving on to discuss the nature of Cook's journals considered as historical sources.

Every naval vessel kept a ship's log as an official record of distances travelled, compass bearings, weather, and significant events relating to the voyage. Such logs, usually written in Cook's day by the master, do not as a rule express opinions, ascribe causes, or make comments of any sort – they merely set out 'the facts'. Officers also sometimes kept their own logs instead of, or in addition to, journals, and the distinction between the two is often blurred, as is borne out by some of Beaglehole's comments, when, for instance, he describes one as 'a log rather than a journal, in spite of the name', and another as 'unambiguously a log, with nothing much in it'.[12] The following is an extract from Cook's log of August, 1764, when, as master and commander of the *Grenville*, he was engaged in a survey of the coastline of Newfoundland and there occurred the accident which permanently scarred his hand:

Sunday 5th   Cape Norman SW 1 Mile

The first part strong gales and very hard squalls, the middle fresh gales and Cloudy, Later moderate. at 3 pm wore and stood to the Northward, found the Lining of the Foresail gone, hauld it down, mended it, Close Reeved it and Set it. at 8 Cape de Grat on the Island of Quirpon SWbS, the white Island SbW¼W, the middle of Belleisle NEbN. at 8 Cape Norman WSW, middle of Belleisle EbN.

Monday 6th   At anchor in Noddy Harbour, the Island NNE¾E

Moderate Breezes and fair w. at 2 pm came on board the Cutter with the master who unfortunately had a Large Powder Horn blown up and Burst in His Hand which shatter'd it in a Terrible manner, and one of the people which was hard by Suffered greatly by the same accident, and having no Surgeon on board Bore away for noddy Harbour where a French fishing ship Lay at anchor in Noddy Harbour.

Tuesday 7th   D°

Fresh gales and fair w. Employ'd getting water on board and making Nettles and gaskets for the sails.[13]

The account of the accident given here is about as descriptive and as close to narrative, as this particular log ever gets. On the whole, ships' logs tend to consist of a series of disconnected statements, related to each other only by chronology, and to this extent they might be compared to those early medieval chronicles which merely list battles, epidemics and the succession of kings, without further commentary. Both ship's log and monkish chronicle are un-processed records containing separate fragments that require to be knit together through some enabling pattern before they can become interesting and meaning-ful to us. In themselves they may contain much potentially useful information, but this potential can only be realized when they are processed and converted into narrative form. Logs, along with other official documents, together with images and other types of artefact, come into Arthur Marwick's well known category of 'unwitting' sources, in other words, objects which may well prove of use to future historians but which were not created with posterity in mind.

To illustrate this point with another example from the same category, one might quote a brief letter from Cook:

Cook to Admiralty Secretary, 14 December 1771.

Having some business to transact down in Yorkshire as well as to see an Aged father, please to move my Lords Commissioners of the Admiralty to grant me three Weeks leave of absaance [*sic*] for that purpose.[14]

By itself this letter is mute. To become part of history it needs to be embedded by a historian into an interpretative reading along with other similar documents, and in his biography of Cook, Beaglehole performs this task. He quotes the letter, inserts it into his narrative, explains about Cook's father, and how as a widower he was now about to move to his married daughter's house. He also discusses Cook's mode of transport, whom else he might have wanted to visit in Yorkshire, and whether or not he might have been accompanied on this trip by his young wife.[15]

We now move on to consider the role of a journalist such as Cook, who, in a comparable way to the subsequent historian, performs an interpretative function by extending the ship's log into a journal, in other words, into a coherent narrative. It is true that the journal still employs the day-to-day chronology of the log, and may contain many statements which are not incorporated into any general pattern, but nevertheless it differs from the log in that much of its content has been shaped with the help of bridging passages. These typically involve explanations, causal linkages, passages of speculation, references to other parts of the journal, and so forth. 'The diary', says Robert Latham, the most recent editor of Pepys's *Diary*, 'has the effect of imposing a factitious order on the succession of often random events that make up each day's experience' and the same applies to the journal of a voyage of discovery.[16] Latham might have added that the order imposed will necessarily concern only a tiny selection of the day's random events. There is an additional issue here about the suitability of writing, which is a relatively slow and cumbersome process, as a medium for recording real events. It stands to reason that no diarist can begin to record literally everything that happened during his day. In fact, he could hardly record truthfully the events of one hour – perhaps not even of one minute. This failure to record, or represent, the totality of experience has been a source of anxiety for diarists and others at least since Rousseau.

The author of a journal makes his own selection of events to be recorded and the linkages he makes between these events are also his own interpretation, which necessarily depends on his personal position and motives. There must therefore always exist the possibility of other selections, and other alternative readings, from different standpoints. The past and its traces may be mute until processed, but they are then open to infinite reprocessing and re-description. Cook's particular standpoint as the author of his journals is clear, although his motives for writing might have altered from voyage to voyage. On his first voyage he is producing, for his superiors at the Admiralty, a report which justifies his actions, and explains how he has fulfilled their original instructions. On the second and third voyages he is doing the same, but there is an additional function, in that he now has it in mind to publish his journals, in order to make them accessible to the general public. Consequently, he is concerned to fashion them into lively and readable travel narratives. Above all, he is, throughout all the journals, presenting not only his voyages but also a portrait of himself – as unchallenged commander, as successful explorer and navigator, as sympathetic humanist. This concern with self-presentation is of course not something peculiar to Cook. It can surely be argued that those who write about themselves in any context are inevitably involving themselves in some kind of public relations exercise, whether aimed exclusively at their contemporaries, or also with an eye to posthumous reputation.

When composing his journals Cook is thus in some sense taking on the role of a historian, and seeking to impose a particular pattern on the evidence available. Through his choice of language and the structure of his narrative he gives a meaning to the events of the voyage, and in this fashion he is performing a function which is also to some extent subsequently elaborated and repeated by the various editors of his journals – including Beaglehole two centuries later. To put this in another way, one might argue that any post-Beaglehole commentator on Cook's voyages is confronted, not so much with the unvarnished facts involving any particular sequence of events, but rather with the literary efforts of two editor/historians, Cook himself and Beaglehole, to render those facts meaningful.

However, while the modern historian's version of events can always be challenged by someone writing from a different perspective, the author of a historical journal is in a more privileged position. The journal, with its personal testimony, has itself turned into an item of historical evidence, a treasured relic of the past, and the version of history enshrined within it has become, as it were, crystallised. And when the main source for a voyage of discovery is the captain's own account, there is an additional difficulty. Alternative source material has often been controlled, or is unavailable. Take, as an example, the voyage of the *Endeavour*. On this voyage, eleven other officers or crew members also kept journals, and these have mostly found their way to the National

Archives at Kew, where anyone can read them and compare them with Cook's version of events. But this exercise turns out to be hardly worth doing. The other journals tend to be highly uniform in style and content, copied as they are from each other and from the ship's log. To take a trivial example, on 1 October 1769 the log records, 'Saw a seal asleep in the water, holding one of its fins up, it appearing like a crooked Billet' (i.e. a log of wood), and it turns out that most of the journals record the same seal, in very much the same wording. As Beaglehole comments, 'this, one is persuaded, was the most observed seal, and this the most overworked simile, in the entire South Pacific'.[17]

These authors were naval personnel with their careers to consider, and all knew that their efforts would be handed in to the Admiralty at the end of the voyage. They – the officers among them at least – had been instructed to keep a journal, but most of them were not particularly proficient at the task. There was, too, a need for caution. It might well be true, as Beaglehole points out, that probably no official person ever bothered to read any journal but Cook's, but who could be sure of this?[18] All in all, they were unlikely to come up with anything very different from their captain – and certainly not anything critical or derogatory.

True, there were also three civilians on board who kept journals and who were not bound by the same rules as the naval personnel. These were the artist, Sydney Parkinson, the astronomer, Charles Green, and the rich young botanist, Joseph Banks. Of these, Green tends to concentrate on scientific issues, such as his attempts to teach midshipmen how to calculate longitude. Parkinson is readable, but brief, and only Bank's journal – lively, perceptive, and quarter of a million words long – is worthy of comparison with Cook's own. Banks is particularly good on Tahiti because he had the time and energy to make friends among the islanders, while Cook was preoccupied with other matters such as refitting the ship and organising observations of the Transit of Venus.

However, it seems clear that Banks and Cook always cooperated closely when it came to writing journals. So closely, in fact, that Cook incorporated considerable portions of Banks's journal into his own.[19] And usually their versions of events totally coincide. However, as any reporter can verify, when it comes to a complex event, especially one involving large numbers of people, there is often a problem working out exactly what happened, and eye-witnesses' accounts do not always match up. Take, for instance, a fairly common scenario during the voyages. A crowd of natives confronts Cook and his men. There is a problem of communication, and the behaviour of the crowd is unpredictable. The two groups mingle, there is much shouting and confusion and suddenly some incident occurs – perhaps a gun is fired and someone wounded or killed. Human nature being as it is, probably no two independent sources would subsequently agree about exactly what happened in a case like this and there will be conflicting accounts. Yet frequently we have in effect only Cook's version – the official version – of such events. There may be accounts in other journals, but in describing a sensitive episode like this, the others are hardly likely to diverge from Cook. Very likely, Cook would have held a *post mortem* on the event with those most concerned, so that an agreed version of the facts could be arrived at. This agreed version, later to be handed to the Admiralty, might describe how the unfortunate incident occurred, and how it was that the behaviour of the islanders left little alternative but for the commander to take the course of action he did. It would show that he was fully in command throughout, and explain the logic of his decisions.

Yet in spite of Cook's close collaboration with Banks it is sometimes possible to detect small contradictions or gaps between the two accounts, and this is the case with the fracas at Poverty Bay in October 1769, shortly after Cook's first landing on New Zealand soil. Here is the account from Cook's journal:

Mr Banks Dr Solander and my self at first only landed and went to the side of the river, the natives being got together on the opposite side. We call'd to them in the George Island Language [i.e. the language of Tahiti] but they answered us by flourishing their weapons over their heads and dancing, as we supposed the war dance; upon this we retired untill the marines were landed which I order'd to be drawn up about two hundred yards behind us. We then went again to the river side having Tupia Mr Green and Dr Munkhouse along with us. Tupia spoke to them in his own language and it was an [a]greeable surprise to us to find that they perfectly understood him. After some little conversation had pass'd one of them swam over to us and after him 20 or 30 more, these last brought their arms with them which the first man did not, we made them every one presents but this did not satisfy them they wanted but everything we had about us particularly our arms, and made several attempts to snatch them out of our hands. Tupia told us several times as soon as they came over to take care of our selves for they were not our friends, and this we very soon found for one of them snatched Mr Greens Hanger [i.e. small-sword, worn at the hip] from him and would not give it up, this encouraged the rest to be more insolent and seeing others comeing over to join them I order'd the man who had taken the hanger to be fired at, which was accordingly done and wounded in such a manner that he died soon after.[20]

For this episode it so happens that we also possess not only Banks's account but an earlier, fragmentary draft written by Cook. On comparing the three versions, certain discrepancies become apparent:

1. How many were in the group that confronted the natives near the river bank? Cook says six, and names them, but Banks writes, 'we were only five in number'.
2. How far away from this group were the marines drawn up? Cook says 'about two hundred yards', yet in his draft he says 100 yards, and Banks gives it as 50 yards. Of course, the further away the marines were, the more isolated was the group, and hence perhaps the more justified in taking the action they did.
3. Were the muskets loaded with small shot, or the more lethal ball? Cook says that only Monkhouse's musket had ball, the rest shot, but Banks says two of the muskets were loaded with ball.
4. Who gave the order to shoot? Cook says he did, but Banks's version is as follows:

> It now appeard necessary for our safeties that so daring an act should be instantly punishd, this I pronouncd aloud as my opinion, the Captn and the rest Joind me on which I fird my musket which was loaded with small shot, levelling it between his shoulders who was not 15 yards from me. On the shot striking him he ceasd his cry but instead of quitting his prize continued to wave it over his head retreating as gently as before; the surgeon who was nearer him, seeing this fird a ball at him at which he dropd.[21]

This fourth point is perhaps the most significant, as Banks's account seems to suggest that members of the group took action on their own initiative, thus calling into question Cook's general command of the situation. However, I list these discrepancies not to suggest that Cook's final version is necessarily inaccurate, but merely to show that, when we do happen to have additional contemporary accounts of a particular event, such discrepancies are likely to arise. It goes without saying that if we had a Maori account of the same encounter there would be far more discrepancies. Unfortunately, for much of the narrative of Cook's voyages we have to rely mainly on the captain's final and official version. As Edward Said might have put it, the power to narrate belonged to Cook. *The Odyssey* comes to us courtesy of Odysseus.

In the end we may just have to accept this version as authoritative, but on the way we can always interrogate it a little. For example, is Cook's account of the first voyage relatively comprehensive, or did he edit his narrative by leaving out certain important events, perhaps because they reflected badly on his status as commander? According to James Magra, a midshipman on the *Endeavour*, a mutiny was projected 'by most of the people' during their stay at Tahiti. It is true that Magra seems to have been disliked by Cook, who described him as 'one of those gentlemen, frequently found onboard Kings Ships, that can very well be spared, or to speake more planer good for nothing'.[22] Nevertheless, he later had a distinguished career, and was British consul in Tangier at the time he wrote about the mutiny. Together with Joseph Banks, he is credited with having first persuaded the British government to dispatch convicts to Botany Bay. Beaglehole dismisses Magra's statement as 'a vague story', but it is fairly specific. For instance, he gives the names of two ring-leaders, as well as the reason the scheme failed, which was the general fear of catching 'the Pox' if they stayed on the island. But there is no mention of mutiny in Cook's journal.

Take another example from the first voyage, the curious case of Patrick Saunders, the midshipman who jumped ship in Batavia shortly before the end of the voyage, and was never heard of again. He was the only member of the crew, officers or men, to desert during the entire three years of the voyage (others tried − in Tahiti − but were recaptured). According to Parkinson, Saunders left because he was suspected of having cut off part of the ears of Richard Orton, Cook's clerk, as he lay in his cabin in a drunken stupor. This episode occurred seven months earlier, but Cook had never discovered the culprits though he obviously felt strongly about it because he offered a reward for information. The question here, however, is not why Saunders chose to quit, but why Cook does not mention his departure (he does not mention about offering the reward either). On the day that Saunders left, Cook writes at length on other matters, such as the loading of stores on board the *Endeavour*, and also a dispute he was having with the Dutch authorities concerning an Irish seaman who had volunteered to join the ship, but there is no mention of Saunders.[23] Nor is there any reference to him in the ship's log, or in the other journals (except Parkinson's). He seems to have been air-brushed from history.

About the other two voyages, and especially the third, it is sometimes easier to balance Cook's account with evidence from the journals of other officers, which tend to be more independent, and even sometimes more critical of Cook, than is the case during the first voyage. Why this might be so is uncertain, but possibly it was felt there was more to criticise, particularly during the third voyage, and perhaps also by this time officers were becoming aware of the commercial possibilities of a lively narrative of exploration. For whatever reason, it is possible to use the other journals of the later voyages to fill in gaps in Cook's account, or to question it, in a way that is not possible for the earlier voyage. An obvious example is the question of punishment. In the journal of the third voyage – unlike in the others – Cook rarely mentions punishing anyone, either natives or crew, and the official ship's log of the *Resolution*, which might have noted punishments, has not survived. However, Anne Salmond has calculated, using the journals of the other officers and midshipmen, that there were seventy-one floggings of seamen from the ship during the voyage – a much higher number than for the other two voyages.[24] Clearly, Cook felt it unnecessary to mention such unpleasant events in a book aimed at the general public, but their omission tends to bring into question the authenticity of the journal as a true record of the voyage.

To sum up, journals are problematical texts due to their dual nature as historical sources or traces of the past on the one hand, and as themselves examples of history-making on the other. Cook's journals in particular are awkward to assess, for reasons connected with their official status, as well as with the constant revision to which they have been subjected. Not only all that, but also these journals are today presented to us cocooned by the formidable scholarship and strong opinions of a second historian, John Beaglehole, who has formed a powerful alliance with the original journalist. In spite of such obstacles no doubt those interested in Cook will continue to form their own judgements, however subjective, bearing in mind that in history the possibility of alternative readings can never be excluded, even though the freedom to make them may at times seem unwarranted, or even subversive.

Chapter 5

Journals as Narrative

I want to say a little more about the nature of Cook's journals and in particular about their process of composition. Consider this typical passage from the second voyage:

> Tuesday 4th [Jan.1774] Fresh gales and Clowdy with some Showers of Sleet. In the pm saw a few more of the small divers, and some small pieces of weed which appeard to be old and decayed and not as if it had lately been broke from rocks. I can not tell what to think of the divers, had there been more of them I should have thought them signs of the vicinity of land . . . As the wind seems now fixed in the western board, we shall be under a necessity of leaving unexplored to the west a space of Sea containing 40° of Longitude and 20° or 21° of Latitude, had the wind been favourable I intended to have run 15° or 20° of longitude to the west in the Latitude we are now in and back again to the East in the Latitude of 50° or near it, this rout would have so intersected the space above mentioned as to have hardly left room for the bare supposission of any large land lying there. Indeed as it is we have no reason to suppose that there is any for we have had now for these several days past a great swell from west and NW, a great sign we have not been covered by any land between these two points. In the AM saw some Pie bald porpuses.[1]

There is a freshness and immediacy about this passage which strikes home. The self-questioning and the tenses used ('I cannot tell what to think'; 'we have no reason to suppose') seem to show these were the actual words Cook wrote on or near that particular date. Perhaps we can visualize James Cook sitting down at his candle-lit table of a tropical evening in the Great Cabin at the stern of his ship, dipping his quill in the ink and setting about composing his entry for the day, an entry which we, two and a half centuries later, are privileged to be able to read. No doubt memories flooded into his mind and were committed to paper – events and scenes he had witnessed or been told about during the day, encounters with natives or conversations he had held with his officers, or – as here – debates with himself as to what to think and where to go next. However, many other entries in the journals lack that sense of immediacy, and instead there are clear signs of hindsight and redrafting. For instance, in December 1773, when the ice forced them back, having reached as far as 67° South, Cook justifies his decision in terms which strongly suggest the entry was written some time later. Here we seem to see a later self reflecting on what an earlier self did:

> Under all these unfavourable circumstances it was natural for me to think of returning more to the North, seeing there was no probability of finding land here nor a possibility of getting farther to the South and to have proceeded to the east in this Latitude would not have been prudent as well on account of the ice as the vast space of Sea we must have left to the north unexplored, a space of 24° of Latitude in which a large track of land might lie, this point could only be determined by making a stretch to the North.[2]

A few weeks earlier there is a small phrase that seems to prove a revision of the entry took place long after the event. Cook is at Queen Charlotte Sound in New Zealand, having recently lost touch with his sister ship, the *Adventure*. He writes, 'I dispair of seeing her any more but am totally at a loss to conceive what is to become of her till now.'[3] This passage was allegedly written in November 1773, but the words, 'till now', imply that Cook revised it sometime after he heard, sixteen months later, in March 1775, that in fact the *Adventure* was safe. Other small phrases which are clear signs of revision occur throughout the journals (e.g. 'Cape Farewell (afterwise so called)'; 'it was at this time thought that').

This evidence of hindsight is due to the journals' process of production. That peaceful image of Cook composing his day's entry in the tropical evening, while possibly realistic, is far from being the whole story, and the journals as we have them today were the product of a lengthy genesis. If we take, for instance, the journal of the second voyage, which admittedly is, of the three, the one most worked over and revised, we may infer that the finished journal emerged from the following stages:

1.   The master, Joseph Gilbert, is responsible for composing the ship's log-book, into which are entered daily details of weather, courses, rigging, etc. plus any special events such as accidents or punishments.

2. Cook keeps his own log, again with daily navigational detail on one side of a double open page, and any 'remarkable occurrences' briefly noted on the other side. No doubt he has access to the ship's log when making his entries.

3. At intervals he writes up his log entries into a longer journal, in which the navigational details were reduced and accounts of events greatly expanded. At this stage he might borrow, both as to style and content, from other journals, especially, on this voyage, that of William Wales, the astronomer on the *Resolution*.

4. At some point during the voyage Cook starts a second, revised version of his journal in which he makes further changes, once more expanding his accounts of events, particularly regarding transactions with islanders. This version has entirely disappeared, but a copy of it made by Cook's clerk, William Dawson, which was dispatched from the Cape to the Admiralty in March 1775, has survived.

5. Not content with this, Cook starts a third version of the journal in which he retells the entire story of the voyage as he hopes to have it printed. He does this either in the latter stages of the voyage, or on land after it finishes. This is the version given to Canon Douglas to edit.

6. Douglas makes numerous minor changes to format and style, and the journal is eventually printed in May 1777.

Another, related, issue connected with Cook's need to produce journals which justified his role, is that of plagiarism. Cook borrowed extensively from other people's journals when compiling his own. His borrowings were quite reasonable, given that, as captain, he often did not have the time to examine some of the places visited as closely as some of the others could, especially civilians like Banks. Hence, if Cook were to produce anything like a comprehensive picture of the various islands and their peoples, as was expected of him, he occasionally needed to acquire information from his colleagues. On the *Endeavour* voyage he tends to look to Banks for this service, on the second voyage to the astronomer William Wales, a well-read young man who quotes Shakespeare and Milton in his own journal, and on the third to William Anderson, surgeon on the *Resolution*, who was also a gifted naturalist and linguist.

Cook not only borrowed content from these other writers but sometimes also their style. As Beaglehole remarks with reference to the journal of the second voyage, if Cook comes up with a surprising and uncharacteristic image one can often discover its origin in the pages of Wales.[4] For instance, when describing the reaction of Oediddee, the young Tahitian who was on board the

Resolution during part of the second voyage, to the sight of New Zealand natives cooking and eating human flesh. Cook writes:

> Oediddee was so affected with the sight as to become perfectly motionless and seemed as if metamorphosed into the Statue of horror: it is, utterly impossible for Art to depict that passion with half the force that it appeared in his Countenance when roused from this state by some of us, he burst into tears, continued to weep and scold by turns; told them they were Vile men, and that he neither was nor would be no longer their friend.[5]

Wales's version is as follows:

> . . . when he saw the piece cut off, and the Man eat it, he became perfectly motionless, and seemed as if Metamorphised into the Statue of Horror: it is, I believe, utterly impossible for Art to depict that passion with half the force that it appeared in his Countenance. He continued in this situation untill some of us roused him out of it by talking to him, and then burst into Tears nor could refrain himself the whole Evening afterwards.[6]

These borrowings by Cook from other journalists are rarely acknowledged, although in the third journal he does mention his debt to Anderson when it comes to descriptions of plants. The result of this lack of acknowledgement is that the journals appear as if composed by a single pen, but are in fact to some extent the result of a team effort. The team on the first voyage certainly included Banks and the clerk, Richard Orton, and perhaps, too, the master of the *Endeavour*, Robert Molyneux, who may have been responsible for the ship's log.[7] According to A. M. Lysaght, the editor of the facsimile edition of Banks's *Endeavour* journal, 'the fact that Cook retained the first person singular in plagiarised passages has suggested to many of us through the years that he is recording his own original observations and this has led to an extraordinary under-assessment of Banks's contribution to the voyage and a very consider-able over-assessment of Cook's general knowledge'.[8] In view of all this, it is rather ironic that one of the main criticisms of the editor of Cook's first journal, John Hawkesworth, has always concerned his technique of creating a single ostensible narrator while in fact combining information and ideas from Cook, Banks and himself. It is quite true that Hawkesworth put words into Cook's mouth which Cook never uttered, and that he was therefore guilty of 'the homogenization of the accounts which is so distressing, the smothering of the individuality of the voices of those who were actual witnesses',[9] but could the same not be said about Cook himself? In his recent book, *The Sea Voyage Narrative*, Robert Foulke quotes an important passage from Cook's first journal in which is described the *Endeavour*'s narrow escape from being wrecked on a coral reef. 'The literary qualities of passages such as this are self-evident', according to Foulke, and so they may be, but he omits to point out that many of the more striking phrases in this particular extract ('a dismal valley' between two waves; 'a wall of Coral Rock rising almost perpendicular out of the unfathomable Ocean') are taken directly from Banks.[10]

There are important differences in style between Cook's three journals. When completing his *Endeavour* journal he probably had no idea of writing for the general public, nor of doing more than was expected of any naval commander in producing a journal for official inspection by the Admiralty. He knew, of course, that this voyage was somewhat special, and that he was expected to record as much as possible about the newly discovered lands and their inhabitants. But the journal nevertheless takes the conventional naval form, with daily details of winds, courses sailed, distance run, and latitude and longitude as recorded at noon daily. These facts were originally set out on one side of a double page spread, with brief notes of any unusual occurrences during the day on the other. The day was a naval one, running from noon one day until noon the following day. However, in the case of his second and third journals he was more conscious that he was composing for the public. He inserts phrases through which the author, as it were, addresses the reader directly, for example: 'It may be worth remarking that'; 'A circumstance which I shall now mention'; 'Before I quit New Zealand it will be necessary to give some account of . . .'. And among his potential readership Cook clearly envisages many who may not be conversant with the ways of the sea. He inserts explanations, as in this example from the second journal: 'Some readers that are unacquainted with the manner of Victualing the Navy may wish to know what is meant by whole allowance, which is a daily allowance of Provisions allowed to each person without distinction.' He seems, too, to have a clear idea in his mind as to what might interest his readership. For instance, at another point in the second journal he writes: 'We will now leave the sloops for a while and take a short view of the isles we have lately touched at, for although I have been pretty minute in relating our transactions while among them, so things rather intresting have been omitted.'

As Beaglehole says, referring to the second journal, it is a far cry from the first journal to this sophisticated document. Cook now omits much daily nautical detail, and in the third journal he even gives up on the daily record and spans his narrative across several days, relegating dates to the margin. The later journals are also more personal, with more use of the first person ('I gave the order to'; 'We sought for a suitable anchorage'). Gone are the passive expressions typical of an official report, which are common in the first journal ('Intending to get under sail at high water the Long boat was sent to take up the Kidge anchor'). Characteristic of the later journals are long blow-by-blow accounts of events in which Cook participated personally. A good example is his 4,000 word account of the *inasi* ritual of Tonga, when he stripped to the waist and let his hair down (and in so doing also let himself down, according to one of his officers) in order to be allowed to be present at this secretive religious ceremony. There is nothing in the *Endeavour* journal comparable to this detailed narrative.

There is no doubt that Cook's narrative style improves with practice. In the first journal he often uses words in a repetitive fashion which detracts from the interest of the story. We might, for instance, like to know a little more about what kind of dances and songs were practised by young girls in Tahiti than is told us by the repetition of the word 'indecent' in this extract:

> The young girls when ever they can collect 8 or 10 together dance a very indecent dance which they call Timorodee singing most indecent songs and using most indecent actions in the pratice of which they are brought up from their earlyest Childhood.[11]

Compare this with the far more circumstantial account of the same dance offered on a later occasion by Anderson:

> Most of these were young women, who put themselves into several lascivious postures, clapp'd their hands and repeated a kind of Stanzas which every now and then began afresh. At certain parts they put their garments aside and exposd with seemingly very little sense of shame those parts which most nations have thought it modest to conceal, but in particular a woman more advanc'd in years who stood in front & might properly be calld the tutoress or prompter of the rest, held her cloaths continually up with one hand and dancd with uncommon vigour and effrontery, as if to raise in the spectators the most libidinous desires.[12]

Or take this lively episode involving pick-pocketing in Tahiti, and notice how the word 'thing' is used by Cook to cover not only what was thrown, but also what had been stolen, and even what was offered by Lycurgus as recompense:

Notwithstanding the care we had took Dr Solander and Dr Monkhouse had each of them their pocket pick'd the one of his spyglass and the other of his snuff Box, as soon as Lycurgus was made acquainted with the theift he dispers'd his people in a Moment and the method he made use of was to lay hold of the first thing that came in his way and throw it at them and happy was he or she that could get first out of his way; he seem'd very much concern'd for what had happened and by way of recompense offer'd us but every thing that was in his House, but we refus'd to except of any thing and made signs to him that we only wanted the things back.[13]

In the later journals Cook takes more trouble to expand his vocabulary and make his style more entertaining. He also occasionally employs direct speech when reporting a conversation in order to make the narrative more dramatic, a technique totally absent from the *Endeavour* journal, where he usually uses indirect and more official-sounding constructions ('Mr Banks being of opinion that'; 'Mr Hicks returned with a favourable account of'). An instance of the increased liveliness that results from repeating – or inventing – the actual words spoken is the anecdote concerning an artful Tahitian chief named Tu (or 'Otoo'):

Amongst other things I had at different times given this Chief was a Spy-glass; after he had had it two or three days, and probably fin[ding] it of no use, he carried it privately to Captain Clerke and told him that as he had been his very good friend he had got a present for him which he knew he would like, but says Otoo, "you must not let Toote know it because he wants it and I would not let him have it" and then he put the glass into Captain Clerks hands at the same time assuring him that he came honestly by it. Captain Clerke at first was not for having it, but Otoo insisted upon it and left it with him. Some days after he put Captain Clerke in mind of the Glass, Captain Clerke tho he did not want the glass, being willing to Oblige Otoo and thinking a few axes would be of more use than the Glass, got out four to give him in return which Otoo no sooner saw than he said "Toote offered me five for it" well says Captain Clerke "if that is the case, your friendship for me shall not make you a losser there['s] six for you", these he accepted of but desired again that I might not be told what he had done.[14]

Cook sometimes employs specifically naval terms, which were inevitably ironed out later by his editors. An example, which occurs quite frequently in the *Endeavour* journal but not subsequently, is the verb *shoalden*, meaning 'to become shallow', or 'to find one's soundings becoming shallower', as here: '[26 August 1770] In standing to the NW we began to Shoalden our water from 9 to 7 fathom.' Hawkesworth alters this sentence to read: 'Our depth of water, from the time we weighed till now, was nine fathom, but it soon shallowed to seven fathom'. The linguistic historian, Carol Percy, suggests that *shoalden* was in fact a standard expression for contemporary sailors, and she comments, 'How can one accuse Captain James Cook of using a nautical verb 'incorrectly'?'[15]

Dialect expressions also occasionally make their appearance in the journals, again invariably to be replaced by the editors. Examples of dialect can even be found in the second journal when Cook knew he was writing for the general public. For instance, during a detailed account of a banquet he was given by Oreo, a chief from Raiatea, he writes:

> . . . the chief then asked me if the Victuals should be brought, I told him yes and presently after one of the Pigs came over my head souce upon the leaves and immidiatly after the other, both so hott that it was scarce possible to touch them . . .[16]

Johnson defines 'souse' as 'With sudden violence. A low word.' A few lines later occurs another example of non-standard usage:

> There were several Women at table and no doubt some of them might be in a longing condition but as it is not the Custom here for the Women to eat with the men, we were not delayed or the victuals suffered to cool by carving out their longing bits.

This vivid idiom was admired by Beaglehole, who suggests it might be local to the North Riding of Yorkshire, where Cook was brought up.

The spelling in the *Endeavour* journal is idiosyncratic and weak though it should be pointed out that when it came to weak spelling Cook was in august company. Joseph Banks, who had received an expensive private education and been to Oxford, was not much of a hand at spelling either. But the interesting point is that Cook's spelling definitely improves with practice, and perhaps with exposure to the more secure spellers among his colleagues. It is possible (though tedious) to make quite a long list of words that are spelt wrongly in the *Endeavour* journal, and correctly by the third voyage. Such a list would include: musquet (musket); sellery (celery); viset (visit); corral (coral); shoar (shore); smook (smoke); ax (axe); earbs (herbs) seveliz'd (civilized).[17] Cook's punctuation also becomes more orthodox as time goes on and the passages of twenty or more lines without a full stop which are typical of the first journal, tend to die out later on.

Carol Percy has scanned electronically and analysed the Beaglehole editions of Cook's first and third journals in order to investigate the linguistic differences between the two.[18] One example she gives is of better subject-verb concord in the third journal; for example, the virtual disappearance of 'we was'. Another is the elimination of the *-th* inflection in the third person singular present tense (hath, doth, riseth). A third example is a reduction in the use of 'flat' adverbs identical in form to adjectives; for example, 'the land is tolerable high and hilly', 'the Bay affords plenty of exceeding good wood and water'.

These various improvements in spelling, punctuation and style show Cook's determination to write a 'correct' form of English, as do also his letters to Douglas in the spring and summer of 1776 describing his approval of editorial amendments.[19] It might also be true that the changes noted had something to do with the degree of literacy of the clerks on board Cook's ships, whose tasks included making copies of his successive drafts of the journals, copies which he himself might have copied in later drafts. Beaglehole reckons, for instance, that William Dawson, Cook's clerk on the second voyage, was more literate than Richard Orton on the *Endeavour*. Nevertheless, the main impetus towards linguistic correction must surely have come from Cook himself. As Percy says, he had always been a reader. During his years in America he had read books on astronomy and surveying, and on the first voyage he would have had access to the many volumes of travel and natural history brought on board by Banks. All these could have been models for his own authorial style.

Evidence of how Cook's spelling and style improved as between the first and third journals can perhaps be seen by taking a brief extract from each which happen to be more or less on the same topic. After they had quitted a particular island or coast it was Cook's practice to give a description of the place and its inhabitants, but when it came to saying something about religion he invariably had to admit a degree of ignorance, given the difficulties of language as well as the shortness of their stay. Here is Cook on the religion of the New Zealanders, from the first voyage:

> With respect to Religion I believe these People trouble themselves very little about it. They however beleive that there is one Supream God whome they call Tawney and likewise a number of other inferior Deities, but whether or no they Worship or Pray to either one or the other we know not with any degree of certainty. It is reasonable to suppose that they do and I beleive it, yet I never saw the least action or thing a mong them that tended to prove it. They have the same

notions of the Creation of the World Mankind etc as the People of the South Sea Islands have, indeed many of there Notions and Customs are the very same, but nothing is so great a proff of they all having had one Source as their Language which differs but in a very few words the one from the other . . .[20]

And here is Cook eight years later on religion at Nootka Sound:

I saw nothing that could give us the least insight into their Religion, unless the figures before mentioned called by them Kulmina were really idols as some imigined, but as they frequently mentioned the word Ackweek when they spoke of them they might probably be Monuments of some of their ancestors, and even in this case they may pay them some kind of adoration. But all this is mere conjecture, as may well be supposed, for we never saw any kind of homage paid them and we could gain nothing from information, as we had learnt little more of their language than to ask the names of things and the two simple words yes and no.[21]

To summarize the argument of this chapter: Cook's journals, especially the second and third, are in fact not really journals at all, but rather, carefully crafted accounts of the respective voyages. For the most part they were not composed at the time of the events described, or at least the version which reached publication (either in Cook's time or as recently edited by Beaglehole) was not the same as the version written at the time described. To compensate for this, however, there was a gain in literary sophistication, especially between the first and second journals, as the author gained in experience, and also took vast amounts of trouble over his composition because he was seeking publication. Among Cook's greatest achievements, and one for which he has perhaps not been given enough credit, is his successful apprenticeship in the trade of authorship. How many long, and possibly painful, hours must he have spent at his table 'facing sheets of paper, trying to get the better of recalcitrant words',[22] when he would much rather have been out on his quarterdeck scanning the horizon?

Part II

Cook's Relations with his Colleagues

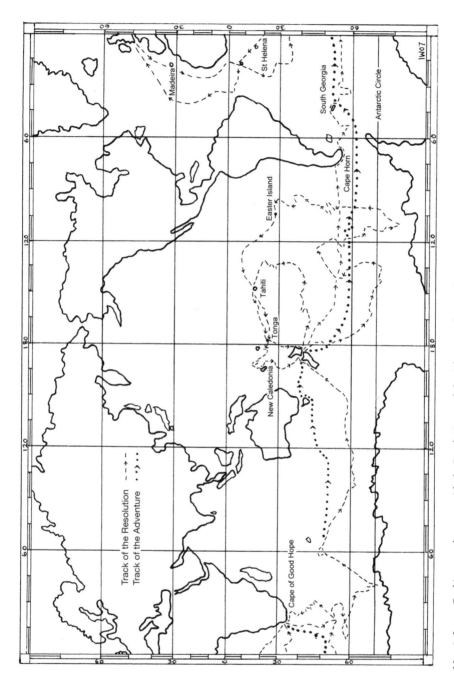

Map 2 *James Cook's second voyage with the Resolution and the Adventure (1772–5)*

Timeline of the
Second Voyage

The Voyage of the *Resolution* and *Adventure*, 1772–5

28 November 1771 Minutes of the Board of Longitude

That the sending out persons in the two ships intended to make discoveries in remote parts and furnishing them, as well as the officers of those ships with astronomical instruments to make observations will render the said expedition more serviceable to the improvement of geography and navigation . . .

That the watch made by Mr. Kendall by order of this Board and now in the possession of the Astronomer Royal be sent out for trial in one of the above ships.

30 November 1771 Admiralty to Cook

Having appointed you Commander of his Majesty's Sloop Drake at Deptford, which we have ordered to be Sheathed, filled, fitted, and Stored at that Place for a Voyage to remote parts, Manned with one Hundred and Ten Men, agreeable to the Scheme here unto annexed, & Victualled for twelve Months for the said Complement with all Species of Provisions except Beer of which she is to have as much as she can conveniently Stow; You are hereby required & directed to use the utmost dispatch in getting her ready for the Sea accordingly, & then falling down to Galleons Reach take in her Guns & Gunners Stores at that place thence proceed to the Nore for further order.

20 December 1771 Lord Rochford to Lord Sandwich

My dear Lord/ I, as well as many others, have been struck with your naming the two ships that are going out the *Raleigh* and the *Drake*; for be assured, though a mere trifle, it will give great offence to the Spaniards. They hold in detestation those two names, and will believe we do it on purpose to insult them.

3 January 1772 Cook to Captain William Hammond, Hull

I am inform'd by letter from Lieut Cooper that the Admiralty have altered the names of the Ships from Drake to Resolution and Raleigh to Adventurer [*sic*] which, in my opinion are much properer than the former.

6 February 1772 Cook to Sandwich

My Lord/ I beg leave to lay before your Lordship . . . my opinion respecting the rout to be pursued by the Resolution and Adventure . . . Upon due consideration of the discoveries that have been made in the Southern Ocean, and the tracks of the Ships which have made these discoveries; it appears that no Southern lands of great extent can extend to the Northward of 40° of Latitude, except about the Meridian of 140° West, every other part of the Southern Ocean have at different times been explored to the northward of the above parallel. Therefore to make new discoveries the Navigator must Traverse or Circumnavigate the Globe in a higher parallel than has hitherto been done, and this will be best accomplished by an Easterly Course on account of the prevailing westerly winds in all high Latitudes.

19 May 1772 Cook to Admiralty Secretary

In concecuence of Lieut Cooper representing to me that the Resolution Sloop under my command was found, upon tryal, to be so Crank [top-heavy] that she would not bear proper sail to be set upon her; I gave it as my opinion that it was owing to the additional works that have been built upon her in order to make large accomodations for the Several Gentlemen Passengers intended to embark in her, and proposed that she might be cut down to her original state, which proposeal I laid before you in my letter of the 14th Inst and likewise attended the Navy Board who were pleased to inform me of the alteration they proposed to make – which alteration, I am of opinion will render her as fit to perform the Voyage as any Ship whatever.

24 May 1772 *Journal of Captain Cook*

M[r] Banks and D[r] Solander came down to take a view of the Sloop as she was now altered and return'd to town again the same even[g] and soon after M[r] Banks declared his resolution not to go the Voyage, aledging that the Sloop was neither roomy nor convenient enough for his purpose, nor noways proper for the Voyage, these were the principal reasons M[r] Banks assign'd for giving up a Voyage the preparing for which had cost him about five Thousand pounds, he probably had others which he did not care to declare, at least whoever saw the Sloop and the apartments that were alloted to him and his people could not help but think so.

3 June 1772 *Navy Board Memorandum*

M[r] Banks seems throughout to consider the Ships as fitted out wholly for his use; the whole undertaking to depend on him and his People; and himself as the Director and Conductor of the whole; for which he is not qualified, and if granted to him, would have been the greatest disgrace that could be put on His Majesty's naval officers.

10 June 1772 *Journal*

Having some business to settle in London I set out for that place in the Even[g] and upon my arrival learnt that M[r] John Reinhold Forster and his Son M[r] George Forster were to imbark with me, gentlemen skill'd in Natural history and Botany but more especially the former, who from the first was desireous of going the Voyage and therefore no sooner heard that M[r] Banks had given it up then he applied to go.

13 July 1772 Journal

Every thing being at length completed we on *Monday* the 13th at Six o'Clock in the morning left Plymouth Sound with the Adventure in Company and stood to the SW.

23 November 1772 Journal

Made several trips to get out of the Bay [Table Bay] which we accomplished by 7 o'Clock at which time the Town [Cape Town] bore SE Distant 4 miles. After having got clear of the land I directed my Course for Cape Circumcision. [an alleged sighting of land thought to be part of the Southern Continent].

3 January 1773 Journal

Lat. In South 59° 18´. I am of opinion that what M. Bouvet took for Land and named Cape Circumcision was nothing but Mountains of Ice surrounded by field Ice.

18 January 1773 Journal

At ¾ past Six, being then in the Latitude of 67°15´S, the Ice was so thick and close that we could proceed no further but were fain to Tack and stand from it. From the mast head I could see nothing to the Southward but Ice . . . I did not think it was consistant with the safty of the Sloops or any ways prudent for me to persevere in going farther to the South as the summer was already half spent and it would have taken up some time to have got round this Ice, even supposing this to have been practicable, which however is doubtful.

10 February 1773 Journal

The Weather was hazey with rain, but towards evening it cleared up so as to see 3 or 4 Leagues [12 to 16 miles] round us and in this state it continued all night, we however kept burning false fires at the mast head and fireing guns every hour, but neither the one nor the other had the desired effect for altho we laid too all the morning we could see nothing of the Adventure which if she had been within 4 or 5 Leagues of us must have been seen from the mast head. Having now spent two Days out of the three assign'd to look for each other, I thought it would be to little purpose to wait any longer.

17 March 1773 Journal

We continued to steer to the East inclining a little to the South till 5 o'Clock in the am at which time we were in the Latitude of 59°7′ S, Long 146°53′ E. We then bore away NE and at Noon steer'e North inclining to the East with a resolution of making the best of my way to *New Holland* or *New Zealand*. If the reader of this Journal desires to know my reasons for taking the resolution just mentioned I desire he will only consider that after crusing four months in these high Latitudes it must be natural for me to wish to injoy some short repose in a harbour where I can procure some refreshments for my people of which they begin to stand in need of, to this point too great attention could not be paid as the Voyage is but in its infancy.

18 May 1773 Journal

At Daylight in the Morn we were the length of Point Jackson at the entrance of Queen Charlotte Sound [on the South Island of New Zealand] and soon after we discovered the Adventure in Ship Cove by the Signals she made.

3 June 1773 Journal

Both Sloops being now ready to put to Sea I gave Captain Furneaux [captain of the *Adventure*] an account in writing of the rout I intended to take which was to proceed immidiately to the East between the latitudes of 41° and 46° untill I arrived in the Longitude of 140° or 135° West and then, providing no land was discovered, to proceed to *Otaheite* [Tahiti], from thence to return back to this place by the Shortest rout, and after takeing in wood and Water to proceed to the South and explore all the unknown parts of the Sea betw^n the Meridian of New Zealand and Cape Horn . . . It may be thought by some an extraordinary step in me to proceed on discoveries as far South as 46° in the very depth of Winter for it must be own'd that this is a Season by no means favourable for discoveries. It nevertheless appear'd to me necessary that something must be done in it, in order to lessen the work I am upon least

I should not be able to finish the discovery of the Southern part of the South Pacific Ocean the insuing Summer.

[The above plan was followed. Cook sailed to Tahiti and the Society Islands, and then returned to New Zealand in October. However, during several days of storms he lost sight of the *Adventure*, and from then on the two ships went their separate ways.]

25 November 1773 *Journal*

This morning before we sailed [from Queen Charlotte's Sound] I wrote a memorandum seting forth the time we arrived last here, the day we sailed, the rout I intended to take & such other information as I thought necessary for Captain Furneaux to know and buried it in a bottle under the root of a tree in the garden in the bottom of the Cove in such a manner that it must be found by any European who may put into the Cove.

30 January 1774 *Journal*

A little after 4 AM we precieved the Clowds to the South near the horizon to be of an unusual Snow white brightness which denounced our approach to field ice, soon after it was seen from the Mast-head and at 8 o'Clock we were close to the edge of it which extended East and West in a straight line far beyond our sight . . . The outer or Northern edge of this immence Ice field was composed of loose or broken ice so closely packed together that nothing could enter it; about a Mile in began the firm ice, in one compact solid boddy and seemed to increase in height as you traced it to the South; In this field we counted Ninety Seven Ice Hills or Mountains, many of them vastly large . . . Sence therefore we could not proceed one Inch farther South, no other reason need be assigned for our Tacking and stretcing back to the North, being at that time in the latitude of 71°10′ South, Longitude 106°54′ W. [This was farther south than any ship in history had yet sailed]

6 February 1774 *Journal*

I now came to a resolution to proceed to the North and to spend the insuing Winter within the Tropick, if I met with no employment before I came there I was now well satisfied no Continent was to be found in this Ocean but what must lie so far to the South as to be wholy inaccessable for Ice . . . But for me at this time to have quited this Southern Pacifick Ocean, with a good Ship, expressly sent out on discoveries, a healthy crew and not in want of either Stores or provisions, would have been betraying not only a want of perseverance, but judgement, in supposeing the South Pacific Ocean to have been so well explored that nothing remained to be done in it, which however was not my opinion at this time; for although I had proved there was no Continent, there remained nevertheless room for very large Islands in places wholy unexplored and many of those which were formerly discovered, are but imperfectly explored and there Situations are imperfectly known; I was of opinion that my remaining in this Sea some time longer would be productive of some improvements to Navigation and Geography as well as other Sciences.

[As envisaged, Cook now sailed north to the tropics, and spent the next few months investigating islands 'imperfectly known' including Easter Island and the New Hebrides, as well as discovering others such as New Caledonia. By October 1774 he was back at Queen Charlotte's Sound preparing for one final search for the elusive Southern Continent]

---

11 November 1774 Journal

At 7 o'Clock in the evening the Snowey Mountains bore WBS and Cape Palliser [the southernmost point of the North Island of New Zealand] North ½ west dis^t 16 or 17 leagues. After a few hours calm a breeze sprung up at North with which we steered SbE all sails Set, with a view of getting into the Latitude of 54° or 55°. My intention was to cross this vast Ocean nearly in these Parallels, and so as to pass over those parts which were left unexplored last summer.

---

17 December 1774 Journal

The land now before us can be no other than the west Coast of Terra del Fuego and near the West entrance to the Straits of Magelhanes [Magellan] . . . I have now done with the SOUTHERN PACIFIC OCEAN, and flatter my self that no one will think that I have left it unexplor'd, or that more could have been done in one voyage towards obtaining that end than has been done in this.

---

21 February 1775 *Journal*

As we were now no more than two degrees of Longitude from our rout to the South after leaving the Cape of Good Hope, it was to no purpose to proceed any farther to the East under this parallel, knowing no land could be there . . . I had now made the circuit of the Southern Ocean in a high Latitude and traversed it in such a manner as to leave not the least room for the Possibility of there being a continent, unless near the Pole and out of the reach of Navigation; by twice visiting the Pacific Tropical Sea, I had not only settled the situation of some old discoveries but made there many new ones and left, I conceive, very little more to be done even in that part. Thus I flater myself that the intention of the Voyage has in every respect been fully Answered, the Southern Hemisphere sufficiently explored and a final end put to the searching after a Southern Continent, which has at times ingrossed the attention of some of the Maritime Powers for near two Centuries past and the Geographers of all ages.

29 July 1775 *Journal*

After leaving the Islands [the Azores] I made the best of my way for England. On Saturday the 29th we made the land near Plymouth and the next morning anchored at Spit-head. Having been absent from England Three years and Eighteen Days, in which time lost but four men and only one of them by sickness.

14 August 1775 *Solander to Banks*

Our Expedition down to the Resolution, made yesterday quite a feast to all who were concerned. We set out early from the Tower, reviewd some of the Transports; visited Deptford yard; went on board the Experiment, afterwards to Wolwich, where we took on board Miss Ray & Co [Lord Sandwich's mistress] and then proceeded to the Galleon's where we were wellcomed in board of the Resolution – and Lord Sandwich made many of them quite happy. Providentially old Cap^n Clements died 2 or 3 days ago, by which a Captains place of Greenwich was made Vacant – This was given to Capt Cook – and a promise of Employ whenever he should ask for it. Mr Cooper was made Master and Commander – Mr Clerke was promised the command of the Resolution to carry Mr Omai home; Mr Pickersgill to be his 1st Lieutenant. 3

Midshipmen were made Lieutenants viz Smith, Burr &^c . . . The Master Mr Gilbert is made Master Attendant at Sheerness. All our friends look as well as if they had been all the while in clover. All inquired after you. In fact we had a glorious day and longed for nothing but You and Mr Omai. Mr Edgcomb & his Marines made a fine appearance. Most of our time, yesterday on board, was taken up in ceremonies, so I had not much time to see their curious collections . . . There were on board 3 live Otaheite Dogs, the ugliest most stupid of all the canine tribe. Pickersgill made the Ladies sick by shewing them the New Zealand head of which 2 or 3 slices were broiled and eat on board of the Ship. It is preserved in spirit and I propose to get it for Hunter [John Hunter, the anatomist], who goes down with me to morrow on purpose, when we expect the Ship will be at Deptford.

Chapter 6

The Ships' Companies: Officers

No doubt the Admiralty chose Cook to command the *Endeavour* because he had established a reputation as a highly successful navigator and surveyor of unknown waters and coastlines in Canada. However, he had never been in charge of a ship anything like the size of the *Endeavour*, with its complement of 85 seamen and marines. His previous command, the *Grenville*, in which he had surveyed the coasts of Newfoundland over several seasons, held a crew of 18. Also, he had never been to the Far East or the Pacific whereas his two lieutenants on the first voyage, Zachary Hicks and John Gore, were more experienced, and Gore had already been round the world twice, under two different captains, Byron and Wallis. It would hardly be surprising if Cook was, to start with, sometimes over-shadowed by these two, and there is some evidence that this was in fact the case. Daniel Solander, who accompanied Banks on the *Endeavour*, and later became a fount of chatty reminiscence about the voyage, told Charles Blagden that Cook had been jealous of Gore's experience, and that Gore was sometimes in a position to be able to disobey him, and make his own decisions.[1] There is no evidence of any rivalry with his captain in Gore's *Endeavour* journal, nor would one expect to find any, but it may be significant that after the voyage Gore chose to accompany Banks to Iceland rather than to sail again with Cook. However, he did decide to accompany him on the third voyage, as Cook's first lieutenant in the *Resolution*.

Solander's statement is mere unsubstantiated gossip, but another witness may carry more weight. William Perry had been assistant surgeon on the *Endeavour*, and became surgeon after the death of William Monkhouse. Cook thought highly of him, describing him as 'equally well if not better skilled in his profession' [than Monkhouse].[2] In a letter to *The Gentleman's Magazine*, published in 1807 (admittedly, long after the event), Perry writes:

> I sailed with Capt. Cook in the *Endeavour*. At that time my knowledge
> of naval matters was very limited. Experience since empowers me

to say farther, that never, through many years service on-board his Majesty's ships, or on board any ship of any nation, has it fallen to my lot to observe any Officer so completely lost as to presence of mind in the moment of imminent danger. On-board the *Endeavour*, upon such occasions, Lieut Zachary Hicks (who died on our return after leaving the Cape of Good Hope) naturally took the lead, insomuch that a stranger must have concluded such were the rules of the Navy. I leave this trait to Capt. James Cook's future Biographers: should a proof be demanded, there yet survive shipmates enough to be referred to.[3]

Zachary Hicks was Second Lieutenant of the *Endeavour*, in other words, second in command under Cook and above Gore. As far as I know, none of Cook's biographers have ever picked up Perry's challenge, and the best known amongst them, Beaglehole, dismisses Hicks in a few words as 'an invaluable man . . . but perhaps born to be a lieutenant'.[4] The charge of occasional irresolution on the first voyage is repeated by a brief entry in the anonymous journal which has been attributed to the midshipman, James Magra. Here Cook is accused of indecisiveness in treacherous waters in Cook Strait, New Zealand in January 1770:

> . . . the captain who was about to give orders of a different kind became irresolute; and during the dispute with the officer of the watch which this contrariety of opinion occasioned we were carried so near the rocks that our preservation appeared almost impossible.[5]

Yet even if it is true that Cook occasionally lost his presence of mind on the first voyage, and relied on his officers to take decisions, it is highly likely that by the second voyage he had so gained in experience and confidence that this was no longer so. However, it should also be stressed that throughout his journals Cook very rarely makes personal comments about his colleagues, and therefore we know little of the relationships between him and individual officers – less, in fact, than we sometimes learn about his relations with certain chiefs on the islands he visited.

It may well be that a man from a less humble background than Cook would have regarded his orders from the Admiralty more lightly as some of his predecessors had done. Cook's personal background may also have made it more difficult for him, as it was for Bligh a few years later, to impose his will on his officers and crew. Eighteenth-century sailors looked up to officers of superior social status. Perhaps Cook had to work harder than most to counteract this disadvantage, and to cultivate the stern, omniscient image which he presented to his colleagues on the *Resolution* during the second and third voyages. On the *Endeavour* voyage he certainly seems to have taken his officers into his confidence more than he ever did later on. There is the famous occasion described in his journal when, having completed the circumnavigation of New Zealand, he actually asked their advice as to what to do next. Should they return home eastwards, via the Horn, continuing the search for a southern continent as they went, or should they sail west for the Cape of Good Hope? And if the latter, by which route? It was finally decided to go westward, but only until they fell in with the coast of New Holland, which they would then explore to the north, returning home by way of the East Indies and the Cape.[6] Such obvious examples of consultation between Cook and his colleagues seem rarer after the first voyage, and instead he kept his own counsel, and gained a reputation for excessive secrecy, something that George Forster, for one, thought unnecessary and bad for morale. He writes, 'nothing could be more dejecting than the entire ignorance of our future destination, which, without any apparent reason, was constantly kept a secret to every person in the ship'.[7] There was a moment during the second voyage when, according to midshipman John Elliott, they all thought they were going home after months of privation and icy conditions, but then Cook suddenly changed course to the south:

> We all experienced a very severe mortification, for when we were steering East, we had all taken it into our heads that we were going streight for Cape Horn, on our road home, for we begin to find that our stock of Tea, Sugar etc began to go fast, and many hints were thrown out to Captn Cook, to this effect; but he only smiled and said nothing, for he was close and secret in his intentions at all times, that not even his first Lieutenant knew, when he left a place, where we should go to next.[8]

There may, however, have been more discussion and consultation between officers than is admitted in the journals. Cook, after all, was writing primarily for his superiors at the Admiralty, and would have been expected by them to justify and take responsibility for his decisions as commander. He may not have felt it always appropriate to reveal any collective thinking behind such decisions. Nevertheless, there are clearly occasions when discussion, and even disagreements, did take place. One such occurred on the second voyage when Cook, faced by the contrary opinions of other officers, modified his punishment of the marine, William Wedgeborough, who had shot an islander.[9] Another, from the third voyage, was when Cook decided, in deference to Gore's opinion, to further explore Prince William's Sound on the coast of America in search of the elusive north-west passage.[10] And a third occurred in March 1775 when it was decided finally to end exploration of the high southern latitudes, and head for home. Cook writes:

> Every one was impatient to get into Port and for good reasons, as we had nothing but stale and Salt Provisions to live upon for a long time and for which every one had lost all taste. These reasons induced me to yield to the general wish and to Steer for the cape of Good Hope.[11]

The 'every one' mentioned here presumably refers only to the officers. Nevertheless, such examples of others influencing Cook's decision-making are very likely only the tip of the iceberg, and the voyages must surely always have involved a considerable degree of teamwork, even if the team was confined to a small handful. According to Andrew Lambert, who participated in the cruise of the *Endeavour Replica* in 2001, one of the main lessons he took away from the experience was the necessity for cooperation in the running of the ship, leading to a feeling of shared companionship. 'If we felt like this after a week', he writes, 'how much closer were Cook's men after three months, or three years?'[12]

In his journals Cook frequently compliments his officers collectively for their composure under danger, and also for their willingness to carry out his instructions. Occasionally this praise rings a little hollow, as when, less than three weeks after Elliott says how mortified they all were at the decision to return to the icy Antarctic seas, Cook writes:

> Great as the design appeared to be, I however thought it was possible to be done and when I came to communicate it to the officers I had the satisfaction to find that they all heartily concur'd in it. I should not do my officers justice if I did not take some opportunity to declare that they allways shewed the utmost readiness to carry into execution in the most effectual manner every measure I thought proper to take.[13]

But this stern, secretive disciplinarian came to be held in great affection as well as awe by his brother officers. In their journals, especially those of the third voyage, they occasionally criticise particular decisions by Cook, or refer ironically to his moods of bad temper, but admiration for his qualities as commander and explorer is rarely in doubt. There was one officer on the *Resolution*, however, who was more critical than the others and this was Lieutenant

John Williamson, by all accounts a prickly character and not particularly popular with his colleagues, even before his rather inglorious role at Kealakekua beach on the morning of Cook's death.[14] From the surviving fragments of Williamson's journal there are accounts of two incidents over which he strongly disagreed with his captain. The first was at Tonga when his musket, a personal possession, was stolen, and he blamed Cook for not making any effort to ensure its return. He writes that Cook would go to any length to reclaim items that belonged to himself, but was indifferent to the theft of others' property.[15] The second incident was at Kauai in January 1778 when Williamson shot dead a Hawaiian who was one of a crowd obstructing his attempt to land on the beach. In his journal he composed a long-winded defence of his action in which he argues that it was preferable under extreme provocation to shoot to kill rather than to use small shot, as recommended by Cook, which might only infuriate an angry crowd still further. Cook himself says little about either incident, but Beaglehole comes down strongly against Williamson.[16]

Among the officers, the ones who probably gave Cook much satisfaction, but who also could be a source of considerable worry, were the 'young gentlemen'. This was the term for the midshipmen and masters' mates – a group whose status hovered uneasily on the dividing line between the quarterdeck and the lower deck. Some had been particularly entrusted to Cook's care by relatives or other persons of influence, and many of them were ambitious and reliable, such as Isaac Smith, the 16-year-old cousin of Cook's wife, who ended his naval career as an admiral, or George Vancouver, who later charted the American coast from California to Alaska. Cook clearly took much trouble over the training of these young men, as reported by Elliott:

> In the Early part of the [second] Voyage, Capt[n] Cook made all us young gentlemen, do their duty aloft the same as the Sailors, learning to hand, and reef the sails, and Steer the Ship, E[x]ercise Small arms thereby making us good Sailors as well as good officers.[17]

The training received under Cook was highly regarded, and when Elliott later applied to the East India Company he reports that his preliminary interview with the directors 'consisted in their saying that they suppos'd I had been with Cook, that having been a pupil of his, I must be a good sailor.'[18] Many of those trained by Cook, including William Bligh, George Vancouver, James Colnett, Nathaniel Portlock and George Dixon, went on to achieve fame in their own right. As the statesman William Windham once exclaimed to another Cook veteran, James Burney, 'But what officers you are, you men of Captain Cook; you rise upon us in every trial!'[19] David Samwell enthuses over the success and shared camaraderie of those who had served with Cook on the third voyage:

> we find no small Satisfaction in talking over the eventful History of our Voyage and are happy beyond measure when any of our old Companions come to see us from other Ships which they do as often as they can; no less than 17 Lieutenants have been made out of our two Ships; We are perhaps somewhat partial to one another, for it is an article of Faith with every one of us that there never was such a Collection of fine Lads take us for all in all, got together as there was in the Resolution & Discovery.[20]

Others, however, among the young gentlemen drank too much, indulged in horseplay and were generally a nuisance. One such was James Magra of the *Endeavour*.[21] On the second voyage there was a generous complement of wild young gentlemen. One incident involving two of them shows the sort of issue with which Cook sometimes had to cope, as a distraction from running the ship:

> Mr Charles Loggie, a Midshipman, and the Son of a very old Post Captain in the Navy, had for some time taken to drinking, a thing that he of all young Men should not have done, as he had when a child most unfortunately cut his head, and had been trapanned. Consequently, when he got liquor, he was a Mad Man – at other times as good a tempered young Man as any in the Ship. His infirmity was sometimes taken advantage of, and by none more than by Mr Maxwell, who made complaints of him to Capt. Cook.
>
> One day Cook had him put in Irons, drunk, on the Quarter deck, where he abused Capt. Cook, and called him every thing, which he bore for a time, and then ordered him to be taken away. Not many days after, Mr Maxwell came to Cook on the Quarter deck, greatly heated, and complained that Loggie had attempted to stab him with a knife, and shewed a scratch in his hand, which he said he had got in saving himself from a worse injury.
>
> Now the fact was, Loggie was in liquor, and at dinner, when they got into an altercation, Maxwell made an attempt either to take the knife from him, or to turn him out of the Birth. Loggie, in holding up the Knife to defend himself, touched Maxwell's hand. But Cook, probably recollecting his conduct to himself so lately, instantly ordered him up to the Gangway, and there flogged him like a common Sailor, and then turned him before the Mast.

> But every body pitied Loggie, while they execrated Maxwell, as a
> wining hypocrite, and we had every reason to think that Capt. Cook
> was very sorry for the hasty step he had taken, as he soon after took
> Loggie on the Quarter deck again.[22]

Midshipmen were not supposed to be punished by flogging like the men, but
could be 'mastheaded', i.e. sent to sit on the upper cross-trees some fifty feet
above the deck, for a few hours. In severe cases they could be reduced to the
status of ordinary seamen which then made them liable to corporal punishment
if the occasion arose, as in Loggie's case.

When Cook comments on someone's character in his journals, their
relationship to drink is often the first thing that comes to his mind. Sometimes
the reference is oblique, as with Charles Green, the astronomer who died in the
Batavia epidemic on the first voyage. Green, according to Cook, 'lived in such a
manner as greatly promoted the disorders he had had long upon him'. Usually
the comment is more direct. Robert Molyneaux, the master, who died about the
same time, had 'unfortunately given himself up to extrevecancy and intem-
perance'. On the second voyage there were the midshipmen Willis and Coghlan,
both of whom were 'wild and drinking', and Joseph Price, who was 'unsteady
and drinking'. There was also Pickersgill (later in his career court-martialled
for drunkenness), who was 'likeing ye Grog' and Daniel Clerk, 'clever but liking
Grog'.

On the other hand, Cook's coded term for those who could hold their liquor
is 'steady'. On the second voyage no less than 13 officers and petty officers on
board the *Resolution* receive this appelation. Robert Cooper, First Lieutenant,
is 'a sober steady man'; the surgeon and his two mates are all 'steady', and so is
the lieutenant of marines, the master, and the botanist, Anders Sparrman.
Clearly for Cook, as no doubt for other naval captains, this distinction between
'steady' men and 'drinking' men was crucial. As for Cook himself, no one
ever implied that he drank too much. He was certainly not a teetotaller – this,
given the circumstances, would probably have been impossible – but he was, by
all accounts, abstemious and self-controlled, just as he was when it came to
women.

As has been said, comments by Cook on his fellow officers are rare, and
almost invariably cautious, and one effect of this is to reinforce the impression
given in the journals that all important decisions were in the hands of one man.
This tendency to downplay the roles of Cook's brother officers, part of the
process of Cook's elevation to hero status, was taken further by the editors
of Cook's journals, Hawkesworth and Douglas, and also by his first biographer,
Andrew Kippis, who very rarely mentions by name any officer except Cook

himself.[23] It is also true that in all the other journals there are surprisingly few comments by his colleagues concerning their relationship with the captain. One midshipman who did write something on this theme was James Trevenen, who was on the *Resolution* during the third voyage. Trevenen, a fervent admirer of Cook, recalls him as somewhat of a tyrant in his behaviour towards the midshipmen, but he also remembers with pleasure outings at Nootka Sound when the harshness was relaxed:

> I with several other of our Midshipmen attended Captain Cook in this expedition, in which we rowed him not less than 30 miles during the day. We were fond of such excursions, altho' the labour of them was very great, as, not only this kind of duty, was more agreeable than the humdrum routine on board the Ships, but as it gave us an opportunity of viewing the different people & countries, and as another very principal consideration we were sure of having plenty to eat & drink, which was not always the case on board the Ship on our usual allowance. Capt. Cooke also on these occasions, would sometimes relax from his almost constant severity of disposition, & condescend now and then, to converse familiarly with us. But it was only for the time, as soon as we entered the ships, he became again the despot.[24]

The respect and awe in which Cook was held by his brother officers is clear from the various tributes paid him after his death. Henry Roberts, master's mate on the *Resolution*, speaks for them all on that melancholy morning when they:

> returned on board not being able to get the body of our lost Commander, whose death occasioned, concern, & sorrow, in every countenance; such an able Navigator, equalld by few and excelled by none, justly stiled father of his people from his great good care and attention, honored, & beloved by those who knew, or ever heard of him.[25]

Chapter 7

The Ships' Companies: Men

We now come to the crews themselves, the inhabitants of the lower deck. Eighteenth-century seamen were a race apart, and even their clothes, both ashore and afloat, were distinctive. A typical sailor wore a short, blue jacket over a waiscoat, with a handkerchief knotted round his neck, and loose-fitting canvas trousers instead of the landsman's tight breeches. But it was not only the clothes. According to the magistrate, Sir John Fielding:

> The seamen here are a generation differing from all the world. When one goes into Rotherhide and Wapping, which places are chiefly inhabited by sailors, but that somewhat of the same language is spoken, a man could be apt to suspect himself in another country. Their manner of living, speaking, acting, dressing, and behaving, are so very peculiar to themselves.[1]

When at sea sailors lived by a network of rules, boundaries and hierarchies, all ruthlessly enforced by their superiors. As Greg Dening explains:

> The hours of their watch, the inches of their hammocks, the ounces of their food, the pennies of their expense and fines, the glasses of grog at noon, the lashes for their offences were not only known and counted constantly but were ceremonially measured that all might see the different boundaries around their lives . . . In the total institution of a ship, persons were owed little. Role and rule were owed everything.[2]

Cook's ships in this respect were no different from others. In his journals he occasionally gives his crew a collective pat on the back, as when the *Endeavour* narrowly escaped being wrecked on the Great Barrier Reef and he writes, 'I must say that no man ever behaved better than they have done on this occasion . . .

every man seem'd to have a just sence of the danger we were in and exerted himself to the very utmost.'[3] But this was at a special moment of obvious peril. Generally, the lower deck were not put in the picture regarding the long-term aims and achievements of the voyages they were on, and were assumed not to care. One has to distinguish here between the efficient day-to-day running of the ship, and a genuine, overall sense of community on board, which did not naturally exist.[4] It would be a mistake to imagine that Cook's crews volunteered themselves for his voyages because they understood, and wanted a share in, his ambitions. Traditional accounts of the voyages tend to locate the sailors within a greater group identity, but this is misleading. If they did have some sense of community and loyalty, it was probably to their own companions rather than to the ship as a whole. As George Forster writes, 'Though they are members of a civilized society, they may in some measure be looked upon as a body of uncivilized men, rough, passionate, revengeful, but likewise brave, sincere, and true to each other.'[5]

To Cook and his officers, the 'people' were like children, needing to be motivated by short-term, physical rewards and punishments, and incapable of taking in a wider view. They needed constant supervision, and would be lost on their own – as actually happened to the two sailors who somehow managed to get themselves lost, and nearly died, on Christmas Island, even though the island was less than three miles across. Cook thought this behaviour quite typical: 'Considering what a strange set of beings, the generality of seamen are when on shore, instead of being surprised at these men lossing themselves we ought rather to have been surprised there were no more of them.'[6]

In the journals the aspirations and feelings of the crew tend to be invisible – until, that is, they conflict with Cook's own goals. One such conflict was over food. At the beginning of the first voyage Cook had difficulty getting the men to eat sauerkraut, of which he had brought on board large quantities, believing it to be good against scurvy.[7] He explains that it was only when the men saw the officers apparently enjoying it day after day that they changed their minds and demanded sauerkraut be put on the menu.[8] There were similar problems on the second voyage, especially when it was reported that the crew of the *Adventure* were not eating their vegetables as they should. Cook suspected this was the fault of Furneaux and his colleagues in not setting an example:

To interduce any New article of food among Seamen, let it be ever so much for their own good, requires both the example and Authority of a commander, without both of which, it will be droped before the People are sencible of the benefits resulting from it; was it necessary I could name fifty instances in support of this remark.[9]

As was usually the case on smaller naval ships, Cook was his own purser. This meant he was personally responsible to the Admiralty for the entire value of the stores on the ships, which included not only food but also many other items classed as 'necessaries', which ranged from clothing to candles, and barrels to brooms. In his book on the Georgian navy, *The Wooden World*, N.A.M. Rodger has several pages on the dangers and difficulties of a purser's life. He was expected to keep highly detailed accounts of what each man ate every day, and what stores perished for whatever cause. If he made a mistake it could cost him dear, although he could sometimes recoup by selling the men items such as tobacco. He was rarely a popular figure. It is of course likely that as a purser Cook received special consideration, given the nature of his voyages. It is also true that he always had a clerk on board with him to handle the recording side. Even so, there is no doubt he had a pecuniary interest in how much was consumed on board, and how savings could be made. Whenever fresh food – whether turtles, shellfish or green vegetables – could be had for free Cook made sure it was distributed evenly among the various messes:

> Whatever refreshment we got [referring here to turtles] that would bear a division I caused to be equally divided amongest the whole company generally by weight, the meanest person in the ship had an equal share with myself or any one on board, and this method every commander of a ship on such a Voyage as this ought ever to observe.[10]

However, when it was a question of food that had been acquired from natives by trade, and had to be paid for, the rule was different, and on these occasions any mess wanting a share was expected to pay, as was the case when, towards the end of the first voyage they bought some local produce at Princes Island, near Batavia:

> The Natives seem'd inclined to supply us with Turtle Fowles etc, Articles that I intended laying in as great a stock as possible for the benefit of the sick and to suffer everyone to purchas what they pleased for themselves . . . the Trade on our part was carried on chiefly with mony [Spanish dollars] such of our people as had not this article traded with old shirts etc at a great disadvantage.[11]

Disputes about food or drink became more bitter if there was any suspicion that Cook was making a profit from his actions, and some of those who kept journals during the voyages, including Pickersgill on the first voyage and Ledyard on the third, refer critically to this role of their captain. The worst such dispute occurred on the final voyage during the seven weeks that the ships were circling the island of Hawaii, trading for food with natives who came out in their canoes (nobody knew why Cook was refusing to land, which certainly made the dispute worse). Cook's report of the quarrel in his journal is fairly brief:

> Having procured a quantity of Sugar Cane and had upon trial made but a few days before, found that a strong decoction of it made a very palatable beer, which was esteemed by everyone on board, I ordered some more to be brewed, but when the Cask came to be broached not one of my Mutinous crew would even so much as taste it. [Therefore] I gave orders that no grog should be served in either Ship.[12]

We learn more about the dispute from other journals. Midshipman Watts tells us that even before the cane beer was produced the men were on short rations due to some earlier dispute. They sent up a letter to Cook to say they disliked the beer, and asking for their provisions to be restored. Cook called a meeting of the whole crew, and told them that their letter was highly mutinous, and that if they refused to drink the cane beer 'the Brandy Cask should be struck down into ye hold & they might content themselves with Water'. They did continue to so refuse and it was struck down.[13] He also awarded the cooper 12 lashes for deliberately opening a cask of cane beer to make it sour. According to Watts, Cook ended his speech about the brandy by saying 'He did not chuse to keep turning & working among these Isles without having some Profit' – a clear reference to his role as ship's purser.

Alcohol was crucial to the functioning of the eighteenth-century navy – for officers and men alike. The amount of beer, wine and spirits that Cook thought necessary to take on board seems astonishing to us, even given the fact that at this time beer was a safer drink than water and could be kept for longer. The men were allowed eight pints a day, plus their much-prized grog ration. Grog, a mixture of brandy, water and sugar said to have been devised by the late Admiral Vernon, was dispensed each morning with some ceremony. A bell brought men running from every part of the ship, to stand in line and receive a mugful from a barrel set on the deck. Most were said to down it in one go, crying as they did so, 'The King, God bless him', but some kept theirs for barter, or for special occasions. The most special occasion in the calendar was Christmas, when, according to George Forster, the entire crew were 'solicitious to get drunk, though they are commonly solicitious about nothing else'.[14]

Cook went along with this system, while criticising its worst abuses in his journals. He winked at the excesses of Christmas, which he probably disapproved of, but could hardly prevent. For example, he writes in his entry for 25 December 1772, 'At Noon seeing that the People were inclinable to cele-brate Christmas Day in their own way, I brought the Sloops under a very snug sail least I should be surprised with a gale of wind with a drunken crew.'[15] Drunkenness, or at least the lack of awareness and slowness of reaction due to alcohol, must have been very common, but drunkenness itself went unpunished, unless it led on to other problems. For instance, John Readon, boatswain, was found dead in his hammock, having drunk three half pints of rum the previous evening, and John Ravenhill, sailmaker, and said to be the oldest sailor on board the *Endeavour*, was 'generally more or less drunk every day', yet there is no mention of either sailor ever being punished for drunk-enness.[16] But Stephen Forward, the ship's gunner, was flogged for stealing ten gallons of rum from a cask on the quarterdeck during his watch. 'Forward', writes Cook, 'is from his Drunkenness become the only useless person on board the Ship.' Nevertheless, he was recommended for promotion after the voyage.[17]

Cook's crews may have been little different from the normal run of sailors, but they faced some extra challenges. One was the issue of collecting 'curi-osities', another example of their irrational behaviour, according to Cook. A curiosity was the term for any kind of native artefact, ranging from spears and fish hooks to cloth, as well as natural objects from the islands, such as shells. The problem cropped up on the second voyage, when Johann Forster was trying to make a collection of such items in the interests of science. But word got round, and sailors started trading on their own account, much annoying Forster, who saw prices escalating as a result, and thought they were doing it merely to irritate him (which may also well have been the case). Cook, too, remarks on the stupidity of sailors who would part with what they really needed, including the clothes off their own backs, for things which were of no use to them and which they had nowhere to store. In Tongatapu, he writes:

> It was astonishing to see with what eagerness everyone catched at every thing they saw, it even went so far as to become the ridicule of the Natives by offering pieces of sticks stones and what not to exchange, one waggish Boy took a piece of human excrement on the end of a stick and hild it out to every one of our people he met with.[18]

Nicholas Thomas, however, makes the point that collecting curiosities was perhaps an attempt to show some initiative by those who usually had every decision made for them. They were demonstrating a certain independence of authority, and at the same time they were also, paradoxically, complying with one of the major objectives of the voyage – to develop new forms of trade in the Pacific.[19] It is also true that back in England some of these curiosities fetched a good price.

Another burden facing Cook's men when the ships arrived at particular islands was the need to prevent theft. It was extremely difficult to watch out for pilferers when large numbers of exuberant islanders clambered on board, many of them feeling entitled to remove from the ship any objects not firmly nailed down. Armed guards stationed on deck often had to make instant decisions as to whether to shoot, or be held responsible for allowing theft. Either way they risked punishment. It was often the same at night, when guards were stationed on land to watch over valuable equipment including astronomical instruments and weapons.

We usually know very little about individual crew members unless they did something wrong and were punished for it. Floggings, with their leisurely, public ritual, were the main punishment, and Cook's floggings were apparently no more or less numerous than the average. Greg Dening has calculated that he flogged more than Bligh but less than Vancouver.[20] No doubt more casual corporal punishment – rarely mentioned in the journals – was also sometimes inflicted. Georg Forster witnessed Cook hitting out on one occasion, and he implies it was a fairly common occurrence:

> After a short stay [on Takaroa], our party prepared to return to their boat. One of the sailors, having been inattentive to his duty, received several blows from the captain. This trifling circumstance would not deserve a place in this narrative, but for the observation, which the natives made upon it. As soon as they saw it, they shewed it one to another, and exclaimed tape a-hai te tina, 'he beats his brother'.[21]

Drink was very important to sailors, and hence could be used as a sanction, as when Cook withheld the daily grog ration because they would not touch his home-made beer.[22] Yet these short-term methods of control – flogging and drink – were never wholly effective. Cook could not prevent, for instance, sex between sailors and islanders, or, indeed, drunkenness. Sometimes he could not even breach sailors' reluctance to inform on comrades, as towards the end of the first voyage, when he unsuccessfully offered a reward for information about the episode of Orton's ears. Any really effective system of control would have involved the hearts and minds of those controlled, and not merely their bodies, but this was hardly the style of the eighteenth-century navy.

To us the 'people' must remain mysterious, partly owning to lack of documentation, and partly perhaps because their lives are so remote from all our twenty-first century experience. Even when we do have evidence about a particular individual the facts are often inconclusive, and tell us nothing about what really happened, or about personalities or motives. Why, for instance, did Cook decide to be lenient in the case of John Marra, a twenty-five year old Irishman who, in May 1774, tried to desert the *Endeavour* at Tahiti? This offence was usually punished severely, and Marra had already been in trouble several times. He was born in Cork, and had been one of the thirteen sailors from the *Endeavour* who had volunteered to join the *Resolution*. He was at that time promoted from able seaman to gunner's mate, but apparently then thought better of his decision to join, because, before the ship set off, in April 1772, he was confined, and then awarded twelve lashes for 'mutiny and desertion'. Three months later he received another twelve for 'insolence to his superior officer', and one year later, another twelve for 'insolence'. Cook's explanation for letting him off after he was recaptured at Tahiti does not explain very much. He writes:

> When I considered the situation of the Man in life I did not think him so culpable as it may first appear . . . I never learnt that he had either friends or connection to confine him to any particular part of the world, all Nations were alike to him, where than can Such a Man spend his days better than at one of these isles where he can injoy all the necessaries and some of the luxuries of life in ease and Plenty.[23]

Perhaps Cook forgave Marra because he remembered his original decision to volunteer, or possibly his words here are an echo of primitivist thinking, and he was imagining himself in Marra's shoes, contemplating the delights of Tahiti. In any case, the story continues with Marra once more trying to jump ship in pursuit of one of the 'young, red-painted, blue-lipped cannibal ladies of Queen Charlotte Sound', New Zealand.[24] This time Cook was not so lenient, and he was flogged. When the voyage was over Marra showed some initiative, by getting a publisher to rush out a book based on a journal which he had managed to smuggle off the ship. The reference to the cannibal lady is from his own journal.

Consider, too, the brief career of the marine, William Wedgeborough, about whom we know only the following – negative – facts:

18 March '74 He was given 12 lashes for drunkenness and for 'easing himself between decks'. There was some dispute about the evidence, as the lieutenant of marines at first objected, though later the sentence was confirmed.

2 Aug '74	He fell overboard when drawing water to wash the deck. The ship was brought to, and he was dragged out and revived with rum.
19 Aug '74	When on sentry duty he shot a native of Tanna who had pointed a bow and arrow at him. Cook called him a 'rascal', and wanted him flogged, but the other officers all believed him justified in shooting, so instead he was put in irons, and kept a prisoner for several weeks.
22 Dec '74	At Tierra del Fuego he fell out of the heads, possibly when drunk, and was drowned.[25]

None of this appears particularly commendable, and Beaglehole calls Wedgeborough, 'a not very attractive person', but on such fragmentary and selective evidence, how can he be so sure?[26] If more were known, and especially something positive or even neutral, his personality and career might appear very different to us. But as far as the journals are concerned, positive behaviour by common seamen was hardly noteworthy.

Wedgeborough was a marine, and marines were somewhat of an anomaly among the ships' companies. They were unskilled landsmen who could pull ropes but not be ordered aloft, and they were soldiers whose standards of drill and musketry were often lamentable. Their status was low amongst the crew, and at sea their only real function was to guard the captain's cabin and other sensitive areas in the ship. Theoretically, they could be used as a bulwark against the common sailors if mutiny threatened, though in practice this might have been a dangerous and doubtful expedient.[27] Yet the number of marines on Cook's ships was increased – from twelve on the *Endeavour*, to 21 on the *Resolution* and twelve on the *Adventure* on the second voyage and to 20 and twelve again on the third. Presumably Cook felt he needed marines, with their uniforms, their drill and their potential firepower, to overawe potentially hostile Pacific islanders, and on landing on a strange beach they were usually among the first to disembark. Nevertheless, the marines were often a nuisance on board ship and according to Anne Salmond they tended to attract more than their fair share of punishment. Of seventeen marine privates on the *Resolution* during the third voyage, eleven were flogged during the voyage, one four times, one three times and two twice, with a total of 216 lashes. Salmond goes so far as to suggest that one of the factors leading to Cook's isolation and death on Kealakekua beach may have been the disinclination of the marines to risk their own lives for a commander who had treated them so harshly.[28]

There are several statements in the journals and memoirs of his colleagues to show that, to his officers and midshipmen, Cook was a revered figure.

Whether the common sailors who sailed with him shared these opinions is not so easy to judge. Captains, especially successful ones, acquired their own followers who would accompany them from ship to ship and often looked to them for pecuniary help when the time came to retire. Apart from these personal followings, it was always difficult for the Admiralty to recruit enough men, qualified sailors or otherwise, to man a ship, especially for such lengthy voyages. Cook was no different in these respects from other captains. Five men out of the 18 on the *Grenville*, the schooner he had commanded for the survey of Newfoundland, transferred with him to the *Endeavour* and out of the 41 that survived that voyage, 20, including officers, volunteered for the *Resolution*. On the other hand, 48 of the sailors allocated to the *Resolution* in 1772 'ran' before she could set sail, and at Madeira Cook was forced to hire boatmen to patrol the ship, to prevent more from deserting.[29] For years Joseph Banks continued to receive letters from sailors who had been on the *Endeavour* requesting his help with money or places, and no doubt if Cook had survived he would have received many more such letters from those who had served with him, and now hoped for his patronage.

Chapter 8

Men of Science

This chapter has two inter-related themes – firstly, the role played by science in Cook's voyages and second, Cook's relationship with the various civilian experts who accompanied him. The great Polish-English novelist Joseph Conrad judged that the era of Cook ushered in modern, disinterested, scientific exploration as contrasted with the bad old days of blatant acquisitiveness:

> The voyages of the early explorers were prompted by an acquisitive spirit, the idea of lucre in some form, the desire of trade or the desire of loot, disguised in more or less fine words. But Cook's three voyages are free from any taint of that sort. His aims needed no disguise. They were scientific. His deeds speak for themselves with the masterly simplicity of a hard-won success. In that respect he seems to belong to the single-minded explorers of the nineteenth century, the late fathers of militant geography whose only object was the search for truth.[1]

There are indeed good grounds for seeing Cook's voyages as enterprises of scientific discovery. It was, after all, scientific progress that made them possible in the first place. Developments in celestial navigation – first, the use of lunar tables and later, the newly invented chronometers – meant that it became possible for the first time to calculate longitude accurately.[2] To confirm this one has only to compare Cook's experience with that of George Anson thirty years earlier. Anson had to rely on dead reckoning, and hence made several disastrous errors during his circumnavigation of the globe. An even more dramatic example of the failure to determine longitude occurred when Admiral Sir Clowdisley Shovell lost four ships and 2,000 men off the Scilly Isles one foggy night in October 1707. Errors in dead reckoning combined with strong tides and foul weather to wreck the squadron. It was this catastrophe that eventually led to the passing of the Longitude Act of 1714 which offered a prize to anyone who could solve the problem.

As regards Cook's first voyage, it is also true that a scientific objective long preceded other factors in the planning of the voyage. For well over a year the Royal Society had been considering the need to send astronomers to the Pacific to observe the transit of Venus across the face of the sun, and a secondary motive for the voyage – to discover, if possible, the elusive southern continent before other powers did so – arose at a much later stage. In fact, it was probably only the return of the *Dolphin* under Wallis in May 1768, with his report of the possible sighting of a continental coastline near Tahiti, that led the Admiralty to amend Cook's instructions so as to include a search for the supposed continent.[3]

Further evidence for seeing the voyages in terms of their scientific impulse resides in the fact that persons qualified in astronomy and natural history accompanied Cook in all three of his voyages. On the first voyage it is true that the provision of scientific specialists was left partly to private initiative, in the persons of Joseph Banks and his team, and partly to a non-governmental organization, the Royal Society, which enlisted and subsidized two astronomers for the voyage, Charles Green and Cook himself. However, on the second voyage the government itself played an important role in this respect. The natural historian, Johann Reinhold Forster received a parliamentary grant of £4,000 to join the voyage, and he was accompanied by his son, George, and another naturalist, Anders Sparrman. A professional astronomer, William Wales, also sailed on the *Resolution*, and another, William Bayly, on the *Discovery*.

On the third voyage Cook's difficulties with Forster led to his insistence on relying on naval personnel for specialist expertise, and the scientific aspects of the voyage were catered for by Lieutenant James King, an excellent observer of nature and an astronomer, and William Anderson, surgeon on the *Resolution*, who possessed a range of scientific interests, and who was described by Beaglehole as 'one of the best minds of all the three voyages'.[4] In spite of this, it is clear that, from the 1770s, concrete support for science on voyages of exploration was seen as a proper object for the expenditure of public or royal patronage, and this was true not only of the British state. The French explorer, La Pérouse, is said to have had 17 scholars on board with him on his voyage of 1785 and D'Entrecasteaux took ten in 1791.[5] This is in contrast to the voyages immediately preceding Cook's, those of Byron (1764) and of Wallis and Carteret (1766), neither of whose expeditions included experts funded by government. Furthermore, the instructions given to Cook by the Admiralty at the beginning of each voyage clearly show the importance of science in the official view of the voyages. The specialists on board were required to make all manner of astronomical, geographical, meteorological and oceanographic observations, as well as to acquire ethnographic artefacts, comment on the islanders encountered, and collect and describe new species of plants and animals.

Nevertheless, this new scientific orientation and state sponsorship does not prove that Cook's voyages were primarily undertaken for scientific reasons, as opposed to strategic or economic motivations related to British interest in the Pacific Ocean. Disinterested scholarship and scientific curiosity may have been significant factors, but the enhancement of national power and prestige was probably the overriding consideration. According to Marshall and Williams:

> The motives for the Pacific expeditions after 1763 were not simply, nor even primarily, scientific. This second New World promised resources of such potential that its discovery and control might tip the commercial balance of power in Europe – for Britain confirm the overseas superiority brought by the wartime conquests, for France redress the humiliations of an unsuccessful war.[6]

Some recent commentators have gone further, suggesting that science may have served as a pretext for other motives. One recent account of Cook's voyages has it that the observation of the Transit of Venus, the main scientific impulse for the first voyage, merely 'offered a useful excuse for a government-sponsored expedition, because England's earlier voyages had excited the suspicions of the French and Spanish, who feared, not without reason, that these voyages of exploration were merely a cover for attempts to expand the nation's influence in the Pacific'.[7] The scientific motives for the second and third voyages – the search for a southern continent and for a north-west passage respectively – might also be seen in terms of offering plausible excuses for voyages which were principally driven by more material interests. 'Despite their pretence of disinterested scholarship', argues the Swiss historian Urs Bitterli, 'the eighteenth-century explorers were chiefly concerned with the enhancement of national prestige'.[8] Explorers' journals, not excluding Cook's, reveal that opportunities were often seized to spy on other naval powers, including, for instance, the making of detailed notes of their fortifications and the dispositions of their forces.

However, the main historiographic tradition regarding Cook has always tended to emphasise disinterested science as opposed to strategic or imperial interests. Cook's editor, John Douglas, in the introduction to his edition of Cook's third journal, lists what he considers were the four main benefits of the voyages. They were:

1. accessions to geographical knowledge.
2. commercial advantages.
3. improvements in science (including knowledge of tides, currents, the earth's magnetism, botany, and health on long voyages).
4. philosophical and religious speculation (including the study of human nature in various situations).[9]

Today we might well class items (1) and (4) alongside (3) as largely scientific. With hindsight we can now see, too, that Douglas's second benefit, commercial advantage, was somewhat doubtful, as little new trade followed on directly from Cook (apart from a modest fur trade in the North Pacific). What can therefore be said is that Douglas's summary is clearly weighted towards a view of the voyages as highly successful efforts to acquire objective knowledge for the benefit of humanity.

A more detailed analysis of Cook's achievements is made by George Forster in his essay of 1787, *Cook the Discoverer.* Forster lists what he believes to be the twenty major results of Cook's three voyages, and of these, no less than sixteen turn out to be scientific, if one includes anthropology, geography and natural history in this category. Of the remaining four, one is about 'new prospects for commerce' (without mentioning Britain), and the other three involve vaguely philosophical statements, such as that Cook's findings show that absolute equality among men is morally impossible, and a state of nature, inconceivable.[10] This emphasis on the impartial and disinterested nature of Cook's activities was no doubt shared by those who gave him expert advice. Daines Barrington, of the Royal Society, was indignant that news of the forthcoming third voyage to search for a north-west passage was viewed with suspicion by the Spanish. He thought foreigners really ought to grasp that 'the English Nation is actuated merely by desiring to know as much as possible with regard to the planet which we inhabit.'[11]

At the other end of that long historiographical tradition, Beaglehole, too, prioritises the scientific dimension of the voyages above strategic, political, or even commercial considerations. Vanessa Agnew has analysed Beaglehole's very full index to his edition of the second voyage, and concludes that references to scientific aspects of the voyage are emphasized at the expense of other, perhaps more controversial, aspects. She comments:

> For all its wide-ranging scope, the bias in the index is clearly towards the scientific. In particular, it is the maritime and ethnographic accomplishments of the voyage which Beaglehole brings out as he emphasizes Cook's interactions with the islanders and his prowess on

the sea. On the other hand, indexal references dealing with phenomena less directly related to navigation, natural history and ethnography are given less thorough treatment: Cook's possession of new islands and his use of force, for example, hardly warrant an entry. Thus, whereas it is possible to gain an overview of the Europeans' commercial trans-actions at any given island, one cannot readily trace the sometimes frail impact of commerce on the indigenous inhabitants, since the index does not include entries which deal specifically with the number of islanders killed as a result of the Europeans' market activities. The superimposition of a critical framework which depends on an 'apolitical' or 'disinterested' notion of the scientific means that the Cook voyage tends not to be viewed within the context of the history of appropriation and colonization in the region.[12]

One technique which Beaglehole uses when annotating Cook's journals of the third voyage is to interpolate his own sub-headings into Cook's descriptions of the islands he visited, such as '*Arts and Manufacture*'; '*Disposal of the dead*'; '*Food and cookery*'. These, together with copious footnotes, and the annotation of Cook's remarks with reference to modern systems of botanical and zoological systems of classification, all tend to heighten the impression that one is reading a scientific treatise.

To turn now to my second theme in this chapter, one of Cook's greatest achievements is surely the close working relationship he formed with Joseph Banks in the *Endeavour* during the three years of the first voyage. This was a union between apparent opposites, which might easily have gone badly wrong, jeopardising the entire voyage. Banks was a gentleman of leisure with an interest in natural history, who had never in his life gone short of anything he wanted. He was 25-years-old when he joined the *Endeavour*, a wealthy young man whose father had died when he was 18, leaving him ancestral estates in Lincolnshire. He had been educated at Eton and Harrow and then Oxford, where he had not worked very hard, except at botany, which became his lifelong passion. He was good-looking, charming, exuberant, occasionally arrogant. Cook was taciturn, cautious, and dour, a 40-year-old professional sailor who had worked his way up from nowhere. Between them they were expected to share this ambitious voyage, with its multiple objectives and hence, there was ample opportunity for clashes of interest and personality. One of Cook's biographers makes the point that very few other naval commanders apart from the recently promoted Cook would have been prepared to share their work-space with Banks, whose instruments and specimens took up so much room.[13] Furthermore, Banks did not arrive alone, but brought with him a retinue of artists, secretaries, servants (eight persons altogether), and dogs (two). A contemporary letter by a friend to the Swedish botanist, Linnaeus, who was Banks's hero, lists some part of the equipment Banks took on board:

> No people ever went to sea better fitted out for the purpose of Natural History, nor more elegantly. They have got a fine library of Natural History; they have all sorts of machines for catching and preserving insects; all kinds of nets, trawls, drags and hooks for coral fishing; they have even a curious contrivance of a telescope, by which, put into the water, you can see the bottom to a great depth, where it is clear. They have many cases of bottles with ground stoppers, of several sizes, to preserve animals in spirits. They have the several sorts of salt to surround the seeds; and wax, both beeswax and that of the Myrica . . . in short Solander assured me this expedition would cost Mr Banks £10,000.[14]

And yet, the arrangement seems to have worked smoothly. Banks's lively and enthusiastic personality comes over in the pages of his journal and it seems clear he had excellent relationships with Cook and his other colleagues. He also enjoyed the opportunities for botanizing that the voyage presented:

> Now do I wish that our friends in England could by the assistance of some magical spying glass take a peep at our situation; Dr Solander setts at the Cabin table describing, myself at my Bureau Journalizing, between us hangs a large bunch of sea weed, upon the table lays the wood and barnacles; they would see that notwithstanding our different occupations our lips move very often, and without being con-jurors might guess that we were talking about what we should see upon the land which there is now no doubt we shall see very soon [the *Endeavour* was approaching the coast of New Zealand].[15]

No doubt Banks admired Cook as a consummate navigator and explorer, but it is more remarkable that the older man was also prepared to learn from the younger. Perhaps at first Cook resented having to share his cabin space with the experimental gentlemen, but very likely he soon realized how much he might gain from the contact. Harold Carter, the biographer of Banks, has described him as 'Cook's Oxford tutor', and by comparing the two journals it is easy to see how closely the two cooperated. Not only did Cook incorporate into his own journal much of the factual material which Banks had written about Tahiti and other islands, but also many of the ideas that surface in Cook's journal clearly originate from liaison with Banks. Likely candidates are: the views Cook expresses about natives needing to 'improve' after contact with Europeans; his admiration, nevertheless, for the simplicity of the Australian aborigine lifestyle in comparison with European materialism; his general contempt for 'superstition' in native religions. All these can be found in both journals, often with very similar wording. It would be most surprising if Cook had managed to develop such views by himself before the voyage started, considering his demanding career at sea. Another advantage for Cook of Banks's participation in the voyage was the library of works of travel and natural history that Banks brought onto the *Endeavour*, and to which Cook would have had access. And a further fact that must have ingratiated Banks to Cook was the profile his presence gave the voyage – a profile much higher than that of recent expeditions by Byron, Wallis and Carteret. Cook was certainly not unaware of the implications of such public attention on his future career.[16]

Banks was accompanied on the *Endeavour* by the hard-working naturalist and disciple of Linnaeus, Daniel Solander, whose reputation among historians has been somewhat eclipsed until recently by that of Banks, but who must also have had a considerable influence on Cook. Solander was not only a learned scholar but also a witty conversationalist and he was ten years nearer Cook's age than the 25-year-old Banks. Between the two of them, Banks and Solander must surely over three years have had a crucial role in refining Cook's sensibilities, expanding his vocabulary and imbuing him with many of the values of the Enlightenment.[17]

Preparations were underway from the latter part of 1771 for Cook's second voyage, and it was assumed that Banks and Solander would again be the naturalists accompanying the voyage. However, Banks now proposed to take an even larger entourage, and in order to house them he required alterations to be made to the *Resolution*, which were effected but which were then found to render the ship unseaworthy. When the vessel was put back into its original state he took umbrage and refused to have anything more to do with the voyage. He wrote a long letter of passionate self-justification to Lord Sandwich, the First Lord of the Admiralty, a letter which contained the suggestion – one that Beaglehole calls 'the least generous and most foolish thing that Banks ever said' – that there were other naval commanders who would be happy to sail with him if Cook would not.[18] The affair ended with Banks taking himself off to Iceland instead of accompanying the voyage, but it is perhaps a tribute to Cook that, although he disapproved of Banks's conduct he did not allow the episode to destroy their relationship. When the *Resolution* reached the Cape of Good Hope he wrote an emollient letter to Banks:

> Dear Sir
>
> Some Cross circumstances which happened at the latter part of the
> equipment of the Resolution created, I have reason to think, a cool-
> ness betwixt you and I, but I can by no means think it was sufficient
> to me to break off all corrispondance with a Man I am under m[a]ny
> obligations too.[19]

We are told that when Lieutenant James King was appointed to the *Resolution*
for the third voyage, he called on Cook to pay his respects, and in the course
of conversation mentioned his regret that no scientists were going on the expedition. He was much taken aback when Cook allegedly replied, 'Curse the
scientists, and all science into the bargain.' If this story is true it would be
surprising on two counts: firstly, because the cautious and methodical Cook
himself seems to us to personify many of the attitudes characteristic of modern
scientists; secondly, because at that date the term 'scientist' had not been
invented. According to the *Oxford English Dictionary* it appeared first in 1840
when William Whewell wrote: 'we need very much a name to describe a culti-
vator of science in general. I should incline to call him a scientist'. But in any
case what is the evidence that Cook used these actual words? The report seems
to have originated with J. R. Forster who wrote in German, and the words said
to have been spoken by Cook are given as, 'Verflucht sind alle Gelehrten und
alle Gelehrsamkeit oben drein', which could equally well be translated as
'Cursed be all philosophers and philosophy.'[20] In the journals of Cook's voyages
a number of equivalents for 'scientist' are used, including 'philosopher', 'natural
philosopher' and 'man of science', and the sailors were also fond of the phrase
'experimental gentlemen' (who tried to persuade them to eat 'experimental
food' which was good for them, and drink 'experimental water' distilled from
sea water). The term 'science' was itself relatively uncommon, and is not
used by Cook in his journals, although it was by both the Forsters, father
and son. It was just starting to take on its modern sense of the theoretical and
methodical study of nature, whereas earlier it had meant any kind of theoretical
study, even including theology, as well as subjects now classified under the
humanities.

Cook's outburst against scientists was probably the result of his unfortunate
experiences with Johann Forster during and after the second voyage. The
Forsters had been appointed to go with Cook at the last minute when Banks
and his team, including a certain Dr. James Lind decided not to go.[21] The elder
Forster is an interesting character who has had a bad press from historians. He
was born near Danzig in 1729, was educated at German universities, and then
trained to be a Lutheran pastor. In 1765 he obtained a year's leave of absence

from his church to travel to Russia, where he was employed by Catherine the Great to make a survey of her new Volga colonies. However, because his report was critical of the way the colonies were administered, the Russian government never paid him, and as he had also been dismissed from his post as minister, having overstayed his leave, he decided to try his luck in England. He found himself a job teaching languages at the dissenting academy at Warrington, Lancashire, but this, too, did not last, and he moved to London, finding it a struggle to maintain himself, his wife and young son by writing pamphlets and making translations. When his friends told him of the opportunity to go on the *Resolution* he jumped at the chance.

Forster was an Enlightenment scholar, a true man of science in the sense that he possessed vast learning and was curious about everything, from botany and medicine to ethnology and linguistics. Beaglehole, Cook's biographer, clearly disliked him intensely, calling him 'dogmatic, humourless, suspicious, pretentious, contentious, censorious, demanding, rheumatic'.[22] However, he has recently been re-assessed, and his latest biographer, Michael Hoare, is much more generous.[23] Nevertheless, he was clearly a prickly, quarrelsome character, quick to take offence, and inclined to believe the whole world was against him – not the ideal companion for a three-year voyage of exploration. His journal contains many passages of self-justification over his quarrels with various members of the ship's company, and on several occasions he berates Cook for being lukewarm in his enthusiasm for science because he did not allow enough opportunities for botanising on the islands they visited. For instance, Cook's decision in July 1774 not to explore a particular island in the Tonga group owing to the dangers of reefs led to a typical outburst in Forster's journal:

Either we stay but a day or 2 on one place, go late ashore, come early off again, are hindered to ramble about by the carelessness of people in guarding their Arms . . . People who know nothing of Sciences & hate them, never care whether they are enlarged & knowledge increases or not.[24]

At one point on the voyage Forster and Cook had a bitter exchange when Cook reprimanded him for peppering with small shot a native whom he had discovered attacking his son. According to Forster:

Then the Captain began to reflect upon my conduct; he arrogated to himself an Authority which he had not, & I supported my Independency of him, with a Spirit which becomes a Man of honour; the Dispute went however too far, & though I had once desired to drop the affair as insignificant, Capt Cook however went on, having been exasperated by some false insinuations from his first Servant who is Stewart to our Mess; & so some hot & unguarded Expressions came out on both sides & he sent me by Force out of his Cabin, the Use of which he had originally agreed upon, I should have.[25]

This exclusion must have been particularly galling for Forster because the so-called great cabin in the stern of the ship was the only place where scientific work could effectively be carried out. Apart from this relatively large space, with its long, fixed table, comfortable settees, and store cupboards along the walls, there were only the various tiny sleeping cabins, in which it would have been quite impossible to spread out books and papers, or examine plants and animals. The great cabin was also the captain's workroom; it was chart room, library, writing room and mess room all combined. Hence it was always busy, and, according to Forster, not always particularly salubrious: 'in the Captain's Cabin there are broken panes, the apartment full of currents & smoke, a parcel of damp Sails spread, & a couple of Sailmakers at work, now & then discharging the mephitic Air from the pease & Sower-krout they have eaten, & besides 5 or 6 other people constantly in it.'[26]

The bouts of ill feeling between Forster and Cook are particularly regrettable because each had much to offer the other, and a partnership between them could produce dividends. If one compares Cook's passages of deductive reasoning on the origins of various groups of Pacific islanders with Forster's own thoughts on the subject, as outlined in his later *Observations*, published in 1778, one realizes that, at times when their relations were relatively cordial, such topics must often have come under discussion.[27] According to Forster there were times when Cook took his advice; for example, to fumigate the ship in the interests of hygiene by regularly burning smoky fires between decks. And when Cook became dangerously ill of the 'Billious colick', Forster made a generous sacrifice on his behalf:

When I began to recover, a favourite dog belonging to Mr Forster fell a Sacrifice to my tender Stomack; we had no other fresh meat whatever on board and I could eat of this flesh as well as broth made of it, when I could taste nothing else, thus I received nourishment and strength from food which would have made most people in Europe sick, so true is it that necessity is govern'd by no law.[28]

Forster and Cook were both men of science, and Cook's second voyage is the richer for Forster's presence, but there was one essential difference between them in their attitudes to scientific knowledge. The two Forsters 'were in part men of the philosophical Enlightenment, in part inheritors of a German moralizing pietistic tradition.'[29] The journals of both Forster and his son, George, demonstrate clearly that they saw themselves as 'natural philosophers' whose ultimate concern was to look at nature and the world as created by God, and thus as capable of revealing God's powers and purposes. This vindication of providence as a unifying motif for a travel journal was not calculated to appeal to the secular-minded Cook, whose own journals only pay lip service to this narrative code.

When the *Resolution* reached England in July 1775, another more serious argument blew up, this time over who had the right to publish the official account of the voyage, which Forster claimed he had been promised. After Lord Sandwich, on behalf of the Admiralty, had rejected a sample of Forster's writing, Cook was authorised to go ahead with the publication of his own journal, edited by Douglas. This was much to the chagrin of Forster, who was perpetually broke, and had hoped to make his fortune from the book. Such was the background to Cook's remark about scientists which had so shocked King, and it was also why Cook was determined not to have any more 'experimental gentlemen' (with the exception of astronomers) on his ships. It was this absence of civilian restraint on board the *Resolution* that was later given by J. R. Forster as one reason for Cook's allegedly irrational and tyrannical behaviour during the third voyage.[30]

Relations between Cook and the professional astronomers who sailed with him seem to have been excellent. On the first voyage there was Charles Green, son of a Yorkshire farmer, who had worked at Greenwich with Maskelyne, the Astronomer Royal, with whom he had made trials of John Harrison's fourth chronometer in Barbados. Green and Cook successfully observed the 1769 transit of Venus in Tahiti, and later Cook wrote of him that he was:

> . . . indefatigable in making and calculating these observations [for latitude and longitude] which otherwise must have taken up a great deal of my time . . . Not only this, but by his instructions several of the petty officers can make and calculate these observations almost as well as himself.[31]

Nevertheless, when Green died at sea of fever Cook's journal comment was critical:

> He had long been in a bad state of health, which he took no care to repair but on the contrary lived in such a manner as greatly promoted

the disorders he had had long upon him, this brought on the Flux which put a period to his life.[32]

On the second voyage the astronomer on the *Resolution* was William Wales. There was also William Bayly, who served on the *Adventure*, and again on the *Discovery* during the third voyage. As has already been mentioned, Cook received considerable help from Wales in the writing up of his own journal. He also relied on him heavily for all matters astronomical and navigational – for ascertaining geographical position, making scientific observations ashore and afloat, instructing junior officers. Again, as with Green, he was complimentary about him in his journal.[33] Nevertheless, it was after his experience with the Forsters on the second voyage that Cook must have taken the decision not to have any civilian experts with him on board ship.[34] He therefore relied for astronomical help during the final voyage on Lieutenant James King, a highly qualified young man and also a subordinate naval officer.

Cook himself was a naval officer, under orders from the Admiralty, and the role of science during his voyages was, of course, inextricably meshed with the commercial and national interests of his country. Since the nineteenth century, science has been the universal creed, and even today there is perhaps at the back of our minds a vision of the scientist as someone engaged in an objective and pure – almost spiritual – search for truth. But in the eighteenth century the scientist had not yet been put on his pedestal, and the pursuit of science was mixed up with other priorities. Just as the various modern disciplines which then were subsumed within the global umbrella of 'natural philosophy' had not yet become distinguished, so also the modern requirement for a divorce between the objective search for knowledge and any vested interests had not yet been recognized. Certainly, Cook and his colleagues were, as Conrad suggested, in search of the truth, but they were also concerned to make discoveries that would be useful, and would in the first place increase the wealth and power of Britain and her empire. As Johann Forster states when summarizing his own objectives: 'The thirst of knowledge, the desire of discovering new animals, & new plants & to be happy to find perhaps one or more substances that might be useful to mankind in general & to the Dominions of Great-Brittain in particular, were the motives that animated me to go on this Expedition'.[35] Cook's voyages took place at a time when imperial impulses were indistinguishable from the advancement of knowledge itself, and there seems no doubt that he would have shared Forster's hybrid ambitions.

Chapter 9

Health Among Seamen

One essential requirement for any explorer is good health, and to start with Cook fitted the bill. He possessed two important physical advantages: firstly, to be capable of going without sleep for a considerable time and snatching brief periods of sleep when he had the chance; secondly, being able to eat and digest practically any food that was put in front of him.[1] 'His stomach', said Lieutenant James King, 'bore without difficulty the coarsest and most ungrateful food'. On the third voyage, for instance, they came across an abundance of 'Sea Horses' (i.e. walruses) on the rocky islands off Alaska, and these proved easy to catch. Cook therefore insisted that fresh walrus meat be served to all on the *Resolution*. He optimistically wrote in his journal, 'few on board did not prefer it to salt meat', but the midshipman Trevenen told a different story: 'Captain Cook here speaks entirely from his own taste which was, surely, the coarsest that ever mortal was endured with.' Trevenen went on to explain that most did eventually eat the walrus meat, but not because they enjoyed it:

> ... that was only because he would let us have nothing else to eat, having put a stop to the usual allowance of Ship's provisions. By this many who absolutely could not eat the sea horses, because it produced purgings and vomitings, were reduced to live on their scanty allowance of bread, till at last the discontents rose to such complaints and murmurings that he restored the saltmeat.[2]

Cook's gastronomic ability was particularly useful when it came to fraternising with natives who might easily take offence if one refused to accept their hospitality. Cook could usually swallow – and keep down – whatever was on offer, whether kangaroo, antarctic penguin or Tahitian roast dog. As his obituary in one newspaper (probably written by Banks) joked rather feebly, 'he eat constantly at his own table the usual food of the inhabitants of the country he was in, except when he was amongst the cannibals of new Zealand'. During the several weeks spent touring the Tonga group on the second voyage, the local chiefs held a number of receptions for Cook and his officers. An important element of these was the ritual production and consumption of *kava*, a drink made by a group of natives all sitting round chewing portions of the root of the *kava* plant and spitting the results into a bowl, the liquid from which was then strained off and served up. One officer described the resulting concoction as tasting like a combination of quinine and dishwater, but Cook managed to drink it – in fact he developed rather a taste for it. The others, however, could not, as he reports:

> . . . pieces of the root was first offered to us to chew, but as we excused ourselves from assisting in the operation it was given to others to chew which done it was put into a large wooden bowl and mixed with water . . . and as soon as it was properly strained for drinking, they made cups of Green leaves which held near half a pint and presented to each of us a Cup of the liquor, but I was the only one who tasted of it, the manner of brewing had quenished the thirst of every one else.[3]

Although at 39 Cook was almost the oldest person on board the *Endeavour*, he seemed to possess an iron constitution, and as far as we know went through the rigours of that voyage without a day's illness. But on the second voyage he was not so lucky and had more than his share of medical problems, although in his journal he makes light of these. For instance, in May 1773 there is a small aside: 'myself being confined on board by a cold',[4] whereas, according to J.R. Forster it was rather more than a cold: 'The captain was taken ill of a fever and violent pain in the groin, which terminated in a rheumatic swelling of the right foot, contracted probably by wading too frequently in the water, and sitting too long in the boat after it, without changing his cloaths.'[5]

Soon after this Cook started having recurrent stomach pains, which went on for months, although, stern stoic that he was, he did as much as possible to conceal his symptoms from the others. But in February 1774, he became really ill, as even he admits in his journal: 'I was now taken ill of the Billious colick and so violent as to confine me to my bed, so that the Management of the ship was left to Mr Cooper my first Officer.'[6] Before being forced to take to his bed Cook had still tried to make light of his condition. Forster takes up the story:

> The warm weather . . . proved fatal to captain Cook's constitution. The disappearance of his bilious complaint during our last push to the

south, had not been so sincere, as to make him recover his appetite. The return to the north therefore brought on a dangerous obstruction, which the captain very unfortunately slighted, and concealed from every person in the ship, at the same time endeavouring to get the better of it by taking hardly any sustenance. This proceeding, instead of removing, encreased the evil, his stomach being already weak enough before. He was afflicted with violent pains, which in the space of a few days confined him to his bed, and forced him to have recourse to medicines. He took a purge, but instead of producing the desired effect, it caused a violent vomiting, which was assisted immediately by proper emetics. All attempts, however, to procure a passage through his bowels were ineffectual; his food and medicines were thrown up, and in a few days a most dreadful hiccough appeared, which lasted for upwards of twenty-four hours, with such astonishing violence that his life was entirely despaired of. Opiates and glysters had no effect till repeated hot baths, and plasters of therica applied on his stomach, had relaxed his body and intestines. This, however, was not effected till he had lain above a week in the most imminent danger.[7]

During the second voyage they entered the Antarctic Circle three times in search of the elusive southern continent – each time being ultimately forced back northwards by the ice. Consequently, the voyage consisted of bitterly cold spells punctuated by periods of warmer, even tropical, conditions, and it appears that Cook's symptoms improved with the cold and deteriorated with the heat. The medical historian W. R. Thrower has diagnosed an acute gall-bladder infection, but more recently another expert, Sir James Watt, has offered a more complex thesis, that he was suffering from a roundworm infestation of the intestine, acquired from eating native food. In hot weather this could apparently produce the alarming symptoms described by Forster.[8] Watt goes on to argue that the more subtle, long-term effects of the infestation included interference with the body's ability to absorb vitamin B, especially niacin and thiamine. He suggests that Cook was never cured of the roundworm, so that the various symptoms which many biographers argue he exhibited on the third voyage, such as irritability, fatigue, loss of initiative and depression, and 'change of personality', are all, according to this theory, ascribable to increasingly severe vitamin B deficiency. If this is true, his medical condition may have been largely the cause of his eventual death at Kealakekua Bay.

The Royal Society's Copley Medal was awarded to Cook in 1776 after his second voyage, for fostering the health of his crews. Cook's journals show his concern for their fitness, diet and general welfare. Several measures contributed towards his achievement, including making sure that the ship was properly ventilated and fumigated, that the crew had warm, dry clothing, and that whenever possible they had adequate rest under a system of three watches per day rather than two, in order to relieve undue stress. And during the more peaceful periods, Cook was equally skilled at making sure the men were occupied, which also contributed to their well-being, as John Marra, author of a journal of the second voyage, explains:

> Another necessary precaution was that when the weather was fine, and the breeze steady, he never suffered any of his men to be idle but constantly employed the armourers, the carpenters, the caulkers, the sailmakers, rope-makers, the other tradesmen on board, as well as the foremastmen and professed navigators in doing something each in his own way, which though not immediately wanted, he knew there would be a call for before the voyage was completed. Having by this means no time for gaming, quarrelling, or rioting among them, he kept them in action and punished drunkenness with the utmost severity: and thus by persevering in a steady line of conduct he preserved their health.[9]

Great emphasis, too, was placed on cleanliness, and on one occasion we read that Cook inspected the men and fined with a day's loss of grog those with dirty hands.[10] None of this was particularly original. According to N.A.M. Rodger naval officers throughout the eighteenth century paid 'fanatical attention' to the cleanliness of their ships and men, since prevailing medical opinion held that disease was transmitted by 'corrupted air', as indicated, for instance, by bad smells.[11] Nevertheless, Cook's persistence and his attention to detail over long periods were probably what led to success in these matters.

The prevention of scurvy comes high among any list of Cook's achievements. It is probable that no one actually died from scurvy during any of the three voyages, although cases did occur, and it is possible that some died from other causes because they were already weakened by scurvy.[12] According to Rodger the significance of scurvy in this period has been greatly exaggerated, and contemporary doctors tended to use it as a catch-all term for anything they could not identify or cure. It is also true that scurvy was not something that any naval officer wanted to admit ever occurred on his ship, hence the difficulty for historians in estimating its frequency. When Francis Cuppage, the author of a recent book on the subject, suggests that over a million naval personnel might have died from scurvy between 1600 and 1800, Rodger comments sarcastically that this would mean every man who ever served in the navy died of scurvy approximately twice over.[13] To add to the problems of identification, the symptoms varied widely, ranging from putrid gums and body sores to a pervasive melancholy and sense of depression.

Until the very end of the eighteenth century there was little understanding of the cause of scurvy, or how to prevent it, although it was generally accepted among seamen that fresh meat and vegetables helped ward off its onset. During the Seven Years War, when much of the navy was engaged in long blockades of French ports, the naval Victualling Board went to great lengths to supply these commodities to ships at sea as regularly as possible. The Board also insisted that naval captains replace salt meat with fresh, and biscuit with baked bread, whenever they could. There were, too, a number of items held to be anti-scorbutic which were supplied to ships setting out on long voyages. However, many of these contained little or no ascorbic acid (vitamin C), which was only isolated in the twentieth century as the key factor preventing scurvy. Occasionally, trials were made by individuals of particular remedies, but such trials usually lacked scientific rigour, and the results were inconclusive. For instance, a young doctor, James Lind, published in 1754 some useful observations about the efficacy of lemon juice, but then, having been appointed physician to the new Haslar naval hospital at Portsmouth, he steadily moved away over the years to a more generally accepted position.[14] It may be, too, that some captains were aware from practical experience that lemon juice could cure scurvy. This seems to have been true for instance of Philip Carteret, who sailed across the Pacific in 1767, and on finally reaching the East Indies specifically demanded lemons for his sickly crew.[15]

Such was the situation regarding scurvy when Cook was getting ready to embark on the *Endeavour*. Consequently, he was supplied with a range of alleged anti-scorbutics, and requested to make trials of them during the voyage. The same occurred during preparations for his other voyages. The letters that Cook exchanged with the Victualling Board, and also the Sick and Hurt Board, which dealt with anti-scorbutics, show that he was not merely the passive recipient of stores, but had a considerable say in what he accepted, and in what quantities.

One commodity which Cook thought important was sauerkraut (i.e. pickled cabbage) which, although it may have been useful as a way of varying a monotonous diet, actually contained very little vitamin C, especially after prolonged storage.[16] Before each voyage he ordered large quantities of sauerkraut; for instance, on the second voyage he took 31,000 pounds of it, packed in 98 barrels, along with a lesser quantity of salted cabbage, which may have been more efficacious. The sauerkraut was served up on beef days, and in his *Endeavour* journal Cook congratulated himself on persuading the crew to eat it:

The Sour Krout the Men at first would not eate untill I put in pratice a Method I never once knew to fail with seamen, and this was to have some of it dress'd every Day for the Cabbin Table, and permitted all the Officers without exception to make use of it and left it to the option of the Men either to take as much as they pleased or none atall; but this pratice was not continued above a week before I found it necessary to put everyone on board to an Allowance.[17]

Something else Cook had great faith in was portable soup, which consisted of blocks of dried beef stock. The recipe for this was to mix it with either pease or oatmeal and boil it up with water. It was served on the three meatless, or 'banyan', days in the week (the word came via the East India Company, and originally meant a Hindu, i.e. a vegetarian). Portable soup was really intended only for the sick, but Cook arranged for enough of it to supply the whole crew.

Another anti-scorbutic Cook received, although in small quantities, was rob of lemon and orange, made by converting juice to a syrup by continuous boiling. He reported after the second voyage that 'The dearness of the rob of lemons and oranges will hinder them from being furnished in large quantities, but I do not think this so necessary; for, though they may assist other things, I have no great opinion of them alone.' He was right about the expense of the rob, as most citrus fruits had to be bought from Spain or her colonies, and large numbers of lemons or oranges were needed to produce the concentrated rob. Furthermore, the process of its manufacture removed much of the original vitamin C, although enough would have remained to make the rob a reasonably effective antidote to scurvy.

The anti-scorbutic in which Cook had the most faith, and which was recommended to him by the Admiralty before his first voyage, was malt (i.e. malted barley). Unfortunately, this, too, contained no vitamin C (though it might have had some vitamin B, which the normal sea diet was also deficient in). Philip Stephens, the Admiralty secretary, explained that 80 bushels of malt were to be packed in small casks and stored in the *Endeavour's* hold. The malt was to be under the charge of the ship's doctor who was to convert it into 'wort' when required, by mixing it with boiling water, and administer it to anyone showing the least signs of scurvy, at the rate of at least a quart per person per day. The use of malt for this purpose had been recommended by Dr. David Macbride (1726–78), an Irish medical writer whose views on the causes of scurvy were very influential, and had in fact become by Cook's time part of orthodox thinking on the subject. The opinion of Sir John Pringle, President of the Royal Society, which had been published, was supportive of Macbride, a fact which may well have influenced Cook's verdict.[18] The theory was that scurvy was a disease of putrefaction, or decay, of living tissues, and that the way to inhibit such decay was by ingesting substances such as wort which would ferment in the digestive tract. The fermentation would produce 'fixed air' (later named carbon dioxide), the presence of which would invigorate the tissues and prevent putrefaction.

After the second voyage Cook sent Pringle a highly favourable verdict on wort which Pringle quoted in a discourse to the Royal Society, and subsequently published in the Society's *Philosophical Transactions*:

> I have found the wort of the utmost service, in all scorbutic cases, during the voyage. As many took it by way of prevention, few cases occurred where it had a fair trial; but these, however, I flatter myself, will be sufficient to convince every impartial person, that it is the best remedy hitherto found out for the cure of the sea-scurvy; And I am well convinced from what I have seen the wort perform, and from its mode of operation, that, if aided by portable soup, sour kraut, sugar, sago, and courants, the scurvy, that maritime pestilence, will seldom or never make its alarming appearance among the ship's crew, on the longest voyages, proper care with regard to cleanliness and provisions being observed.[19]

As this extract shows, Cook, while enthusiastic about wort, did not feel able sufficiently to distinguish between the effects of the various anti-scorbutics he had been given. It is somewhat surprising that on the first voyage Cook did not listen to Banks, whose experience during the long, landless haul across the south Pacific towards Tahiti led him to back the rob of lemon as against malt wort. Banks writes:

> Wort was served out almost constantly, of this I drank from a pint or more every evening but all this did not so intirely check the distemper as to prevent my feeling some small effects of it. About a fortnight ago my gums swelld and some small pimples rose in the inside of my mouth which threatned to become ulcers, I then flew to the lemon Juice which had been put up for me according to Dr Hulmes method [i.e. made into rob of lemon] . . . The effect of this was surprizing, in less than a week my gums became firm as ever and at this time [April 1769] I am troubled with nothing but a few pimples on my face.[20]

Of course, if the navy had issued ships with whole lemons or oranges instead of rob, the scurvy problem would have been solved at a stroke, but both of these were costly. This decision by Cook to back malt rather than lemons actually contributed to delaying the search for a satisfactory treatment against scurvy on naval ships for some years. In 1785 a fleet well supplied with lemon juice (preserved in alcohol) reached Madras scurvy-free after nineteen weeks at sea, and a decade after that Sir Gilbert Blane, a prominent naval surgeon, finally persuaded the Admiralty to sanction regular supplies of oranges and lemons for naval ships.[21]

Rather than the use of alleged anti-scorbutic remedies, it was Cook's insistence on fresh food whenever possible that led to his generally successful record against scurvy. At every opportunity, he went to great lengths to find or buy fresh local supplies of fish, meat, and especially fruit and vegetables. In addition, he insisted on collecting edible green plants at any islands they came across. From the evidence of all the journals including Cook's it is possible to list over 50 species of plant which Cook's crews are likely to have sampled in different parts of the Pacific. These included various kinds of scurvy grass, wild celery, watercress, mustards and berries.[22] Alexander Home, master's mate on the *Discovery*, was quite correct when he wrote,

> Scarcly any thing Came wrong to him that was Green and he was as Careful in providing Vegetables for the Messes of the Crews as for his own Table and I do Belive that in this Means Consisted his graund Art of preserving his people in Health During so Many of the Longest and Hardest Voyages that was Ever Made.[23]

Home goes on to explain how all hands soon became aware that this was one of Cook's obsessions, and one way to keep in with him was to go and find something eatable and green:

> Perhaps in Many it Might be with a Veiw of making their Court to him, for they knew it was A great Recommendation to be seen coming on board from A pleasure Jaunt with A Handkerchief full of greens'.

As Beaglehole says, 'one thinks one sees the surreptitious smirk'.[24]

During the second and third voyages, Cook put great emphasis on the brewing of 'spruce beer' as an anti-scorbutic. This was beer based on molasses or sugar instead of malt, together with infusions of the cones, leaves or bark of spruce firs or other conifers. Spruce beer was held to derive its medicinal virtues from the vegetable matter and also, according to the fixed-air theory mentioned above, from the fermentation of the brewing process.[25] Unfortunately, neither was the case. It is true that a simple decoction of spruce would have been anti-scorbutic, as was shown, for instance, by Jacques Cartier in Canada during his 1535 expedition, but fermentation tended to destroy any vitamin C contained in the spruce. Cook's insistence on the crew drinking the spruce beer was no doubt admirable, but led on at least two occasions to altercations with those who could not stand the taste. As already mentioned, he describes one confrontation off Hawaii in December 1778 which led to him cutting off supplies of grog because no one would drink his home-made beer, and in the course of his account he mentions another occasion when there was 'a resolution they took on our first arrival in King George Sound [i.e. Nootka Sound], not to drink the spruce beer we made there'.[26]

To sum up, most, if not all, of the various anti-scorbutic substances used by Cook were ineffective. According to Jonathan Lamb the only truly anti-scorbutic measure he took was his prohibition against the men eating the salt-beef fat skimmed from the ships' boiling pans, as was traditional, since hot salt fat coming into contact with copper acquires a substance which irritates the gut and prevents the absorption of vitamins.[27] Yet Cook's overall record in the prevention of scurvy is impressive. This was because of his insistence on fresh food wherever possible and also perhaps owing to his overall leadership, and his concern for the cleanliness and well being of his crews.

Part III

Cook's Relations with Pacific Islanders

Chapter 10

How to Study Natives[1]

On 12 May 1769, in Tahiti, Cook reported a mysterious event involving Joseph Banks:

> This Morning a Man and two young women with some others came to the Fort whome we had not seen before: and as their manner of introduceing themselves was a little uncommon I shall insert it: Mr Banks was as usual at the gate of the Fort trading with the people, when he was told that some Strangers were coming and therefore stood to receive them, the compney had with them about a Dozn young Plantains Trees and some other small Plants, these they laid down about 20 feet from Mr Banks, the People then made a lane between him and them, when this was done the Man (who appear'd to be only a Servant to the 2 Women) brought the young Plantains Singley, together with some of the other Plants and gave them to Mr Banks, and at the delivery of each pronounce'd a Short sentence, which we understood not, after he had thus dispose'd of all his Plantain trees he took several pieces of Cloth and spread them on the ground, one of the Young Women then step'd upon the Cloth and with as much Innocency as one could possibly conceive, expose'd herself intirely naked from the waist downwards, in this manner she turn'd her Self once or twice round, I am not certain which, then step'd of the Cloth and drop'd down her clothes, more Cloth was then spread upon the Former and she again perform'd the same ceremony; the Cloth was then rowled up and given to Mr Banks and the two young women went and embraced him which ended the Ceremoney.[2]

In his journal Cook offers no explanation for this incident, but Beaglehole speculates that it 'may have been some sort of fertilization ceremony – the plantain was certainly phallic – the intended effect of which was to place the young women of the district at the disposal of Mr Banks'.[3] However, Anne Salmond believes that the ceremony, although a mark of great honour for a distinguished guest, 'carried no implication of sexual availability'.[4] Nicholas Thomas likewise argues that the woman's behaviour merely 'initiated a sort of trading partnership'. She was revealing not her genitals but her tattoos – thereby showing that she was a mature social actor and thus an appropriate person with whom to trade.[5]

Banks was later to make some progress in learning the Tahitian language but at this date he had been on the island for less than a month and consequently failed to understand the 'Short sentence' pronounced by 'the Man' involved in the ceremony. In order to work out what was happening all he had to go by were the various gestures and facial expressions of the participants. Based on these he assumed the women were indicating their sexual availability, and led them to his tent, although apparently they did not stay for long.

Several writers of Cook's day, and earlier, had in fact suggested that signs and gestures might constitute a form of natural communication, a 'universal language' which the whole world could follow. For instance, in 1644 John Bulwer wrote that:

> . . . the hand . . . speakes all languages, and as an *universal character of reason*, is generally understood and knowne by all nations, among the formall differences of their Tongue. And being the onely speech that is naturall to man, it may well be called the *Tongue and generall language of Humane Nature*, which, without teaching, men in all regions of the habitable world doe at the first sight most easily understand.[6]

A corollary of this view, expressed by Condillac and Burke amongst others, was that so-called primitive peoples would be especially proficient in the language of gesture because they had retained faculties of imagination and forceful expression long since atrophied in more sophisticated societies.

Cook and his companions had numerous opportunities of putting these theories to the test. Was there in fact a language of gesture that could be used and understood in first encounters between Europeans and indigenous peoples, or were signs and gestures invariably linked to their respective cultures, and hence incomprehensible to an outsider? In the journals it is easy to find examples to support either case. When the *Resolution* visited Tanna in the New Hebrides in August 1774, they encountered a language (or rather, several languages) completely different to others they had met and therefore were thrown back on Bulwer's 'generall language of Humane Nature'. This sometimes worked but often it did not. For instance, before landing they were confronted by a large, seemingly threatening crowd assembled on the beach, of which:

> . . . not one Was without arms: In short everything conspired to make us believe they intended to attack us as soon as we were on shore . . . one fellow shewed us his back side in such a manner that it was not necessary to have an interpreter to explain his meaning.[7]

So far so good with regard to a universal language of gesture, but very soon the grammar of this language became more opaque. A canoe was rowed out to the *Resolution* and an islander ceremoniously presented Cook with a barn owl – a totally obscure gesture, but clearly of significance.[8] Closer examination of the beach itself revealed some curious arrangements:

> Two divisions of the Natives were drawn up on each side the landing place, the space between was 30 or 40 yards, here were laid to the most advantage a few bunches of plantains, a yam and two Tara roots, between them and the shore were stuck in the sand four small reeds about 2 feet from each other in a line at right angles to the sea shore, for what purpose they were put there I never could learn.[9]

Beaglehole quotes an authority on the New Hebrides who writes:

> I think the explanation is simple enough. They were placed to indicate that the food was *tapu* [taboo]. Moreover, the natives clearly looked upon Cook as a returned ancestor . . . I have a notion, too, that the line of reeds was also designed to discover whose ancestor Cook was – whether that of the party to the left or that to the right. There seem to have been two different clans present.[10]

Such modern elucidations are all very well, but they were hardly likely to occur to Cook, who, having received no grounding in the science of ethnology (because no such science then existed) had to rely on common sense together with his increasing experience of island cultures. His instructions were to observe the 'Genius, Temper, Disposition, and Number of the natives and inhabitants, if there be any',[11] and these he recorded as faithfully as he could, yet where language was totally impenetrable, signs and gestures often proved insufficient except for the most basic communication. Threats of violence and invitations to sex were in the latter category – though even here, as we have seen in the passage at the beginning of the chapter, misunderstandings could occur.

On the third voyage Cook spent six months ranging the coasts of North America, and here, as in the New Hebrides, he came up against peoples whose words were unintelligible. David Samwell, surgeon on the *Discovery*, defines the problem:

> We enquired as well as we could by Signs of these Indians [on the Alaskan coast] whether the two inlets opened into any Sea &c, or whether they were shut, & everyone put what Construction he pleased upon the Signs they made us in return, and 'tis ten to one that the Indians knew no more of what we were enquiring after than we knew of this supposed Passage, in fact there is no dependence to be placed upon the Constructions we may put upon Signs &c. made by Indians where we are totally unacquainted with their Language. In enquiries of this sort it was hardly ever found that two people agreed in the interpretation they put upon the same Signs; upon the whole I am well convinced that no information obtained from Indians of whose Language we are ignorant can or ought in the least to be depended upon.[12]

However, for most of Cook's time in the Pacific he was dealing with the Polynesian language, various dialects of which were spoken from Hawaii in the north to New Zealand, and from Tonga in the west to the Marquesas. Cook had two great advantages here, the first being the three months the *Endeavour* had spent at Tahiti early on the first voyage, a period that allowed some members of the crew to pick up elements of the language, and the second, that he could turn to interpreters in the persons of Tupia on the first voyage and Omai on the third, both of whom acquired some English and had lived on board ship for extended periods. These assets did not mean that meaningful information was always acquired about native politics, culture or religion, as Cook himself was the first to admit. After the three-month stay on Tahiti he writes, 'I have learnt so little of [the Tahitian religion] that I hardly dare touch upon it.'[13] When discussing the 'customs, opinions and arts' of the Tongan people, he says, 'unless the object or thing we wanted to enquire after was before us, we found it difficult to gain a tolerable knowledge of it from information only without falling into a hundred mistakes' and the journals are peppered with similar disclaimers.[14] In the words of James Boswell, who dined with him in 1776, shortly before he set off on the third voyage:

[Cook] candidly confessed to me he and his companions who visited the south sea islands could not be certain of any information they got, or supposed they got, except as to objects falling under the observation of the senses; their knowledge of the language was so imperfect they required the aid of their senses, and any thing which they learnt about religion, government, or traditions might be quite erroneous.[15]

Nevertheless, much could be achieved through a combination of sign language and fragmentary Polynesian/English interchange. An example of what was possible occurs at Queen Charlotte Sound, New Zealand, on 6 November 1774, when Cook wished to discover what had happened to the *Adventure* from which the *Resolution* had been parted in a gale the previous October. Some locals had apparently seen the *Adventure* in the Sound earlier that year, and after two of them had been entertained to a meal in the great cabin, communication was effectively established. George Forster explains how:

We made two pieces of paper, to represent the two ships, and drew the figure of the Sound on a larger piece; then drawing the two ships into the Sound, and out of it again, as often as they had touched at and left it, including our last departure, we stopped a while, and at last proceeded to bring our ship in again; but the natives interrupted us, and taking up the paper which represented the Adventure, they brought it into the harbour, and drew it out again, counting on their fingers how many moons she had been gone.[16]

One strategy at which Cook and his colleagues became relatively proficient – provided the natives stood still long enough to be questioned, which the Australian aborigines, for example, seldom did – was to indicate certain objects or parts of the body and note down a transcription of the terms they were given. The neuroscientist and linguistic specialist Stephen Pinker has wittily described some of the pitfalls in this procedure:

Imagine a linguist studying a newly discovered tribe. A rabbit scurries by, and a native shouts, 'Gavagai!' What does *gavagai* mean? Logically speaking, it needn't be 'rabbit'. It could refer to that particular rabbit (Flopsy, for example). It could mean any furry thing, any mammal, or any member of that species of rabbit (say, *Oryctolagus cuniculus*), or any member of that variety of that species (say, chinchilla rabbit). It could mean scurrying rabbit, scurrying thing, rabbit plus the ground it scurries upon, or scurrying in general. It could mean footprint-maker, or habitat for rabbit fleas. It could mean the top half of a rabbit, or rabbit-meat-on-the-hoof, or possessor of at least one rabbit's foot. It could mean anything that is either a rabbit or a Buick. It could mean collection of undetached rabbit parts, or 'Lo! Rabbithood again!' or 'It rabbiteth', analogous to 'It raineth'.[17]

Apart from the Buick all this could have applied to Cook, and of course when the object under discussion was not immediately visible, or even worse, was abstract, the task became much harder. Cook believed that New Zealand was ruled by a single king named Teratu, because his enquiries as to where the king lived were often answered by a gesture towards the west and the phrase 'to ra to' (i.e. 'to the westward'). Similarly, natives informed Johann Forster that the name of their island was 'Tanna', although this simply meant 'ground' in the local language.[18] In spite of all this, the various island vocabularies collected by Cook and his colleagues are reckoned by modern experts to be remarkably accurate, given the circumstances in which they were collected, and the difficulties involved in transcribing unfamiliar vocal sounds onto paper. Using data from these vocabularies Cook was able to speculate fruitfully about the origins and subsequent diffusion of Polynesian peoples. For instance, about the inhabitants of Easter Island he writes:

> In Colour, Features, and Language they bear such affinity to the people of the more Western isles that no one will doubt but that they have had the same Origin, it is extraordinary that the same Nation should have spread themselves over all the isles in this Vast Ocean from New Zealand to this Island which is almost a fourth part of the circumference of the Globe, many of them at this time have no other knowledge of each other than what is recorded in antiquated tradition and have by length of time become as it were different Nations each having adopted some peculiar custom or habit &c[a] never the less a careful observer will soon see the Affinity each has to the other.[19]

This passage reveals a historical understanding unusual for the era, and which contrasts Cook with, for instance, his rival, Bougainville, whose perceptions were more limited, and who failed to appreciate the possibility of long-term historical changes in the cultures of the islands he visited.[20]

Cook is always particularly good when recording information about material objects or native crafts, as in this description of the seasonal houses of the Chukchi Indians of the north-eastern coast of Siberia. Such extracts illustrate his qualities as an observer – the assurance of personal examination, the precise measurement, the readiness to make comparisons or cautious speculations as to use:

> Here were both their Winter and summer habitations, the former are exactly like a Vault the floor of which is sunk a little below the surface of the earth. The one I examined was of an oval form the length where of was about twenty four feet and the height 12 or more; the framing was composed of Wood and the ribs of Whales, disposed in a judicious manner and bound together with smaller materials of the same sort. Over this framing is laid a covering of strong coarse grass and over it a covering of earth; so that on the outside it looks like a little hillock, supported by a wall of Stone about 3 or 4 feet high which is built round the two sides and one end; at the other end the earth is raised slooping to walk up to the entrance which is by a hole in the top of the roof over that end . . .
>
> The Summer huts were pretty large, and circular and brought to a point at the top; the framing was of slight poles and bones, covered with the skins of Sea animals. I examined the inside of one; there was a fire place just within the door or entrance where lay a few wooden vessels all very dirty; their bed places were close to the side and took up about half the circuit; some privecy seemd to be observed as there were several partitions made with skins, the bed and beding were of dear skins and the most of them were dry and clean. About the habitations were erected several stages ten or twelve feet high, such as we had observed on some part of the American coast; they were built wholy of bones and seemed to be intended to dry skins, fish etc. upon, out of the reach of their dogs, of which they had a great many.[21]

But it was one thing to record a static object, quite another to describe a collection of human beings and how they behaved. Cook ran up against one of the perennial problems of anthropological investigation – the difficulty of observing natives going about their everyday activities, because the European presence was so novel and exciting that everyone gave up what they were doing so as to crowd around the newcomers. 'It was always holyday with our visitors as well as with those we visited', he notes in Tongatapu on the third voyage, 'so that we had but few oppertunities of seeing into their domestick way of living'.[22]

An even more fundamental problem was the virtual impossibility of being able to study a people uncontaminated by contact with strangers. If indeed a particular culture was uncorrupted, that is, not yet subdued by the power of

European weaponry or tarnished through trade with Europeans, then they were also in a position to control their own lives, and, if they so wished, to control their visitors, for example, by not allowing them to go where they liked or inspect what they chose. This was the case, for instance, when the *Resolution* and *Discovery* arrived at Atun, one of the hitherto unvisited Cook Islands, in April 1777. Because the ships' boats were not able to cross the reef that surrounded the island, it was decided that a small group of officers, with Omai as interpreter, would entrust themselves to the islanders' canoes in order to make a landing. William Anderson, surgeon on the *Resolution*, was intensely curious to visit this virgin territory, but he soon discovered that he was not to have things all his own way:

> We regretted much that their behaviour prevented us making any observations on the country, for we were seldom a hundred yards from the place where we were introduc'd to the chiefs on landing and consequently were confind only to the objects that surrounded us. It was an opportunity I had long wish'd for, to see a people following the dictates of nature without being bias'd by education or corrupted by an intercourse with more polish'd nations, and to observe them at leisure, but was here disappointed.[23]

Even when the inhabitants of a particular island had become fully acclimatised to the European presence, there may well have been institutions or ceremonies which they were reluctant to share with outsiders. Cook's brief was to observe every aspect of native life and culture, and he seems to have taken the task especially seriously on the third voyage, possibly because there were no civilian scientists on that expedition. Perhaps the most ambitious piece of research he himself ever undertook, and one which reveals his strengths and weaknesses as proto-ethnologist, was his attendance at the two-day Tongan *inasi* ceremony to which he devotes several pages in his journal. His determination to see and report as much as possible is valuable because he was the sole European ever to view this highly secretive and solemn ritual, which in fact the Tongans only continued to observe for a few more decades. Its precise purpose is still unclear, but it appears to have been a cross between a harvest festival and an affirmation of allegiance to the ruling chief and the son who was to succeed him. Cook's ethnographic curiosity is admirable but his presence deeply displeased the Tongans, who held that by his very presence he was breaking *tapu*, and hence risking the anger and retaliation of the gods. In complying with the local dress code for the ceremony, Cook also managed to offend at least one of his officers' sense of decorum. Lieutenant Williamson writes:

We who were on the outside were not a little surprised at seeing Capt Cook in the procession of the Chiefs, wth his hair hanging loose & his body naked down to the waist; no person being admitted covered above the waist, or with his hair tyed; I do not pretend to dispute the propriety of Cap^n Cook's conduct, but I cannot help thinking he rather let himself down.[24]

One of Cook's main characteristics as an author is that he is on the whole non-judgmental when it comes to recording native customs – this can mean that his journal is less lively than those of others who were less cautious about expressing an opinion. Compare, for example, the entries of Cook and Charles Clerke, commander of the *Discovery* on the third voyage, about the pieces of bone which the Unalaskans inserted into their lower lips. Cook merely says, 'both men and Women bore the under lip to which they fix pieces of bone, but it is as uncommon at Onalaska to see a man with this ornament as a woman without it'. Clerke, typically, adds a personal point of view:

'These people have Holes in their under lip, for the reception of Ornaments, some one, others two, and some few, whom I suppose are the beaux of the Village, have three . . . this is a very foolish, awkward kind of bauble, as it frequently puts them to great inconveniences, for as you may often perceive they are under some embarrassment and trouble to keep their Ornaments in their proper position'.[25]

A further example of Cook's objectivity – and also generosity of spirit – occurs when he found himself forced to sit through three hours of a Tongan singing and dancing ceremony. He is much too cautious to admit how excruciatingly monotonous he probably found it:

These dances vary perhaps much more than we were able to discover, however there appeared a sort of sameness throughout the whole, and so would, I apprehend the most of our Country dances to people as unacquainted with them as we were with theirs.[26]

There speaks the potential ethnologist. About another ceremony in Tonga, during which there were some rather suggestive 'motions of the hands and snaping of the fingers', he was equally understanding: 'these indecent actions few as they are, do not arrise from any wanton ideas, but merely to increase the variety, for it is astonishing to see the number of actions they observe in their dances.'[27]

Prejudiced and sweeping comments on entire groups are rare from Cook. However they do sometimes occur when the group concerned spoke a totally unknown language and also had an unexpected physical appearance. On his first, extremely brief encounter with some natives of Tierra del Fuego in January 1769, he summed them up as 'perhaps as miserable a set of People as are this day upon Earth',[28] and on the second voyage when he met another group whom he took to be from the same tribe, he went further, describing them as 'a little ugly half starved beardless race', and that 'they do not seem to be more nicer in their food than in their persons, in short one sees nothing about them that is not disgusting in the highest degree'.[29] As for the Malekulans of the New Hebrides (who were 'quite a different Nation to any we have yet met with, and speak a different Language'), this 'Apish Nation' had 'flat and monkey faces', and were for Cook 'the most ugly and ill proportioned people I ever saw'.[30] Given such denigrating comments it seems rather odd that he has nothing negative to say about the Australian Aborigines from his first voyage, or the Tasmanians from the third. Each of these might well have appeared to him to be at a roughly similar stage of development to the Fuegans, yet about the Tasmanians he makes no comment at all, and the Aborigines, he thinks, were 'far more happy than we Europeans'.[31] The reason may be that he considered the almost naked Aborigines well adapted to their tropical climate, whereas the Fuegans seemed inadequately clothed and perpetually shivering in their much harsher environment. To sum up, when forced to write something about groups with whom he had little real contact, Cook sometimes forgets his habitual caution, and comes out with exaggerated and ill-founded generalisations, both negative and positive.

Cook's judgments about individuals on the other hand are often penetrating and with certain islanders whom he came to know well – frequently native chiefs – he even developed close personal links (see Chapter 12). By and large he was not given to recording his own feelings in his journals, but very occasionally he does let his guard down and reveal the intensity of a certain relationship. For instance, during August 1773 in Tahiti he met the mother of Toutaha, a chief with whom he had exchanged names on the first voyage:

> She seized me by both hands and brust into a flood of tears saying Toutaha Tiyo no Toute matte (Toutaha the friend of Cook is dead). I was so much affected at her behaviour that it would not have been possible for me to refrain mingling my tears with hers had not Otoo come and snatched me as it were from her.[32]

Cook is also non-judgmental about something which most of his companions viewed with deep horror and disgust. The New Zealanders had a habit of cooking and eating parts of enemies they had killed or captured. Cook had already become aware of this cannibalism on his first voyage, but on his return to England he discovered a degree of incredulity, and many asked him if he himself had actually witnessed the eating of human flesh. Therefore, on arriving at Queen Charlotte Sound on the second voyage he was determined to put the issue beyond doubt. One day Lieutenant Pickersgill bartered two nails for the head of a youth, about 15 years old, killed in battle, and brought it back on board. Strips of flesh were taken off the cheeks, grilled in the ship's galley, and offered to a visitor who, according to Charles Clerke who organised the grilling, ate it with evident pleasure and 'suck'd his fingers ½ a dozen times over in raptures'.[33] After describing this incident, and the onlookers' horrified reactions, Cook adds a lengthy passage in which he explains that cannibalism is not something natural to the Maori, a people whom he generally much admired:

> The New Zealanders are certainly in a state of civilization, their behaviour to us has been Manly and Mild, shewing always a readiness to oblige us; they have some arts a mong them which they execute with great judgement and unwearied patience; they are far less addicted to thieving than the other Islanders and are I believe strictly honist among them-selves. This custom of eating their enemies slain in battle (for I firmly believe they eat the flesh of no others) has un-doubtedly been handed down to them from the earliest times and we know that it is not an easy matter to break a nation of its ancient customs let them be ever so inhuman and savage, especially if that nation is void of all religious principles as I believe the new zealanders in general are and like them without any settled form of government; as they become more united they will of concequence have fewer Enemies and become more civilized and then and not till then this custom may be forgot.[34]

These sentiments reflect one of Cook's basic premises, certainly shared by the vast majority of his contemporaries – a firm belief in the progress of humanity. Peoples living beyond Europe were thought to exist behind Europe in time. Some of them – such as the natives of Tierra del Fuego or the Hottentots of Southern Africa – were a long way behind, in fact, not so far away from the first, natural state of humanity. As Locke once famously remarked, in a phrase that rings curiously today, 'in the beginning all the World was America'.[35] This was the theory generally accepted in Cook's day, that in order to progress from its original, primitive state, all human societies must pass through various stages of development.[36] Some groups were held to be further along this road, others further behind, the main point being that throughout the world there was only one possible set of goals, and every society was advancing, or could advance given the right circumstances, towards them. England, France and a few other European nations, of course, had already passed along the road, and had reached its terminus. So when Cook commented on the natives of the New Hebrides that 'these people are yet in a rude state', the operative word was 'yet'.[37] Charles Clerke is making the same point in his jocular style, when he declares of the Tasmanian aborigines, 'The Inhabitants seem to have made the least progress towards any kind of Improvement since Dame Nature put them out of hand, of any People I have ever met with.'[38]

This notion, that every part of the world had the possibility – in principle, at least – of one day becoming like Europe, was a keystone of Enlightenment thinking, and its optimism was in obvious contrast to the racist theories that succeeded it during the following century. However, it was also a restrictive and Eurocentric concept, in that the European pattern of development was assumed to be the only possible path of progress. On Cook's first voyage, Banks's enthusiastic account of Tahiti is full of suggestions for things that Britain might usefully copy, such as how the Tahitians made fishing nets, or how they wove their cloth from bark ('[here] I shall be rather diffuse, as I am not without hopes that my countrey men may receive some advantage').[39] Cook borrowed much of the information about the island supplied by Banks for insertion into his own journal, but it is striking that he departs from Banks by playing down the future possibilities of the Tahitian economy: 'notwithstanding nature hath been so very bountifull to it [i.e. Tahiti] yet it doth not produce any one thing of intrinsick Value or that can be converted into an Article of trade'.[40] On the later voyages, too, he never suggests that any particular native craft might usefully be imitated back at home. In this sense it was Banks who appears exceptional, and Cook very much a product of his time. He probably never entertained the idea that a certain society could behave in a way wholly different to European norms, yet internally consistent within its own cultural pattern and ethical standards. But in fact it was only a few years later, and in Germany rather than Britain, that this eurocentric vision, so typical of Enlightenment ideals, started to come under fire, to be replaced with the concept of cultural relativity. 'Ye men of all the quarters of the globe, who have perished in the lapse of ages', declaimed Johann Gottfried von Herder, in a work published in 1784, 'ye have not lived and enriched the Earth with your ashes, that at the end of time your posterity should be made happy by European civilization. Let justice be done to other ways of life.'[41] Instead of 'civilization' as a universal goal, Herder developed the novel idea, essential to the birth of the modern intellectual world, that different parts of the globe, and different races, could have their own cultures, each one as valid as the next. It is unlikely that anyone on Cook's expeditions, not even excluding the polymath, Johann Reinhold Forster, ever thought like this.[42]

Attempts to describe and compare different human societies go back a long way – in the West, at least, to the Greek historian, Herodotus, who discusses in his *History* numerous 'barbarian' societies that he had personally encountered, or been told about. However, the modern science of ethnology, with its methodology based on evidence gathered from rigorous field work, only gets underway less than two centuries ago – perhaps with Bronislaw Malinowski and his researches into the life of the Trobriand islanders of the Western Pacific, or slightly earlier, with Tylor and his attempt to set out a taxonomy of culture.[43] There is no doubt that Cook and his companions were not equipped for such investigations, lacking the linguistic skills, the time and opportunities necessary, and perhaps above all the mind-set that would permit them to accept indigenous societies on their own terms.[44] Yet it was Cook's determination to note down as much he could about the various peoples he visited, and to communicate with them as far as possible, that helped create the conditions for the new science eventually to emerge. The journals of Cook's voyages, including his own, were to provide, for several generations of scholars, a unique source of data concerning the islanders of the Pacific, and the nature of their early contacts with Europeans. Cook himself may have not been an ethnologist but his journals are a landmark on the path leading towards this future discipline.

Chapter 11

How to Treat Natives

A major theme of those writing about Cook after his death is his humanity towards the peoples of the Pacific he encountered and his behaviour towards them is often contrasted with contemporary slave-traders, or with the earlier cruelties of Spanish and Portuguese explorers.

> Not like that murd'rous band he came,
> Who stain'd with blood the new-found West;

writes Helen Maria Williams in her poem about Cook[1], and Hannah More, another contemporary, makes a similar comparison:

> Had these possess'd, O COOK! thy gentle mind,
> Thy love of arts, thy love of human kind;
> Had these pursued thy mild and liberal plan
> DISCOVERERS had not been a curse to man![2]

Some commentators go further and imply that Cook's main motive for embarking on his voyages was to befriend and civilise the islanders.

> What Pow'r inspir'd his dauntless breast to brave
> The scorch'd Equator, and th' Antarctic wave?

asks Anna Seward, who composed a lengthy 'Elegy on Captain Cook', and she answers her own question:

> 'It was HUMANITY!'[3]

And Cook's first biographer, Andrew Kippis, makes the same point, more prosaically:

to undertake expeditions with a design of civilizing the world, and meliorating its condition, is a noble object. The recesses of the globe were investigated by Captain Cook, not to enlarge private dominion, but to promote general knowledge; the new tribes of the earth were visited as friends; and an acquaintance with their existence was sought for, in order to bring them within the pale of the offices of humanity, and to relieve the wants of their imperfect state of society. Such were the benevolent views which our navigator was commissioned by his Majesty to carry into execution.[4]

This theme is a major component of the general softening of Cook's image that occurred after news of his death reached England. Cook was now no longer to be seen as a mere circumnavigator like Anson, an intrepid adventurer like William Dampier, or even as someone who lived and died in the service of his country such as General Wolfe, hero of Quebec. Instead, he evolves into an almost Christ-like figure, martyred by those he gave his life to help. As Rod Edmund puts it, he was transmogrified from military to bourgeois hero, and becomes 'a kind of thirteenth disciple embodying the Christian virtues of charity and benevolence, and respecting the common origin of all human-kind'.[5]

It was of course Cook himself who initiated this humanist myth in the first place. Throughout the journals he seeks to explain and justify his conduct to his superiors and to a wider public, and from the start there was pressure on him to present himself as consistently humane. A large part of the 'Hints' composed by Lord Morton, president of the Royal Society, and given to Cook before he set out on the *Endeavour*, concerns the treatment of natives, who were, writes Morton, 'human creatures, the work of the same omnipotent Author, equally under his care with the most polished European: perhaps being less offensive, more entitled to his favour'.[6] The Royal Society was a partner with the Admiralty in the planning of the voyage, and was to pay Cook a gratuity and a salary as one of the two astronomical observers on the *Endeavour*. The 'Hints' therefore carried considerable weight, and were in the nature of additional instructions for this voyage, and by implication also for the later ones. Morton urges that natives are not to be killed, even if they resisted European attempts to land:

sheding the blood of those people is a crime of the highest nature . . . They may naturally and justly attempt to repell intruders, whom they may apprehend are come to disturb them in the quiet possession of their country, whether that apprehension be well or ill founded.

> Therefore should they in a hostile manner oppose a landing, and kill some men in the attempt, even this would hardly justify firing among them, 'till every other gentle method had been tried.[7]

Here speaks, no doubt, the authentic voice of the Enlightenment, though Morton's advice may also have been partly a reaction to the news of Wallis's expedition, and the carnage off Matavai Bay in May 1768. Captain Wallis of the *Dolphin* had circumnavigated the world a year previous to Cook, and had come upon the island of Tahiti where there had occurred a bloody confrontation with the islanders, dozens of whom were slaughtered with grapeshot before Wallis judged it safe to land.

No such 'Hints' were issued before the second and third voyages but by then Cook was well aware of the force of public opinion. He knew that his contacts with Pacific islanders would be avidly read about, and hotly debated, just as had been the case with Hawkesworth. The many occasions when Cook either justifies his own conduct after a violent episode, censures others for shooting natives, or explains that he had rejected advice to be more ruthless, all show his concern to present a humane image to the reader. In his journals Cook is representing not only his voyages but also his own conduct and character.

To dwell on Cook's preoccupation with his humane image is in no way to argue that this image is a false one. Cook did not share the ruthless attitude towards other races shown by many of his contemporaries. This was an age of crude Eurocentric assumptions, and of unthinking cruelty towards less technically advanced peoples, as can perhaps be illustrated by a single notorious example from the lucrative slave trade of the day. In 1783 a certain Captain Collingwood, of the slave ship *Zong* bound for Jamaica, found himself faced simultaneously with an assortment of problems in that his stock of water was running low, his slaves were sickening from an epidemic, and his insurance policy only covered slaves lost at sea. He solved them all at a stroke by throwing 133 sick slaves into the sea in batches, and still wearing their chains.[8]

Before joining the *Endeavour*, Joseph Banks visited Newfoundland, and his diary for August 1765 provides a typical example of the treatment of indigenous people – in this case, the Beothuks – by local traders and settlers:

> Our people who fish in those Parts Live in a continual State of warfare with them firing at them whenever they meet with them & if they chance to find their houses or wigwams as they call them Plundering them immediately tho a Bow & arrows & what they call their Pudding is generally the whole of their furniture.[9]

Cook's predecessors in the Pacific, Byron and Wallis, also had shown little respect for native life, and both had no compunction in using firearms against club-wielding, or stone-throwing, islanders. It is probably true, too, that an endemic racism affected some at least of Cook's own officers and crews, and that many of them, if they had been allowed a free hand, would have dealt more harshly with the natives than Cook himself did. George Forster says as much when commenting on the Grass Cove massacre of December 1773.[10] Forster implies that this tragedy was largely the fault of Jack Rowe, the midshipman in charge, and that Rowe's high handed treatment of the Maori was also typical:

> Mr Rowe, the unfortunate youth who had the command of this boat, combined with many liberal sentiments the prejudices of a naval education, which induced him to look upon all the natives of the South Sea with contempt, and to assume that kind of right over them, with which the Spaniards, in more barbarous ages, disposed of the lives of the American Indians.[11]

Cook, however, did not usually follow the examples of Byron and Wallis, nor did he seem to have acquired 'the prejudices of a naval education' mentioned by Forster. It is also true that some of his colleagues admired his benevolent relationship with natives. George Forster's father who, as we have seen, was a frequent critic of Cook's decisions on the second voyage, nevertheless mentions 'the amiable manner with which he knew how to gain the friendship of all the savage and uncultivated nations',[12] and David Samwell writes:

> Capt[n] Cook ever acted with the utmost Impartiality, being as ready to hear the Complaint of an Indian and to see justice done to him when injured, as he was to any of his own Men.[13]

There are passages in his journals which indicate that Cook was fully capable of putting himself in the place of a native islander, and grasping his point of view. He was prepared to recognise, for instance, that the New Hebrideans, with whom there had just been a confrontation, were justified in trying to protect their islands from strangers:

> When one considers the light in which they must look upon us in, its impossible for them to know our real design, we enter their Ports without their daring to make opposition, we attempt to land in a peaceable manner, if this succeeds its well, if not we land nevertheless and

mentain the footing we thus got by the Superiority of our fire arms, in what other light can they than at first look upon us but as invaders of their Country.[14]

He could also stand back and assess the possible consequences of his voyages on those he encountered. Concerning the natives of New Zealand he writes on the second voyage that Europeans had debauched their morals and introduced new diseases, a passage subsequently deleted by John Douglas, the editor of the journal.[15] He was even, apparently, capable of admiring a people whose values seemed as distant from those of Europe as they could possibly be:

> From what I have said of the Natives of New-Holland they may appear to some to be the most wretched people upon Earth, but in reality they are far more happier than we Europeans; being wholy unacquainted not only with the superfluous but the necessary Conveniencies so much sought after in Europe, they are happy in not knowing the use of them. They live in a Tranquillity which is not disturb'd by the Inequality of Condition: the Earth and sea of their own accord furnishes them with all things necessary for life, they covet not Magnificent Houses, Houshold-stuff etc., they live in a warm and fine Climate and enjoy a very wholsome Air, so that they have very little need of Clothing and this they seem to be fully sencible of, for many to whome we gave Cloth etc to, left it carlessly upon the Sea beach and in the woods as a thing they had no manner of use for. In short they seem'd to set no Value upon any thing we gave them, nor would they ever part with any thing of their own for any one article we could offer them; this in my opinion argues that they think themselves provided with all the necessarys of Life and that they have no superfluities.[16]

It is difficult to believe that Cook based these conclusions about the Australian aborigines on any substantial evidence, since they were the most elusive and shy of all the peoples he met in the Pacific. Such myths of the 'noble savage', quite common in travel narratives of the day, were often not so much about the natives themselves, but rather a coded way of attacking the evils of one's own society – its alleged corruption, materialism, etc. The key to this passage may lie in Cook's statement that the aborigines did not 'covet . . . Magnificent Houses, Houshold-stuff etc'. Do we detect here a sympathy implicitly linked with his own background – the years of spartan living, first with his parents on the farm and later in the comfortable but unostentatious household of John Walker, the Quaker? Perhaps he admired people who could live without material possessions, in contrast to those who wasted their money on luxuries. That his musings were not just a temporary aberration is proved by his writing in very similar vein after the voyage to his old employer, John Walker of Whitby – a letter in which he also describes Tahiti and other South Sea islands as 'Terrestrial Paridises'.[17] On the second voyage, too, there are hints that this enthusiastic attitude towards unspoilt peoples had not been entirely eradicated. He writes, about the natives of Tonga:

> No one wants the common necessaries of life, joy and contentment is painted in every face; indeed how could it be otherwise, here an easy freedom prevails among all ranks of people, they injoy every blessing of life and live in a climate where the extremes of heat and cold is unknown.[18]

There were, however, occasions when Cook forgot his own commitment to sympathy and understanding of the Other, and these were the times when he came up against the contradictions lying at the heart of his entire project. The realities inherent in a voyage of discovery were frequently incompatible with the ideals of Mortonian humanism. For example, a pressing need to land on a particular island in order to replenish supplies of fresh food and water might take precedence over that 'utmost patience and forbearance with respect to the Natives' requested by Lord Morton. Such was the case when the *Resolution* arrived at Erromanga in the New Hebrides during the second voyage. Cook and a boatload of marines tried to land because they needed water but a crowd of natives opposed the landing, so Cook gave the order to fire, killing several. The carnage could have been even worse. In his journal Cook wrote, 'happy for many of these poor people not half our Musquets would go off otherwise many more must have fallen'.[19] But a fortnight later, at the neighbouring island of Tanna, there occurred an event which shows Cook back in humanist mode. As we have seen, he became very angry on hearing that William Wedgeborough, a marine on sentry duty, had fired at, and killed, an islander who had pointed an arrow at him. Cook writes:

> I was astonished beyond measure when the sentry fired for I saw not the least cause . . . The rascal who perpetrated this crime, pretended that a Man had lain an arrow a Cross his bow and was going to shoot it at him, so that he apprehended himself in danger, but this was no more than what they had always done, and I believe with no other view than to shew they were armed as well as us, at least I have no reason to think so, as they never went further.[20]

Wedgeborough was punished, though not as severely as Cook wanted, because other officers pleaded that he had behaved quite properly. Edgcumbe, Lieutenant of the marines, said that 'the man was entitled to believe he was not posted there merely to provide a target for arrows, without the right to defend himself'.[21]

These two adjacent episodes, the one where an unknown number of islanders attempting to defend their own beach were killed because Cook wanted to land, the other when he punished a marine for merely pre-empting a possible attack on himself, show clearly the ambivalence of his position. Whatever his instructions, and his own good intentions, it was simply not possible to avoid violence, or the threat of violence, on first making contact with Pacific islanders. Lord Morton himself had not been anywhere near the Pacific, and his 'Hints' turned out to be the well-meaning advice of an armchair moralist who was acting a similar role to those stay-at-home geographers and savants whom Cook often disparages. An example of the impracticality of Morton's thinking is when he suggests ways to convince natives about the lethal nature of firearms without actually shooting them:

> By shooting some of the Birds or other Animals that are near them;–
> Shewing them that a Bird upon wing may be brought down by a Shot.–
> Such an appearance would strike them with amazement and awe.[22]

Cook may have found this advice laughable. Apart from the fact that when shooting at birds his colleagues usually missed,[23] it was often the case that natives were not even deterred from aggressive behaviour by a peppering of small shot, let alone a sporting demonstration.

First contact with a particular people having been successfully established, a new problem almost invariably cropped up – pilfering. Islanders were often adept at abstracting anything they could lay their hands on, from scientific instruments and weapons, to the personal property and clothing of members of the expedition, and on one occasion even the ships' cats.[24] Cook usually reacted strongly to theft. It was materially damaging, and could even endanger the entire voyage, as in the case of a ship's boat, or a sextant. Furthermore, it was ideologically repugnant and morally reprehensible. Cook and his colleagues tended to assume that the laws of property, as inscribed in the hearts of eighteenth-century Englishmen, formed part of natural law and therefore must surely be acknowledged throughout the world. He often judges a particular group by its propensity to steal, writing of the Tahitians, for instance, 'they are thieves to a Man and would steal but everything that came in their way, and that with such dexterity as would shame the most noted pickbocket in Europe'.[25] The

Hawaiians, however, were very different: 'It is remarkable that they have never once attempted to cheat us in exchanges or once to commit a thieft.'[26]

If someone was detected in an act of theft he was shot at and sometimes killed and those who were caught were punished by floggings. On the third voyage the punishments and reprisals grew ever more severe, culminating in the affair of the stolen goat. Zimmerman relates what happened:

> Cook went ashore . . . when he asked after the goat they mocked him into the bargain and ran with all haste into the bush . . . Cook, possessed of a quick temper, was very indignant over this and for two days he had the marines burn every hut that was to be found inland whilst the sailors practised a like destruction along the shore and also chopped up and completely destroyed all the native canoes which they found. The damage which the inhabitants thereby sustained could scarcely be repaired in a century.
>
> These people had canoes which, after their fashion, were most practical and in some cases very large and constructed with infinite pains. I must therefore disapprove somewhat of Captain Cook's procedure . . . Soon after we returned to the ship on the second day of this devastation the goat was brought back by the natives and turned loose amongst the rest of the cattle which were still at pasture.[27]

It was, however, an open question whether these laws of property were also inscribed in the hearts of Pacific islanders, who had not had the benefit of having been brought up under the strictest criminal code in Europe, or on a diet of weekly Protestant sermons. Islanders tended to live very much in the present, and while they might be aware that stealing was not approved of, they probably did not suffer from the same degree of guilt as would a European. Pacific societies did have private property – Cook corrects a misapprehension by Bougainville that everything in Tahiti was communally owned – but property rules did not play nearly such a central role as they did in Europe, and useful natural objects, such as breadfruit or shellfish, were often publicly available, although chiefs' requirements might take precedence over those of common people.

This relaxed attitude to other people's property can be seen in the case of the man from Kauai (one of the Hawaiian islands) who said plaintively, when he was prevented from removing the *Resolution*'s lead and line, 'I am only going to put it into my boat.'[28] Frequently, it is clear that thieving was seen as an entertaining game in which the objects stolen were not the point. At Queen Charlotte Sound a young man broke into an officer's cabin and took a copy of the novel *Tom Jones*, and at Tongatapu another young man stole from another cabin a volume of Pope's Homer and a Nautical Almanac.[29]

How to stop theft was the problem, and on the third voyage especially, Cook started exacting an irrational revenge. For example, after they had stayed several weeks in Tonga, in June 1777, relations seem to have deteriorated between Cook and the common people so much – due to harsh reprisals against petty theft – that stones were thrown at sailors working near the shore. Edgar, master of the *Discovery*, reports Cook's reaction to one such episode:

Tonga 28 June 1777

About 10 in the Morning those of the old Offenders who had ston'd our Centinels and Wood Cutters were taken prisoners. Captain Cooke punish'd one with 3 dozen lashes, another with 4 dozen and the third with 6 dozen lashes . . . After this a strange punishment was inflicted on the Man which received Six dozen as Captain Cooke said that he might be known hereafter, as well as to deter the rest from theft or using us ill when on Shore – this was by scoring both his arms with a common knife by one of our Seamen, Longitudinally and transversely, into the Bone.[30]

On this occasion Cook himself reports in his journal merely that some natives had been arrested, and that 'I did not then dismiss them without punishment',[31] but, as Beaglehole says, in Tonga there were those who remembered Cook without love.

Often it proved impossible to detect the actual culprits and at such times, as mentioned above, Cook tended to lose patience and embark on collective sanctions, which might result in the return of the stolen property, but which also caused much resentment. Another reaction to anonymous pilfering was to take a chief or his family hostage pending the return of the property. This tactic was employed more or less successfully at Tahiti, Raiatea and Tongatapu, but at Kealakekua Bay, Hawaii, in February 1779, it failed disastrously leading to the deaths of Cook himself and a number of others.

The incompatibility between efforts to treat islanders with benevolence and respect, and the goals of the voyages, was exacerbated by underlying assumptions of superiority, and the need for Europeans to maintain 'face' at all times. When his first efforts to retrieve the goat at Moorea failed, Cook explains his decision to burn houses and canoes. He writes, 'I was now very sorry I had proceeded so far, as I could not retreat with any tolerable credit, and without giving incouragement to the people of the other islands we had yet to visit to rob us with impunity.'[32] This seems an inadequate justification for all the destruction that was to follow, the real motive for which was evidently Cook's perceived loss of credit if the goat was not returned. It was 'face' that determined Cook's decision to fire over the heads of a crowd of Marquesas islanders in April 1774, even though he had already quitted their island of Takaroa:

> As soon as the boats were hoisted in I ordered two or three Guns to be fired over the little isle the Natives were upon in order to shew them that it was not their own Superior strength and numbers which obliged us to leave their isle.[33]

There is an even clearer example of the same attitude from the first voyage, when Cook decided to take prisoner the crew of a fishing canoe in Poverty Bay, New Zealand. The unfortunate fishermen did their best not to be taken, throwing everything they had in their canoe, including the fish they had caught, at the sailors in the pinnace alongside them. Eventually three were captured and three or four killed. After the event, Cook writes:

> . . . had I thought they would have made the least resistance I would not have come near them, but as they did I was not to stand still and suffer either myself or those who were with me to be knocked on the head.[34]

This was disingenuous, as he could easily have sailed away from the canoe once it became evident there would be resistance. In a draft version of this passage in the journal he shows that his real motive was possible loss of face:

> When we was once a long side of them we must either have stud to be knockd on the head or else retire and let them gone off in triumph and this last they would of Course have attributed to their own bravery and our timorousness.[35]

The adjective, 'insolent', quite frequently applied to particular islanders by Cook and his colleagues, is another indication of the same attitude of superiority. He used this epithet to describe, for example, troublesome natives from Poverty Bay on the first voyage, from Tanna on the second, and from Tonga on the third.[36] The dictionary defines insolence as disrespect by an inferior towards a superior, or contempt of rightful authority. It is also what one might describe as a barrier term, the use of which eliminates any need to delve further and discover the cause of the alleged insolence. European *amour propre* (self-esteem), and the perceived need to display superiority over indigenous peoples at all times, were obstacles getting in the way of any genuine or lasting cross-cultural friendship.

Behind these assumptions lay not so much any cultural or moral ascendancy, but simply the possession of firearms. Once, in New Zealand, Gore shot and killed a native for cheating over an exchange of pieces of cloth, and Cook comments:

> I must own that it did not meet with my approbation because I thought the punishment a little too severe for the Crime, and we had now been long enough acquainted with these People to know how to chastise trifling faults like this without taking away their lives.[37]

Gore here was acting as both judge in his own cause, and executioner, but on this occasion he had, in Cook's opinion, picked the wrong option. There was a range of possible punishments available, and death, while perhaps fitting at another time and place, was here inappropriate for such a 'trifling fault'. But whether or not natives were shot on any given occasion, or punished for stealing, was largely irrelevant, since the back-up possibility of overwhelming European firepower was always there. Violence was implicit in every encounter Cook ever had with Pacific peoples, just as it had been with Byron or Wallis, and it preceded and underlay any notions of benevolence, or protestations of undying friendship with particular islanders. It is certainly true that Cook was more humane, more sensitive, in his dealings with the newly discovered peoples of the Pacific than many other Europeans had been or were to be, but nevertheless, his role as 'discoverer', and agent of empire, was not dissimilar to other European travellers, and nor was his weaponry.

Chapter 12

Natives Cook Knew

In this chapter I pick out four Pacific islanders whom Cook met, and whose stories seem to give some insight into his own views and attitudes. The first of these is Tupaia, whose acquaintance represents perhaps the most significant interaction between Europeans and Pacific islanders during all of Cook's voyages.[1] In June 1767, Tupaia had first met British sailors, in the shape of members of Wallis's earlier expedition in the *Dolphin*, who were impressed with his knowledge and apparent status, christening him Jonathan. Two years later he chose to accompany the *Endeavour* when she sailed away from Tahiti in July 1769, and he remained with them until his death in Batavia nearly 18 months later. He was then in his mid-forties, a man of varied talents and in many ways the ideal native companion for Pacific voyaging.

Tupaia was born of a high-ranking family in the island of Raiatea, but he came to Tahiti as a young man after losing his father and his ancestral lands when Raiatea was captured by invaders from neighbouring Bora Bora. He was by birth a member of the peripatetic *arioi*, or priestly caste, and had travelled widely throughout the Society Islands, and even as far as the Tonga group to the west. In Tahiti he became adviser, and also lover, to Oborea (or Purea), the forceful lady whom Cook describes in his journal as queen of Tahiti, although she was not exactly royal, and her political power was already on the decline when he met her, which was probably one reason why Tupaia chose to leave the island.

According to his journal it was actually Banks who persuaded a reluctant Cook to take Tupaia. He writes:

> Tupaia came on board, he had renewd his resolves of going with us to England, a circumstance which gives me much satisfaction. He is certainly a most proper man, well born, chief Tahowa or priest of this Island, consequently skilld in the mysteries of their religion; but what

makes him more than anything desirable is his experience in the navigation of these people and knowledge of the Islands in these seas; he has told us the names of above 70, the most of which he has himself been at. The Captn refuses to take him on his own account, in my opinion sensibly enough, the government will never in all human probability take any notice of him; I therefore have resolvd to take him.[2]

Banks goes on to discuss his own motives for taking him, in rather unfortunate language which suggests it was the result of an aristocratic whim:

> Thank heaven I have a sufficiency and I do not know why I may not keep him as a curiosity, as well as some of my neighbours do lions and tygers at a larger expence than he will probably ever put me to; the amusement I shall have in his future conversation and the benefit he will be of to this ship, as well as what he may if another should be sent into these seas, will I think fully repay me.

Banks's implication that Tupaia was being collected as one might collect animals for a zoo was wide of the mark, since he was actually a strong, independent character quite capable of making his own decisions. His usefulness became apparent soon after leaving Tahiti because Cook decided to spend several weeks touring the Society Islands until his crew, many of whom were suffering badly from venereal disease, were strong enough to face the cold and stormy seas expected on the way to New Zealand. Tupaia not only possessed navigational and interpreting skills but he also, due to his status as high priest and his knowledge of Polynesian cosmology and ritual, made relations with the various islanders much easier than they would have been without him. At the same time he helped Banks compile an account of Tahiti and its inhabitants, a description which Cook largely borrowed for his own journal. He also made for Cook a map showing all the Pacific islands he had visited, or knew about, from Tonga and Samoa down to New Zealand. The map itself has disappeared, but a copy Cook made of it has survived.[3]

Another major achievement of Tupaia's involved an artistic apprenticeship. Recent research has shown that a number of sketches previously attributed to Banks because they were found among his papers were actually by Tupaia.[4] These include scenes from Tahitian life as well as, for instance, the drawing of a European, possibly Banks, exchanging bark-cloth from Tahiti for a New Zealand crayfish, which is reproduced on page 157. These sketches may seem primitive to our eyes but one has to remember that in Tahiti no tradition of realistic or descriptive art existed, although art was used for religious purposes as well as decorating canoes, and tattooing. Tupaia would therefore have had to tackle this western art form entirely from scratch, perhaps by watching and practising with Sydney Parkinson, the young artist on the *Endeavour*. Glyndwr Williams makes the point that when Tupaia took up his paint brush he was crossing a significant intellectual, and even racial, boundary. To record people and their behaviour in this permanent way was to exercise a certain power, of a kind usually reserved for Europeans and quite unexpected from Pacific islanders.[5]

Tupaia's services were still in demand when the *Endeavour* reached New Zealand because it turned out that in language and culture New Zealand was not that dissimilar to the Society Islands, from where the ancestors of the Maori had probably come. However, he was less useful when the expedition reached Australia, since the Aborigines spoke a completely different language, or rather languages, of which no one, including Tupaia, understood a word. Nevertheless, there is no doubt that his presence made a huge difference to the success of the voyage generally, in that contact with the various peoples they met would have been far more awkward, and probably more violent, without him. In his journal Cook notes that 'Tupia always accompanies us in every excursion we make and proves of infinate service',[6] and when speculating about a possible future expedition to search for the Southern Continent he writes:

> Should it be thought proper to send a ship out upon this service while Tupia lieves and he to come out on her, in that case she would have a prodigious advantage over every ship that have been upon discoveries in those seas before; for by means of Tupia, supposeing he did not accompany you himself, you would always get people to direct you from Island to Island and would be sure of meeting with a friendly reseption and refreshments at every Island you came to.[7]

During this second expedition – and long after Tupaia's death – more evidence emerges about his importance, because wherever the *Resolution* went, natives enquired about him, and were sad to hear he was no longer alive. Cook comments that he seemed as familiar to those who had never met him but only heard his name, as to those who had met him, and that 'it would be no wonder if at this time it [Tupaia's name] is known over great part of New Zealand'.[8] It was almost as if many islanders thought of him as the real leader of the expedition because it had been he who had communicated with them, and who had even been able to tell them about the origins of their own religion and customs.

In spite of this evident usefulness all had not been plain sailing between Tupaia and the crew of the *Endeavour*. He was a man who knew his own worth, and made sure others knew it. It may be that sailors and officers resented a native who apparently considered himself so superior. As John Marra, who had joined the *Endeavour* at Jakarta and who also sailed on the second voyage, later reported:

> Toobia . . . was a man of real genius, a priest of the first order, and an excellent artist: he was, however, by no means beloved by the Endeavour's crew, being looked upon as proud and austere, extorting homage, which the sailors who thought themselves degraded by bending to an Indian, were very unwilling to pay, and preferring complaints against them on the most trivial occasions.[9]

Possibly indicative that Tupaia was not entirely popular on board ship is the fact that none of the journals mention his artistic efforts, and also that among all the images that were made during the voyage by Parkinson and others, no portrait of him has survived.

By the autumn of 1770 Tupaia was developing signs of scurvy. The heavily salted meat diet on board ship did not agree with him, and when he had no opportunity, during the long weeks at sea, of collecting his own food in the shape of shellfish or greens, he became progressively weaker. He died during the expedition's stay at Batavia – probably from the effect of malaria on his already weakened constitution. In his journal Cook wrote him an obituary which sounds rather ungracious, and perhaps shows that he, too, resented Tupaia's claims to authority:

> He was a Shrewd, Sensible, Ingenious Man, but proud and obstinate which often made his situation on board both disagreeable to himself and those about him, and tended much to promote the deceases that put a period to his life.[10]

It seems that Tupaia did not conform to the helpful yet deferential role expected of an 'Indian', and this may have been why Cook labeled him 'proud and obstinate'. Perhaps, too, with his geographical expertise, he sometimes questioned Cook's decisions, and if so, this would have been a cardinal sin, a sin of which John Reinhold Forster was also found guilty during the next voyage.[11] The captain's authority was never to be undermined. There may well have been, as David Turnbull suggests, 'an element of ambivalence and patronizing eurocentricity' in Cook's attitude to Tupaia.[12]

My next choice of native known to Cook is very different. Kahura did have his portrait painted, but on the other hand Cook hardly knew him since he only met him quite briefly during a stay at Queen Charlotte Sound in New Zealand during the third voyage. Nevertheless, he is included here as I think his relationship with Cook does reveal something about the latter.

Kahura was a Maori chief who visited the *Resolution* twice, during February 1777. The second time he brought about twenty members of his extended family with him and he (though perhaps not all the others) was entertained in Cook's cabin. There his eye fell on a portrait by John Webber, and he asked if he too could have his portrait painted, so he sat for Webber, who produced the likeness reproduced on the following page. This shows an energetic, youngish man, his face bearded and tattooed in complex patterns, his hair done up in a neat top knot with white feathers. He is wearing a garment made of flax, and there are ornaments – possibly of bone – dangling from his pierced ears. He looks alert, intelligent and poised – altogether a sympathetic portrait. It seems that Kahura made a hit with both Cook and Webber. But this is somewhat strange, considering he was the self-confessed leader of those who, two years earlier, had massacred, and then eaten, a boatload of British sailors.

During the previous voyage, the *Adventure* under Tobias Furneaux, having lost contact with Cook in the *Resolution*, had spent several weeks at Queen Charlotte Sound. One day a boat crew under the command of Jack Rowe, master's mate on the *Adventure*, had visited a certain cove to cut grass for the animals on board. A crowd of islanders gathered round them, some trading took place, and then a quarrel sprang up over an exchange concerning a stone adze for which the owner alleged a sailor had not handed over anything in return. Some of the sailor's bread was then snatched, and when he tried to get it back a scuffle ensued. Rowe fired his musket and killed the native concerned. But before he could reload, the others, led by Kahura, attacked the party, and after a fight they were all killed.

There was another dimension to this story. When a launch commanded by James Burney, the *Adventure's* Second Lieutenant, was dispatched to look for the original boat crew, they discovered at Grass Cove, the scene of the massacre, baskets full of pieces of human flesh, including the tattooed hand of a sailor; while in the adjoining cove a party was still going on, with natives sitting round cooking fires, and dogs busy devouring the roasted remains of heads, hearts and other human parts. In his report Burney described in detail this 'shocking scene of Carnage and Barbarity', and therefore when he met Kahura, Cook not only heard him admit to the massacre, but also certainly was aware of the cannibalism that had accompanied it.[13]

Kahura, the New Zealand chief whom Cook met in February, 1777, and who then admitted being responsible for killing and eating a boatload of British sailors two years earlier. A pen and ink drawing by John Webber.

It seems that practically everyone concerned except Cook thought that Kahura should have been killed rather than having his portrait painted.[14] Other Maoris who visited the ship told Cook that he was a bad man and deserved to die. To their way of thinking, Kahura and his accomplices had eaten parts of the sailors in order to gain their spirit, or *mana*. To kill and ritually eat members of another group was therefore not only the ultimate insult and humiliation, but also meant that the killers acquired some of the power of those humiliated. Thus by visiting the ship Kahura was provocatively flaunting the power he had gained by killing other Englishmen. The Maoris could not understand why Cook was so forgiving, and they interpreted it as a sign of weakness in a leader.

The officers and men under Cook also fully grasped this attitude. James Burney, now second in command of the *Discovery*, and witness of what had occurred at Grass Cove, was speaking for the two crews when he wrote:

> It seemed evident that many of them held us in great contempt and I believe chiefly on account of our not revenging the affair of Grass Cove, so contrary to the principals by which they would have been actuated in the like case.[15]

Another member of the *Resolution's* company was even more perplexed and offended by Cook's attitude. This was Omai, the South Sea islander who had originally been brought back to England by Furneaux, and whom Cook was now returning to his home. When he was asked to bring Kahura to the great cabin Omai exclaimed furiously, 'There is Kahourah, kill him', and later on, when Cook ignored him, he protested:

> Why do you not kill him, you tell me if a man kills an other in England he is hanged for it, this Man has killed ten and yet you will not kill him, tho a great many of his countrymen desire it and it would be very good![16]

Cook wrote in his journal that Omai's argument, 'though reasonable enough had no weight with me'. About Kahura he added: 'I must confess I admired his courage and was not a little pleased at the confidence he put in me'.[17] But why did Cook take this line? The only indication we have from the journal is this statement:

> I had always declared to those who solicited his death that I had always been a friend to them all and would continue so unless they gave me cause to act otherwise; as to what was past, I should think no more of it as it was some time sence and done when I was not there, but if ever they made a Second attempt of that kind they might rest assured of feeling the weight of my resentment.[18]

The operative phrases here are 'a friend to them all', and 'done when I was not there'. Cook always saw himself as the impartial protector of the various Pacific peoples he met, but not as their judge. He was prepared to punish, or even shoot, natives whose actions threatened the goals of his expeditions or his own status as commander, but in this case he did not see Kahura as a threat, or how killing him would help. The Grass Cove massacre had not impinged on his personal authority since the victims had not been under his command, and he himself had been hundreds of miles away at the time. In this particular case, too, he believed there had been faults on both sides, that Jack Rowe's decision to shoot had been hasty, and that Kahura's actions had been impulsive, not pre-meditated. Cook's decision not to punish Kahura was clearly a considered one, since he held to it even at the expense of his own popularity. Anne Salmond argues that resentment over this particular incident was highly significant since it started a gradual process of alienation between Cook and his men which was to lead to a partial breakdown of morale and discipline in the months to come.[19]

Next on my list of natives that were known to Cook is Omai himself, the young Society islander who was brought back to England on the second voyage, lived there for a year and was then transported back home on the third voyage.[20] Cook's relationship with Omai is interesting, since Omai was an example of someone whose good and bad points of character were diametrically opposed to his own. Omai was charming, childish, happy-go-lucky, irresponsible and spontaneous, while Cook was – as we know him. Actually, Cook did not choose to bring Omai back in the first place – this was the decision of Furneaux, captain of the *Adventure*, and it was possibly a decision that Cook resented. Certainly he was not complimentary about Omai after first meeting him, describing him as 'dark, ugly and a down-right blackguard'.[21] Beaglehole, going by Johnson's *Dictionary*, explains the contemporary meaning of 'blackguard' as 'of low social status' rather than criminal, but this hardly makes the comment any politer.

At this time Omai was about twenty-one years old. He was born in Raiatea where his father owned land, and, like Tupaia, he and his family had been forced to flee after an invasion from Bora Bora. Omai then went to Tahiti, and later to Huahine, another island in the Society group, where he met Furneaux and begged him to let him make the trip to England. When he arrived in London, Omai was taken up by Banks and his raffish circle, and he soon learnt the necessary social skills, such as playing backgammon, delivering gallantries to ladies, and holding his wine. According to Samwell, 'he learn't nothing [in England] but how to play at cards, at which he is very expert'.[22] He was received by the king (whom he called Tosh, not being able to pronounce George), entertained by society hostesses and admired by Dr. Johnson, who described

London Mag. Aug. 1774.

OMIAH.

A Native of Otaheite, brought to England by Capt. Furneaux.

Omai or Mai (also spelt Omiah), the young Pacific islander who was brought to England in 1775 and was returned home by Cook on his third voyage after having spent two years mixing in London high society. An engraving by J. Page after the portrait by Reynolds.

him as 'genteel'. Johnson, however, may have been using him as a convenient stick with which to attack social rivals. Once he commented to Boswell:

> Sir, Lord Mulgrave and he dined one day at Streatham; they sat with their backs to the light fronting me, so that I could not see distinctly; and there was so little of the savage in Omai, that I was afraid to speak to either, lest I should mistake one for the other.[23]

In a similar vein, one satirist published a poem ostensibly written by Omai, the unspoilt native, which criticised aspects of English society including the 'English arioi' of Pall Mall. Cook was probably surprised by Omai's social success. He told Boswell that when returned to his home he would soon sink into his former state, and then would probably ask to return to England, but he, Cook, would take care to leave before this could happen. Cook's fairly low opinion of Omai would certainly have been confirmed when he was informed of the list of articles chosen when they asked what he would like to take back with him, which included fireworks, two drums, a suit of armour, regiments of tin soldiers, a barrel organ, and handkerchiefs printed with a map of England and Wales.[24] He may have been an exotic dinner guest within London social circles, but he learned little during his year's stay that would be of use to him when he returned home.

Nevertheless, when the journey started Omai was to prove an asset to Cook, acting as interpreter on the third voyage, especially during the expedition's stay in the Tonga islands, though he was never nearly as effective in this role as Tupaia had been. He frequently revealed his impulsive and immature side by advising Cook to punish severely natives who stole things, or were in any way a nuisance. After the theft of the goat in Moorea, Omai was particularly vigorous in demanding reprisals. He told Cook to head into the country 'and shoot every Soul I met with'.[25] This Cook would not do, though he did destroy numerous native houses and war canoes before the goat was returned.

It was decided to settle Omai in Huahine, rather than his birthplace, Raiatea, in case he tried to exact revenge on the Bora Borans who had once displaced his family. Therefore the carpenters on the *Resolution* were instructed to build him a little house and an enclosed garden by the sea. Cook's journal, however, is full of references to his irritation with Omai's behaviour at this time. According to Cook, he mixed with the wrong sort of people and needlessly gave away many of his gifts from England, failing to placate the powerful chiefs on whom he would be dependent when the British finally left. Cook was disappointed with him, and ultimately glad to see the back of him. After commenting on his failure to profit from his experiences, and his laziness, he sums up:

this kind of indifferency is the true character of his Nation. Europeans have visited them at times for these ten years past, yet we find neither new arts nor improvement in the old, nor have they copied after us in any one thing.[26]

Omai's case thus symbolises for Cook, the dilemma, and ultimately the tragedy, of the Pacific voyages. The natives were incapable of profiting from their encounter with Europeans. They either would not, or could not, learn the various skills that Cook thought they ought to learn, and seemingly refused to take their chance of 'improvement'. Cook's pessimism was no doubt justified in this particular instance. One wonders what would have happened had it been the 'proud and obstinate' Tupaia, rather than Omai, who had been lionised by London society, having survived Batavia, and what Cook's verdict on him would have been. Omai, after all, although immature and unreliable, usually did what Cook told him to do: 'Whatever faults this Indian had they were more than over balanced by his great good Nature and docile disposition.'[27]

Bartering between a Maori and a European, an image from Cook's first voyage. This sketch is now believed to have been made by the skilful and knowledgeable Raiatean priest, Tupaia, who joined the Endeavour at Tahiti.

My fourth choice is a chief from Tongatapu. One day in May 1777, during the eleven weeks the *Resolution* spent touring the Tonga Islands, and when the ships were anchored off the small island of Lifuka, the paramount chief of all the islands in the group, Fatafehi Paulaho, came on board. He may have had some difficulty in doing so as he was, according to Anderson, 'of a monstrous size with fat which render'd him very unwieldy and almost shapeless'.[28] He was invited to dine in the Great Cabin although at first there were problems since his attendants objected on the grounds that people on the quarterdeck might walk over his head, which was strictly *tabu* (forbidden). Nevertheless, he did sit down to eat, but he did not deign actually to lift the food into his own mouth, and it took two attendants to feed him. But all passed off successfully, and in the days to come he returned Cook's hospitality on several occasions. As to Paulaho's character, Charles Clerke thought he was 'an indolent, fat, greasy rogue', but Cook, who may have had more opportunity to cultivate his acquaintance than Clerke, called him 'a sedate sensible man'.[29] He was intrigued when Paulaho asked why the expedition had come to Tonga; few other islanders, thought Cook, had ever shown this kind of curiosity.

Owing to Paulaho's status, Cook went to great lengths to befriend him, an eminently logical policy, as David Samwell, surgeon's mate on the *Resolution*, explains:

> Capn Cook kept up an amicable intercourse with the Chiefs by making them Presents & treating them at all times with Kindness & respect, by which means our market ashore & the Ships were well supplied with provisions but which cannot be the case without the Concurrence of the Chiefs, who have it in their Power to put an interdiction upon all Trade, which they call Taboo.[30]

It was not always easy to know which particular chief was worth putting oneself out for. Tongan society was complex and highly stratified, and the different strands of authority, religious and political, were awkward for strangers to disentangle. It may be, too, that Cook was sometimes over-inclined to accept native protestations of undying friendship at face value. These chiefs were crafty politicians with their own agendas. For instance, before meeting Paulaho, Cook had been under the impression that another chief, Finau, was the most important in the region. Finau seemed very friendly and Cook banqueted with him, and exchanged presents, but we now know – thanks to what Finau's son later told a missionary, William Mariner – that there had been a plot to kill Cook and his officers on the night of the banquet, a plot which was called off by sheer chance. The knowledge that there was such a plot, at a time when Cook imagined he was on the best of terms with his Tongan hosts, comes as a shock to readers of his journal: 'Cook's propensity here, as in many places before, is to play up the sociality and friendliness that he feels subsists between himself and prominent Polynesian men.'[31]

In Paulaho's case there is no evidence that he was not sincere in his offers of friendship, and Cook was highly impressed by his status as 'king' of all the dozens of islands in the Tonga group. Wherever Paulaho went, or rather, wherever he was carted on a species of wheelbarrow, his people greeted him with deep respect, silently bowing down to touch his feet with their heads. Cook writes: 'I was quite charmed with the decorum that was observed. I had no where seen the like, no not even amongst more civilized nations.'[32] Later, Cook's ships left Lifuka for Tongatapu, the largest island in the Tonga group, and Paulaha's home. Here Cook and Clerke were invited to a banquet and kava ceremony, and in his journal Cook again expatiated on his admiration for Paulaha's regal status:

> There is a decorum observed in the presence of their great men and particularly the Kings, that is truly admirable. Whenever he sits down, whether it be in the house or without, all those with him seat themselves at the same time in a semicircle before him; leaving always an open convenient space between him and them, into which no one attempts to come, unless he has some particular business . . . When any one wants to speak with him, he comes and sits down before him, delivers what he has to say in a few words, receives his answer and then retires to the circle . . . In short to speak to the King standing would be here accounted as great a mark of rudeness as it would be with us for a man to speak to his superior seting with his hat on and that superior on his feet uncovered.[33]

There was perhaps something here redolent of the respect shown to a naval captain on his own quarterdeck, only more pronounced, but there was, too, a darker side to this decorum, as noted by Charles Clerke:

> We clearly perceive that Powlahow, Feenow, Mallawogga and any of these principal People, can & will order a Man to be put to death instantaneously, & there is not the least Appeal from their Commands . . . what is very extraordinary on these Occasions, the Standers by look on with the utmost indifference, just as tho' they were Matters of course, and in 5 minutes afterwards are as facetious as if nothing of the kind has happen'd.[34]

In Tonga, Cook himself was treated in royal fashion, and could consort on equal, or even superior, terms with other 'kings'.[35] This, of course, was very different from his status back in England although it is true that this status had risen considerably after the second voyage, when he had lectured to the Royal Society, and been invited to mix with the great and the good of London society. Yet he was still by no means a member of that society's highly class-conscious élite, and given his background, he never could be. In the Pacific things were different, and no doubt Cook enjoyed the difference. But in the Pacific, too, kings were sometimes gods, and gods were kings, and an acceptance of kingly status by a visiting stranger might lead to cultural misunderstanding – with disastrous consequences.

Chapter 13

Sex in the South Seas

One of Cook's biographers, Jillian Robertson, sums him up as 'ambitious, hardworking, clever, clean and quiet '. There can be no dispute about most of these adjectives, but one wonders about 'clean'. Does she mean that when at sea he made the men air their hammocks on deck daily, and had the whole ship fumigated and scrubbed every week? I doubt it. The most likely explanation comes from the source quoted at length a few pages later. This is Zimmerman, a German who served as an able seaman on the third voyage, and who later wrote one of the few personal descriptions of Cook we have. Zimmerman writes: 'all the men allowed themselves to be led astray by the attraction of the native women, he alone remained clean and uncontaminated'.[1]

No writer on Cook has ever suggested the contrary, i.e. that he was 'unclean' in this sense, and nor do the journals of his colleagues. Even the salacious table talk of Daniel Solander, who gossiped in London clubs about the *Endeavour's* three-month stay in Tahiti, has nothing prurient to say about Cook. Solander alleges that other officers and gentlemen took Tahitian 'wives' – including the career officers, Gore and Clerke, the astronomer, Green, and even the ship's artist, that earnest young Quaker, Sydney Parkinson, who was discovered (by Banks) making love in the woods to a lady called Fieri, the sister of Banks's own current flame.[2] But not Cook. And it is not as though Solander idolised Cook. As we have seen, he claimed, for instance, that Cook was jealous of Gore because he was the better seaman.

Whenever Cook comments on the sexual proclivities of other people, he is always careful to distance himself. For example, on the second voyage he writes, '*I have been told* that the Ladies here [New Caledonia] would frequently devert themselves by going a little aside with our gentlemen as if they meant to grant them the last favour and then run away laughing at them'. And again, on the third voyage, 'The Women [of Unalaska] grant the last favour without the least scruple; Young or old, Married or single, *I have been told*, never hisitate a Moment'.[3]

In a later history of Hawaii there is a suggestion, based on oral sources, that Cook was seduced by a certain 'high-born' lady:

> Then a high chiefess, Kamakahelei, the mother of Kaumu-alii, the last king of Kauai said, 'Let us not fight against our god; let us please him that he may be favourable to us'. Then Kamakahelei gave her own daughter as a woman to Lono . . . and Lono slept with that woman, and the . . . women prostituted themselves to the foreigners for iron.[4]

Lono was Cook, and the anthropologist, Marshall Sahlins, jokes – at Cook's expense – that 'if the Hawaiians really did present their sacred woman to Captain Cook because he was a god, we can be sure he refused her – for something like the same reason'.[5] This story, however, lacks any corroborative detail and is, as Anne Salmond says, inherently improbable, given that such an act would have fatally undermined Cook's authority after his frequent admonishments to his crews.

There is only one entry in all of Cook's own journals which might imply a personal sexual encounter, and this was during the second voyage when he met a certain 'well-born' Tahitian female (not named). A rather ambiguous passage in the journal starts:

> This lady wanted neither youth nor beauty, nor was she wanting in using those charms which nature had given her to the most advantage, she bestowed her caresses on me with the utmost profusion and before I could get clear of her I was obliged to satisfy all her demands.[6]

Very likely, this statement does not mean what it might appear to mean to a casual twenty-first century reader, and in fact Cook goes on to imply that while the woman no doubt expected him to demand sex, she might well in the event have refused him.

On the first voyage, when everyone else had their Tahitian 'wives', Cook said that he found most Tahitian women 'very Masculine'.[7] Clearly, he was aware how much this marked him out from all his colleagues. In Tonga he was once berated by an old woman for not accepting the young girl she brought him. He writes, 'I understood very little of what she said, but her actions were expressive enough, and shew 'd that her words were to this effect, Sneering in my face and saying, what sort of a man are you thus to refuse the embraces of so fine a young Woman.'[8] As Beaglehole says, his apparent lack of interest in women was probably attributed by most Pacific islanders to age and impotence because 'The passionately professional man was an idea rather beyond Polynesian conception.'[9]

How today ought we to read Cook's image as a 'passionately professional man' and his apparent ability to look on native females, young or old, without desire? We have to be careful here not to fall into anachronism in attempting to apply post-Freudian insights about sublimation or substitution to people of another age and culture, but it is perhaps in order to look a little harder at Cook's self-imposed role in this context. Perhaps we can assume that he willed himself impervious to sexual blandishments because his ambitions and sense of duty were too intense to allow him to be sidetracked by lust, or the need for female companionship. Certainly, he was a stern and self-controlled man who seems never to have let slip the mask of authority. According to the historian Lee Wallace, Cook is 'the epitome of British imperial collectedness whose every professional competence indexes that masculinist and nationalist order'. She contrasts Cook with Joseph Banks, whose sexual adventures on Tahiti 'captures the essence of the sentimental agent of imperialism'. Banks's charm and informality are said to mask the reality of power, and the two of them, Banks and Cook, thus act in tandem as 'flip sides of the same coin . . . the tough and soft cops necessary for a successful expedition'.[10]

Combined with other factors, Cook's chastity played a crucial role not only in his actual command of his ships but also in his subsequent public image as explorer and harbinger of civilized values. As Bridget Orr explains

> [Cook] embodied a markedly paternalistic form of masculinity that seemed to inform both his public virtues and his private character; thus his stern but careful treatment of his crew and much-lauded sense of responsibility towards the natives was matched by celibacy on board and the generation of a large family at home. The cultural power of this image was not inconsiderable. It provided a model of masculinity that rendered male chastity plausible by combining it with manly action.[11]

The chances of contracting venereal disease may also have weighed heavily for a man with vast ambition and a wife at home, though this fear does not seem to have influenced the other officers. But there may be yet another explanation for Cook's celibacy, as George Forster hints when he claims that 'enjoyment of sensuality meant nothing to him'.[12] Does this imply that Cook was uninterested in sex generally, or merely uninterested in women? There is a heterosexual presumption behind all European accounts of Pacific contact, with their stress on erotic women and priapic sailors, but we are now aware that, in many of the islands, just as on board ship, things were not always that simple. In Hawaii, for instance, there were the *aikane*, young men of influence who acted as political agents, but who also had permanent homosexual relationships with the particular chiefs they served. Such partnerships were publicly acknowledged and sanctioned by custom, and *aikane* were men to be reckoned with, as the British discovered to their cost when they had to deal with Palea, the *aikane* of the chief Kalaniopuu. It was Palea, the journalists agree, who was behind the theft of the *Discovery's* cutter during the night of 13 January 1779, an incident which set off the chain of events that led to Cook's death.[13]

The Hawaiians saw something similar to the aikane relationship among the exclusively male cohorts of their British visitors. Samwell records that 'they have frequently asked us on seeing a handsome young fellow if he was not an Ikany to some of us'.[14] According to the boyish and elegant Lieutenant James King, Kalaniopuu and another of his *aikanes*, Koa, 'asked Captn Cook very seriously to leave me behind'. King adds that he himself 'had had proposals by our friends to elope, & they promised to hide me away in the hills till the Ships were gone'.[15] These Hawaiian overtures raise a possibility about which we can only speculate, that the ostensibly impersonal and professional relationships among Cook's seamen and officers might indeed have had a sexual underside. Clearly, some Hawaiians believed that the British were signaling this particular sexual availability. 'There may have been "something about Bligh"', is Beaglehole's cryptic and intriguing judgement about the *Resolution's* master, the brusque and aggressive William Bligh, who seems to have been unique in his dislike of King. Lee Wallace, admittedly arguing from minimal circumstantial evidence, invokes the possibility of a latent sexual triangle, involving forces of attraction, repulsion and rivalry, between Cook, Bligh, and King.[16]

So much for Cook the man. But for Cook, leader of expeditions, the problems of sex did not go away merely through denial or force of will. During the long weeks of the *Endeavour's* stay in Tahiti – that paradise, or New Cythera, as Bougainville called it, after the island near which Aphrodite is said to have sprung from the sea – it proved quite impossible to segregate 80 young men who had been at sea for eight months from the willing and available women of the island. Cook says as much (this was on the third voyage): 'A connection with women I allow because I cannot prevent it.'[17] He could try and keep his crew occupied in all kinds of activity – refitting and repainting the ship, setting up and guarding a fort, practising musketry drill – but there always came a time when they were free to slip away into the forest with their chosen partners or very often to invite them on board ship for the night. Did this matter? Yes, for several reasons. It was bad for morale and the unity of the ship's company. There were bound to be quarrels over women – mostly unrecorded in the journals, though we do hear about the near-duel between Banks and the ship's doctor, Monkhouse, over one of 'Queen' Oborea's attendants named Otheothea. Parkinson merely says the two had 'very high words' but prudently avoided an actual duel, but another, anonymous journal recounts that 'having furnished themselves with arms and amunition, they landed privately, but after a few discharges they were arrested and reconducted on board, by a party sent for that purpose, before any mischief happened'.[18] As previously mentioned, there may also have been talk of a mutiny by some of the crew who thought they would like to stay permanently on a Pacific island with their partners – just as the crew of the *Bounty* also thought, some twenty years later. And three sailors did try to do precisely that, running away immediately previous to the ship's departure and having to be recaptured with considerable effort.

Then there was the question of nails, a commodity the Tahitians came to prize above everything else, once they realized how much better they were than stone or bone tools when it came to building a house or a boat. It was these nails which were to entirely subvert the stone-age Tahitian economy within a few years, as the old skills came to be devalued and forgotten. Cook knew all about what had happened to the *Dolphin*, the first European ship to visit the island, a year or so before the *Endeavour*. In order to pay for sex, sailors from the *Dolphin* had extracted so many nails from the framework of the ship that not only was there nowhere to hang a hammock, but also the vessel itself was in danger of falling to pieces. Another problem with nails was that they were subject to inflation, especially once the women grasped that longer ones were available. One of the many satirical publications produced after the first voyage put the problem neatly (with a hint of *double entendre* on the word, 'nail'):

With nails we Traffic for the blooming maid
And the ships' planks supply the dangerous trade
At last the fair ones see with strange surprise
Some nails produced of more than common size
The happy females with this treasure grac'd.
Display their triumphs and our coins debased.
In vain we sue, the Nymphs comply no more.
'Give us large nails', reaches from the shore.[19]

Cook was determined to restrict this trade in nails if at all possible, and on arrival in Tahiti he issued a set of strict instructions to govern contact with the natives. The most important of these read:

> No Sort of Iron, or anything that is made of Iron, or any sort of Cloth
> or other usefull or necessary articles are to be given in exchange for any
> thing but provisions.[20]

These rules seem to have operated effectively to some degree, and it was not
found necessary to punish any nail thieves with the extreme penalty of running
the gauntlet, as had happened to one unfortunate from the *Dolphin*. However,
one sailor, Archibald Wolf, was awarded two dozen lashes for breaking into the
ship's storeroom in search of nails.

The other sex-related problem, which caused Cook much anguish, was
venereal disease. There was a suspicion – much debated, hotly denied and yet
lingering – that this scourge had been brought to the island by the *Endeavour*
(the journals are unspecific about the type of venereal disease).[21] But Cook
hoped, and believed, that it might have been brought earlier – either by the
Dolphin, or by the French, who had made a brief visit in between the two British
expeditions. He did what he could to limit the spread of the disease, and one
passage in his journal gives a glimpse of a lonely commander doing his utmost
to contain the problem, while his colleagues selfishly put their pleasures before
their duty:

> I had reason (notwithstanding the improbability of the thing) to
> think that we had brought it along with us which gave me no small
> uneasiness and did all in my power to prevent its progress, but all
> I could do was to little purpose for I may safely say that I was not
> assisted by any one person in the Ship, and was oblige'd to have the
> most part of the Ships Companey a Shore every day to work upon
> the Fort and a strong guard every night and the Women were so very
> liberal with their favours . . .[22]

No one knew how many of the crew already suffered from venereal disease
when the *Endeavour* arrived at Tahiti, but there is no doubt that during their
stay the disease spread rapidly – so rapidly in fact that when the time came
to leave half the crew were infected, and it was decided that in their weakened
state they were in no condition to sail southwards into colder waters. Cook
writes that because of this he had decided to alter the timetable and spend a few
weeks exploring the Society Islands until those affected had recovered.[23]

As regards the Tahitians themselves and their sexual customs, Cook
seems to have adopted an objective, and even liberal, attitude. He reports
without comment behaviour which departed some way from that of polite
society back at home. 'The Tahitians', he says, 'express the most indecent ideas

in conversation without the least emotion . . . Chastity indeed is but little valued especially amongst the middle people . . . the men will very readily offer the young women to strangers even their own daughters and think it very strange if you refuse them.'[24] The women usually went around nearly naked, but this, he tells us, should not be interpreted as lasciviousness, for 'it reckon 'd no shame for any part of the body to be exposd to view except those which all men hide'.[25]

The clearest instance of Cook's attempt to be objective is his restraint when describing the notorious sex ceremony which was to shock Georgian England when they read about it in the pages of Hawkesworth. Here, an audience of Tahitians, together with Cook and some of his crew, watched a young man making love to a little girl of eleven, with shouted instructions and applause from the onlookers, including Oborea. Cook merely records that this was an odd performance, adding that 'it appear 'd to be done more from custom than lewdness'. The report of this scene, which may or may not have been typical of Tahitian culture – Nicholas Thomas thinks it was specially put on for the *Endeavour* crew's benefit, as a satire on the public copulations taking place daily between sailors and Tahitian girls – inevitably caught the attention of the civilized world. John Wesley described it as unbelievable because it appeared to contradict the doctrine of man's shame after the Fall from Eden. But Voltaire saw it as the celebration of the religion of Venus, a once universal faith. 'One can be sure', he wrote, 'that the Tahitians have preserved in all its purity the most ancient religion of the world.'[26]

Incidentally, Cook's description of the copulation scene is one of the rare occasions in the journals that his meaning is ambiguous, possibly the result of some embarrassment, or uncertainty as to how he ought to react. He writes, 'there were several women present . . . and these were so far from shewing the least disaprobation that they instructed the girl how she should act her part, who young as she was, did not seem to want it'.[27] The ambiguity is in the last two words. Does this mean (a) she did not desire instruction, or (b) she did not lack instruction, or (c) she did not desire to carry out her role?

Cook does express a point of view when describing the Tahitian *arioi*, an aristocratic society whose members were in the habit of meeting together regularly for group sex. The babies that were the by-products of such meetings were often smothered at birth because parenthood was incompatible with membership of the *arioi*. Cook first, as usual, takes care to distance himself from the topic ('I never saw one of these meetings. Dr. Monkhouse saw part of one enough to make him give credit to what we had been told.'), but then reveals his abhorrence at this infanticide, grounded as it was upon 'a Custom so inhuman and contrary to the first principals of human nature'. But even in this extreme case he does his best to understand the other point of view: 'They are so far from concealing it that they rather look upon it as a branch of freedom upon which they value themselves.'[28]

Cook's attempts at objectivity are very far from the tone Christian missionaries would adopt when they arrived in Tahiti and met the *arioi* a few decades later. It is likely that his impartiality in regard to a culture so exotic and clearly immoral to Western eyes was borrowed from Banks. While Cook was occupied in the affairs of the ship and the fort, Banks had the time – and the capacity and the energy – to explore the island, anthropologically as well as geographically. He learnt a smattering of the language, became a great favourite of the natives and found himself at least one female partner – even though his fiancée, 'the injured Harriet', as one satirist later called her, was supposed to be waiting for him back at home. It was therefore hardly surprising that when it came to writing up his journal Cook took his cue from Banks, copying out large swathes of what Banks had written on Tahitian life, and including opinions as well as facts. To take one example, Cook took straight from Banks a rather Victorian-sounding theory about 'the inferior sort' [of Tahitian women] who, he said, 'were generally small owing possibly to their early amours which they are more addicted to than their superiors'.[29]

After Tahiti, on the first voyage, questions involving sex are rarely raised in the journal. The New Zealanders were a bellicose lot who usually took care their women did not approach anywhere near the crew of the *Endeavour*, and on the few occasions when they did, it was always possible to know which members of the crew had been exchanging friendly greetings with a woman, i.e. nose-rubbing, owing to the red ochre with which the women powdered their noses, and which came off very easily. In Australia it proved practically impossible to clap eyes on the native women, let alone make love to them.

All changed, however, when Cook returned to England. It turned out that the part of the voyage that most interested the general public was the three-months stay in Tahiti and easily the most fascinating part of that was the sex. Within a fortnight of the *Endeavour's* arrival garbled reports were circulating in the press about a voyage 'from which we expect many discoveries and much entertainment'. The *General Evening Post* wrote 'An Authentic Account of the Nature of Otaheite . . . from __ __ on board the ENDEAVOUR, to his Friend in the Country', which included the following:

> The women are extremely lascivious . . . They are not very decent in their amours, having little regard to either place or person . . . A virgin is to be purchased here, with the unanimous consent of the parents, for three nails and a knife. I own I was a buyer of such

commodities – and after some little time married one of my nut-brown sultans.[30]

Reports like this could hardly have cheered Cook, who naturally expected the achievements of the voyage to be taken seriously and not obscured by irrelevant gossip. Worse was to come. Within a couple of months, and in spite of the rule that all journals were supposed to be handed in before arrival in England, an enterprising publisher brought out the first narrative of the voyage. This anonymous account, which may have been by Magra, the midshipman whom Cook once described as 'good for nothing', included titillating detail about native encounters with the crew, and the Tahitian lifestyle. Some months later, John Hawkesworth started to compose the official version of the voyage, relying heavily on Banks's journal as well as Cook's. It is unclear whether or not Cook saw Hawkesworth's manuscript before leaving on his second voyage in July 1772, but in any case he must by that time have been fully aware of the unwelcome public appetite for what he considered the wrong kind of information. However, it was not until he returned from the second voyage three years later that the full force of the public's reaction to Hawkesworth and to Tahiti really struck him. By then there had been a flurry of publications – satirical letters, poems and lampoons, moralistic and yet prurient, most of them referring to Banks, but also, at least by implication, to Cook himself. Who else, for instance, did the author of these lines have in mind, as a 'tourist', wandering the Southern Ocean with Banks and Solander?

> ATTEND, ye swarms of MODERN TOURISTS,
> Yclept, or Botanists or Florists:
> Ye who ascend the cloud-capt Hills,
> Or creep along their tinkling Rills;
>
> Ye who o 'er Southern Oceans wander
> With simpling B_ks or sly S_r;
> Who so familiarly describe
> The Frolicks of the wanton Tribe,
> And think that simple Fornication
> Requires no sort of Palliation.[31]

The last two lines are clearly a direct reference to Cook's observation, repeated in Hawkesworth, that the public sex he had witnessed was done 'more from custom than lewdness'. Banks had not been present at that particular ceremony, but he was at another one, in which a girl 'displayed her naked beauties' in stripping off and making a present to him of her own clothes.[32] The satirists had a field day:

> While, as she turns her painted bum to view,
> With fronts unblushing, in the public shew,
> They search each crevice with a curious eye,
> To find Exotics – where they never lie,
> O Shame! Were we, great George, thy gallant crew,
> And had we – damn it – nothing else to do,
> But turn thy great design to filthy farce
> And search for wonders or an Indian's a. . . . ?
> But then to print our tale!
> O, curse the thought.[33]

Cook was now preoccupied with turning the journal of the second voyage into a book. He was absolutely determined that this time there would be no opportunity for hack writers and gossips to amuse themselves at his expense. He revised the journal several times until he was satisfied, making sure most of the references to sex were left out. To take an example, when they were at Queen Charlotte Sound in New Zealand, he first writes:

> we were visited by a Number of strangers; they came from up the Sound; and brought with them but little fish, the chief articles of their trade was Women and green stones . . . two articles which seldom came to a bad market.

In the final version the strangers only bring green stones – the women have disappeared.[34] He was now also keen to explain to the public that a false impression had been created by Hawkesworth, and that the natives of the South Seas were in fact fairly respectable in their morals, or at least no worse than Europeans:

> Great Injustice has been done the Women of Otaheite and the Society Isles, by those who have represented them without exception as ready to grant the last favour to any man who will come up to their price. But this is by no means the case; the favours of Married women and also the unmarried of the better sort, are as difficult to obtain as in any other Country whatsoever.[35]

Again, their marriage customs turned out to be no different from those of the civilized world:

I cannot recolect what is said on this subject [polygamy] in the account of my former Voyage, therefore shall now take upon me to say they have no such custom, each man can have only one wife let his rank be ever so much elevated.[36]

And even if some apparent polygamy was practised elsewhere in the Pacific, it was not *real* polygamy. For instance, in Fiji:

Polygamy is allowed to the Chiefs, and it is no uncommon thing to meet with some who will tell us they have got eight or ten wives. Yet Some of us were of opinion, that the most of those which they [the Fijians] called their wives were only concubines, and that there was only one that was looked upon as the wife and who always prepared to be the Mistress of the family.[37]

In New Zealand, according to Cook, it was true that polygamy existed, but in this case it was actually a beneficial institution, and improved the status of women:

The Women are Marriageable at a very early age and I am told that an unmarried Woman is in but a forelorn state and can hardly get a livelyhood at least she is in a great measure without a protector, so that Polygamy is perhaps more justifiable here than in any other part of the World.[38]

The message Cook was now trying to put over was clear. Hawkesworth's account had been tendentious and misleading – the women of the Pacific were on the whole chaste, especially the better sort:

none but common women would yield to the embraces of our people; not one of the gentlemen were able to obtain such favours from any women of distinction, though several attempts were made, but they were always jilted in the end.[39]

Just to make sure nothing had slipped the net, Cook spelt out the message to John Douglas, the newly appointed editor of his journals:

With respect to the Amours of my People at Otaheite and other places; I think it will not be necessary to mention them at all, unless it be by way of throwing a light on the characters, or as Customs of the People we are then among; and even then I would have it done in such a manner as might be unexceptionable to the nicest readers. In short my desire is that nothing indecent may appear in the whole book, and you cannot oblige me more than by pointing out whatever may appear to you as such.[40]

This policy also, of course, implied that Hodges and Webber, the artists who sailed with Cook on his second and third voyages respectively, and whose illustrations were to accompany the published narratives of the voyages, would have to go easy when it came to portraying the breasts and thighs of dancing girls. As Bernard Smith says, 'Webber would not be expected to spend much time drawing naked savages in the Pacific, even though he may have spent time drawing nude men and women in the life class of the *Ecole des Beaux-Arts*.'[41] It was all part of the new image Cook wanted to present to the world, having learnt caution from the public's first exposure to sex in the South Seas. In his third journal, when it came to describing yet another visit to Tahiti, Cook writes cautiously, 'So much, or rather too much has been published of Otaheite and the neighbouring islands already that there is very little room for new remarks.'[42]

Nevertheless, the journals of the second and third voyages make plain that sexual activity continued much as before. J.R. Forster reports that during the *Resolution's* stay at Tahiti in May 1774, there were 30 or 40 women on board every night,[43] and according to David Samwell, surgeon on the Adventure, Hawaii on the third voyage was a kind of sexual paradise (Samwell admittedly, as his journal makes clear, was a young man who always put sex at the top of his list of priorities). He writes:

When any one of us sees a handsome Girl in a Canoe that he has a mind to, upon waving his Hand to her she immediately jumps overboard & swims to the Ship, where we receive her in our arms like another Venus just rising from the Waves; both Men & Women come on board the ships in great Numbers and during the whole time of trafficking with them it is nothing but one Scene of noise & Confusion on board the Ships & all round them . . . The Inhabitants of the Friendly Isles did the same when we were among them.[44]

It turned out that Hawaiian women were even more insistent on clambering on board the British ships and seducing their crews than the Tahitians had been on this, or earlier, voyages. Whether this was because of compulsion from their menfolk, material inducements in the shape of gifts, or, as anthropologists have argued, to capture for themselves the strangers' *mana*, or status, is open to question.[45] On his arrival at Kauai, the first of the Hawaiian islands to be encountered, and which he suspected had not previously been visited by Europeans, Cook once again tried to prohibit sexual traffic, but in his journal he admits the impossibility of such a ban:

> It is no more than what I did when I first visited the Friendly Islands, yet I afterwards found it did not succeed, and I am much afraid this will always be the case where it is necessary to have a number of people on shore; the opportunities and inducements to an intercourse between the sex, are there too many to be guarded against.[46]

It is ironic that one of the major objectives of the voyages was to develop trade with the newly discovered lands in the Pacific, and yet the most successful trade of all, the trade for sex, was one which Cook did his unsuccessful best to suppress, and which produced results that few wanted.

Naturally, too, the accompanying problem of venereal disease failed to go away. Cook's men spread it far and wide, especially in Tonga and also Hawaii. As the surgeon William Anderson said: 'The injury these people [i.e. the Tongans] have receivd from us by communicating this certain destroyer of mankind is not to be repair'd by any method whatever.'[47] When they re-visited the Hawaiian Islands in November 1778, having spent seven months exploring the north-west coast of America, they were met by men who already had the disease and who came on board the *Resolution* to complain about this novel import and to show their swollen, inflamed organs to the ship's surgeon. Cook realized that his attempts to segregate his sailors back in January had indeed failed.[48]

Of all the difficulties that Cook had to contend with in the Pacific, the problems caused by sex were among the most intractable. There was just too much of it available. At Ulieta in the Society Islands on the third voyage, a sailor named John Harrison deserted and the scene at his recapture explains graphically the nature of the challenge that faced his commanding officer:

> The Indians conducted our People to the House where he was & they found him lying down between two Women with his Hair stuck full of flowers & his Dress the same as that of the Indians, that is with some Cloth about his middle & all other parts uncovered; his musket was lying by him, he was much surprised at seeing Captn Cook & gave himself up immediately.[49]

If, indeed, sex was something Cook himself was uninterested in, then no doubt he heartily wished everyone else shared his point of view.

Part IV

Assumptions, Ambitions, Achievements

Chapter 14

Cook and Divine Providence

On 10 June 1770, while traversing the coast of New South Wales, the *Endeavour* struck a coral reef. What happened next is told here using Banks's journal, Cook's description being rather more technical and less dramatic:

> Scarce were we warm in our beds when we were calld up with the alarming news of the ship being fast ashore upon a rock, which she in a few moments convincd us of by beating very violently against the rocks. Our situation became now greatly alarming; we had stood off shore 3 hours and a half with a plesant breeze so knew we could not be very near it: we were little less than certain that we were upon sunken coral rocks, the most dreadful of all others on account of their sharp points and grinding quality which cut through a ship's bottom almost immediately. The officers however behaved with inimitable coolness void of all hurry and confusion; a boat was got out in which the master went and after sounding round the ship found that she had run over a rock and consequently had Shole water all round her. All this time she continued to beat, very much so that we could hardly keep our legs upon the Quarter deck; by the light of the moon we could see her sheathing boards etc. floating thick round her; about 12 her false keel came away.[1]

For the next twenty-three hours the crew found themselves confronting imminent death by drowning. The ship was impaled on a needle of rock, while all around them the lead showed several fathoms depth of sea, with the mainland many miles distant. Everyone could hear the horrible noise of coral grinding against the ship's timbers, as they were dragged from side to side by waves and tide. The pumps were manned to expel the rising waters in the bilge, and everything possible was done to lighten the ship, such as throwing overboard every conceivable heavy object, including six cannon. Luckily, most of this time a dead calm prevailed, otherwise the voyage would certainly have been terminated because there was not enough room for everyone in the ship's boats, and even if some of them had reached the coast they would have starved to death, if not murdered first by the natives.

Eventually, however, another high tide shook the ship free from the rock and out into deeper water. It proved possible partly to seal the gash made by the coral by 'fothering' – a technique which involved covering over the ship's bottom with canvas into which had been sewed tufts of wool and oakum. Cook then sought out a sanctuary on the coast where they could beach and the necessary repairs be carried out. It turned out that a piece of coral had lodged itself in the ship's bottom, greatly reducing the size of the hole. Due to presence of mind, effective leadership, and above all, good luck, they survived.

John Hawkesworth, Cook's editor, chose this episode to illustrate his own opinions in a key eighteenth-century debate over the issue of 'particular providence'. Was there such a thing? In other words, did God sometimes intervene in the world to help people when they particularly needed him? Hawkesworth, as a deist, did not believe so. Why, he asked, should we attribute to providence only what appears to be pleasant or useful for us at the time? Surely God decrees everything that happens in the world, the good and the bad. 'It is true that when the *Endeavour* was upon the rock off the coast of New Holland, the wind ceased, and that otherwise she must have been beaten to pieces' – but was this a natural event, or not? If natural, it could hardly be called providential, any more than the sun rising in the morning could. If not natural, then why did God leave his intervention so late? He could have providentially stopped the ship striking the rock in the first place. All this Hawkesworth analysed at length, taking up three pages of his introduction to the voyages, and in doing so the author himself became impaled – on the wrath of public opinion.[2]

It was a question which not only Christians, but people of all religions and none, have been debating for centuries. Ought we, as the Anglican prayer book suggests, ask God to help us, for instance to bring rain, heal the sick, or preserve the royal family? Is there much point in thanking Him if he does? The deists, who included among their ranks Newton, Pope, Benjamin Franklin and thousands of others, held that God manifests His presence in the world continually. He is responsible for everything that happens – the fall of a sparrow, the wreck of a ship. It is, therefore, hardly up to us, with our puny intellects, to label certain events 'providential'. 'Such thinking', contended Hawkesworth, 'derogates from the honour of the great Universal Cause', a cause which from a wider perspective 'tends ultimately to the good of the whole.' Deists were generally great optimists (and as such were pilloried in Voltaire's *Candide*, published in 1767, the year before Cook's first voyage).[3] They believed in a Newtonian universe, a universe subject to the laws of Nature, in other words, to the laws ordained by the Creator of Nature, and purpose-built for mankind's benefit. God, they argued, does not need to intervene in this best of all possible worlds, and in fact, if he did intervene he would be merely subverting his own rules. The possibility of miracles was therefore not to be entertained, either in the present day, or even in Biblical times, because the real miracle was Nature herself, and the progress of science. Every new species discovered, said the great Swedish botanist, Linnaeus, gives homage to the Creator.[4]

However, a number of Hawkesworth's readers failed to see it his way. Evangelicals, Methodists, proto-Romantics, together with men and women of 'sentiment', as was the fashionable term, all rejected his deterministic and impersonal universe. Their God was a living God who continually watches over us, listens to our prayers, and can and does intervene when we need Him. To deny this fact was to blaspheme against the heart of the Christian religion. After he and Dr. Johnson were nearly wrecked in a small boat off the Isle of Sky, James Boswell wrote:

> I was disturbed by the objections that have been made against a particular providence, and by the arguments of those who maintain that it is in vain to hope that the petitions of the individual, or even of congregations, can have any influence with the Deity; objections which have been often made, and which Dr. Hawkesworth has lately revived in his Preface to the Voyages to the South Seas; but Dr. Ogden 's excellent doctrine on the efficacy of intercession prevailed.[5]

Hawkesworth's theological speculations had become another stick with which to beat him – along with his over-frank discussion of sex in Tahiti, and his £6,000 advance from the publisher.

Of course, these two versions of Providence – the version that God reveals himself through the laws of nature, and the version that God often intervenes in nature to help mankind – were not mutually exclusive. It was quite possible to believe both versions simultaneously, as, for instance, did George Forster who sailed with Cook on his second voyage. Forster recounts several examples during the voyage of 'instances of impending destruction, where all human help would have been ineffectual' had not God directly intervened. He also held that the natural world had been created expressly for man, arguing, for example, that coral insects had built up their structures over many centuries precisely in order that men in historical times could live on the resulting coral islands.[6]

So much for the controversy over providence, but our subject is supposed to be Cook, not Hawkesworth. One has to remember, however, that for eighteenth-century readers Hawkesworth *was* Cook. Only relatively recently have readers been in a position to separate the two, and to interrogate the journals unmediated by their contemporary editors. Regarding Cook's attitude, there is, as is usual with Cook, little direct evidence, though there is Zimmerman, who says that he never mentioned religion and would have no priests on his ship.[7] Zimmerman adds that he 'seldom celebrated the Sabbath', and in fact there is only one mention in all of Cook's journals of his taking the Sunday morning service on board ship, a duty which was supposed to fall to the captain. Very occasionally, a throw-away remark in the journals sheds a faint light on Cook's beliefs. Noticing a decayed *morai* (or burial site) in Tahiti, he says that religious customs there were 'like most other nations now less observed than formerly'.[8] On another occasion he admits to not understanding much about Tahitian religion, adding: 'the Misteries of most Religions are very dark and not easily understood even by those who profess them'[9] – clearly a sally against ministers of God everywhere. He also seems to have a fairly utilitarian attitude towards sin when he explains that 'Incontinency in the unmarried people [of Tahiti] can hardly be call'd a Vice sense neither the state or individuals are the least injured by it.'[10]

Where does Cook stand on *particular providence*? He certainly uses the term 'providence' with relative frequency, but this is hardly significant.[11] 'Providence' in the eighteenth century was not merely a theological term, but also a literary cliché, fulfilling much the same function as 'luck' or 'good fortune' today. The fact that the word comes into the journals a score or more times hardly proves that Cook necessarily believed in any version of it. By the second voyage he was writing a book, and perhaps choosing his terminology to suit his public. There is one example of him specifically altering his draft to make it more 'providential'. Concerning a close shave off New Caledonia he at first writes, 'we perhaps owed our safety to a good lookout and the very brisk manner the Ship was managed'. The final version reads, 'we owe our safety to the Interposition of Providence, a good lookout . . . [etc]'.[12]

There is, however, a counter-example from the first voyage. When describing a near disaster in August 1769, when the *Endeavour* was almost forced onto the Great Barrier Reef by strong currents, Cook writes in an early draft of his journal: 'It pleased GOD at this very juncture to send us a light air of wind which with the help of our Boats carried us near a Cables length from the present danger.' In the final version the reference to God is omitted: 'At this critical juncture when all our endeavours seem'd too little a small air of wind sprung up.'[13]

The jury on this issue, then, is still out, but it seems worth hazarding a guess that Cook, given his scientific bent, might if pressed have admitted to sharing Hawkesworth's assumption concerning a purposeful Newtonian universe without any need for Divine intervention. Most of his colleagues including Banks would probably have gone along with this, although certainly not the two Forsters, whose journals show that they were both committed to a strongly 'providential' line.

Linda Colley points out that Britons in the mid-eighteenth century retained a strong belief in national providence.[14] They attributed their victory in the Seven Years War to Divine favour towards the leading Protestant nation, although, a few years later, it was to be the other side of the coin, defeat in the war against America leading to doubt and self-questioning. Throughout Cook's lifetime, anti-Catholic feeling had a continuing resonance. The Jacobite rebellion of 1745 took place when he was seventeen, and the Gordon riots, the most Protestant and most destructive of all the century's riots, a few months after his death. And if one narrows the focus to the locality in which James Cook grew up, the Protestant connection is even more pronounced. Great Ayton, the Yorkshire village where he lived with his family between the ages of eight and sixteen, possessed a strong and radical Protestant tradition. There were two dissenting places of worship in this village of a few hundred souls. One was a Quaker Meeting House, and the other an Independent chapel, built onto the back of Ayton Hall and owned by Thomas Skottowe, the village's principal landowner. It was Skottowe who employed Cook's father and who paid for James Cook's education at the village school.

The next village to Ayton was Stokesley where there lived an unpopular little community of Catholic recusants. In 1746, not many months after James Cook had left Ayton to become a shop assistant in nearby Staithes, a crowd of Ayton youths staged their own version of the Gordon riots. They marched to Stokesley where they desecrated the Catholic 'mass-house'. When the ring leaders of this episode were arrested, the magistrate before whom they appeared was that same Thomas Skottowe, the Protestant dissenter, or at least sympathizer, with radical Protestantism. History relates that Skottowe merely laughed at the youths' reported antics, and sent them away with a warning pat on the head. As a result of this tacit encouragement, an even larger crowd of youths returned to the mass-house and completely demolished it.[15] Such was the atmosphere in which James Cook grew up, though admittedly there is no special evidence that as an adult he was particularly anti-Catholic, or interested in Protestant dissent.

Five letters by Cook to John Walker, the Whitby ship-owner and his former employer, have survived, and in these the word 'providence' crops up quite frequently. For example, from the Cape of Good Hope in November 1772, Cook tells Walker that 'providence has been very kind to me on many occasions, and I trust in the continuation of the divine protection'.[16] Such sentiments are untypical of Cook, but here he was addressing a Quaker and perhaps trimming his sails to the wind. As a young apprentice Cook had lived for a time in Walker's house and may well have absorbed some of its Quaker atmosphere. Richard Allen, a scholar who has specialized in Quaker history, lists various characteristics displayed by the mature Cook which might possibly be described as Quaker qualities.[17] They include the avoidance of frivolity in dress or behaviour, a solid work-ethic, personal modesty, sexual restraint, and a desire to settle quarrels by conciliation where possible. All these traits, however, might clearly be shared by many non-Quakers. Allen concludes by pointing out that eighteenth-century Quakers formed themselves into separate and distinct communities, and that there is no evidence that Cook was ever part of such a community. Not only that, but he also displayed some rather un-Quakerlike habits, such as a tendency to swear, and also a readiness to use violence to achieve his aims when other methods failed. One could add that he married the daughter of an inn-keeper, an act which would certainly have been frowned on in Quaker circles.[18] It seems, too, that his mentor, John Walker, was himself not a model Quaker. He was frequently criticised by other Quakers for furnishing his ships with guns, and when he died the Quarterly Meeting refused to allow that he was still a member of the Society of Friends, presumably for the same reason.

Cook may have tacitly accepted contemporary assumptions about providence, but what evidence there is tends to show that he was not a particularly religious man, at least not in the sense recognised and sanctioned by contemporary churchmen. Certainly, he showed no desire to preach Christianity to the various peoples he came across. He was very different in this respect from earlier explorers, as well as later missionaries. In previous centuries, religion, along with the search for gold and slaves, had furnished, ostensibly at least, a major pretext for exploration. When Christopher Columbus, after his first voyage, was seeking continued funding from his patrons, Ferdinand and Isabella of Spain, he found it appropriate to stress a religious motive for returning to the New World. He writes:

> I truly believe that given devout religious persons knowing thoroughly
> the language that they use, soon all of them [i.e. the peoples of the
> Caribbean] would become Christians. And so I hope in Our Lord that
> Your Highnesses, with much diligence, will decide to send such
> persons in order to bring to the Church such great nations and to

convert them, just as you have destroyed those that did not want to confess the Father and the Son and the Holy Spirit [i.e. Jews and Moslems].[19]

Explorers of Cook's day may have had their own priorities and expectations regarding Pacific islanders, but religious intolerance and conversion were not among them.

What did good Christian people generally think about Cook during his life, and after his death? In 1796 the first missionary ship sent into the Pacific, the *Duff*, under Captain Wilson, arrived at Tahiti. It was dispatched by the London Missionary Society, an influential organisation which had the backing of the growing evangelical movement back at home. A paradigm shift was now taking place in peoples' attitude to non-Europeans in general, and the natives of the Pacific in particular. Eighteenth-century explorers had been less confident, more critical, of the values of their own civilisation. In his journals Cook more than once criticises British society by implication, the best known example being when he describes the Australian aborigines as 'far more happier' than Europeans because they never seemed to covet any of the material goods he could offer them.[20] He was also prepared on occasion to let his hair down and join in native religious rituals. But the attitude of the missionaries towards their new acquaintances was very different. They had no doubts as to the superiority of Christian values and saw it as their duty not only to spread the gospel but also to eradicate whenever possible all traces of the old religions. Perhaps the nearest a leading missionary ever came to seeing the native's point of view is in John Williams's half-admiring reference to 'the peculiar and intricate character of some ancient images which we were anxious to see abolished'.[21]

Cook was not one of the missionaries' heroes. Some of his defects are listed in an anonymous article about Tahiti from the *The Quarterly Review* of 1809:

How is it, said the natives, that Cook, Clarke, Vancouver, Bligh, and others, that have been here, never told us anything of what you tell us concerning Jesus Christ? It cannot indeed be doubted that the total silence of former visitors upon the subject of Christianity, the complacency with which they assisted at idolatrous ceremonies, and the habits of licentious intercourse to which they abandoned themselves, must greatly have prejudiced the natives against any lessons of religion or morality from the English.[22]

But the major charge made against Cook by those who were 'serious' in religion, the discreet term applied by one evangelical to another, was connected with the final weeks before his death. The accusation was that he had allowed himself to be worshipped as a god by the Hawaiians, and therefore deserved retributory punishment from the Almighty. The best known version of this thesis is contained in a letter written by the poet, William Cowper in 1784 to his friend, the Rev. John Newton:

> The reading of these volumes' [the journal of the third voyage, edited by Douglas] afforded me much amusement, and I hope some instruction. No observation however forces itself upon me with more violence than one, that I could not help making on the death of Captain Cook. God is a jealous God, and at Owyhyee the poor man was content to be worshipped. From that moment the remarkable interposition of Providence in his favour was converted into an opposition that thwarted all his purposes. He left the scene of his deification, but was driven back to it by a most violent storm, in which he suffered more than in any that had preceded it. When he departed, he left his worshippers still infatuated with an idea of his godship, consequently well disposed to serve him. At his return, he found them sullen, distrustful and mysterious. A trifling theft was committed, which, by a blunder of his own in pursuing the thief after the property had been restored, was magnified to an affair of the last importance. One of their favourite chiefs was killed too by a blunder. Nothing in short but blunder and mistake attended him, till he fell breathless into the water, and then all was smooth again. The world indeed will not take notice or see that the dispensation bore evident marks of divine displeasure; but a man, I think, in any degree spiritual cannot overlook them. We know from truth itself that the death of Herod was for a similar offence . . . besides, though a stock or stone may be worshipped blameless, a baptized man may not. He knows what he does, and, by suffering such honours to be paid him, incurs the guilt of sacrilege.[23]

It is impossible to know how many 'spiritual' persons there were in Britain at the time who might have agreed with this judgemental verdict. But the message did find support in Hawaii, where it was endorsed by the missionaries and their native converts. For instance, Hiram Bingham, an American missionary, repeated it in his autobiography, *A Residence of Twenty-One Years in the Sandwich Islands*, a popular work which ran through several editions in the mid-nineteenth century. Bingham's language is more extreme than Cowper's, but the message was similar, and clearly derived either from Cowper himself, or from a common source, since Bingham, too, compares Cook to Herod. Very likely, Cowper and Bingham represented the views of only a small and extreme minority, but such opinions might very well have been shared by that other vociferous minority who, a few years earlier, had berated Hawkesworth for denying a 'particular providence'.[24]

Such were the sentiments of certain evangelicals and missionaries in Britain and abroad. The vast majority of churchmen, however, even including some of an evangelical persuasion, probably held a more positive opinion concerning Cook's role within the Divine scheme of things. It might seem a little odd, given Cook's apparent lack of interest in organized religion, that all his early editors and biographers had clear religious affiliations. Hawkesworth, his first editor, was a doctor of Divinity, Andrew Kippis and George Young, his first and second biographers, were non-conformist clergymen, and John Douglas, editor of the second and third journals, was shortly to become an Anglican bishop. Presumably they all saw Cook, whatever his personal convictions or lack of them, as God's chosen instrument for bringing the light of Christianity to the heathens of the Pacific. Douglas certainly did. He writes about Cook's efforts having resulted 'in rescuing millions of fellow-creatures from their present state of humiliation'.[25] Kippis makes the same point:

> Perhaps, our late voyages may be the means appointed by Providence, of spreading, in due time, the blessings of civilization among the numerous tribes of the South Pacific . . . Nothing can more effectually contribute to the attainment of this great end, than a wise and rational introduction of the Christian religion.[26]

The only member of this quartet who veered towards a more critical stance was the Presbyterian minister, George Young, who wrote:

> It is much to be regretted, that instead of discountenancing the licentiousness of the natives, the seamen of the *Endeavour*, like those of the *Dolphin*, and of the two French ships commanded by Bougainville, disgraced themselves by indulging in illicit intercourse with the females of Otaheite. Such practices are not only highly immoral and degrading, but tend to the subversion of discipline and good order.[27]

Young also goes on to criticise the deification of Cook:

> Besides the general neglect of divine service, too apparent from his journals, he was chargeable with a most glaring deviation from the line of duty, in permitting the inhabitants of Owhyhee to adore him as a god.

Even Young, however, held that on balance, 'the labours of Capt. Cook have been eminently subservient to the progress of Christianity, and to the best interests of mankind.[28] And certainly some of those associated with the London Missionary Society, such as the Rev. George Burder, thought the same. According to Burder:

> Captain Cook and others have traversed the globe, almost from pole to pole, and have presented us, as it were, a new world . . . May we not reasonably hope that a well-planned and well-conducted mission . . . will be attended with the blessing of God and issue in the conversion of many souls.[29]

It seems, therefore, that certain churchmen, including some missionaries, held a somewhat ambivalent view of Cook. On the one hand, they hoped that others might follow in his footsteps, to the places he had opened up, but on the other, they sought to dissociate themselves from the alleged errors of judgement he had made in his relations with Pacific islanders. God moves in mysterious ways, they may well have argued, and on balance Cook ought to be recognized as an agent of divine providence, in spite of any personal failings.

Chapter 15

Nation and Empire

In October 1928 ceremonies to honour the bicentenary of Cook's birth were held at Marton and Great Ayton, the villages in North Yorkshire where he was born and grew up. At Stewart Park, Marton, the atmosphere was distinctly militaristic, with the dignitaries, from various parts of the British Empire, enclosed in a hollow square made up of several ranks of soldiers and sailors, with their officers out in front. One of the speakers was Sir George Fuller, Agent General for New South Wales, who was reported in the local press as wishing that the spirit of Cook could wing its way back to earth and see the wonderful developments which had taken place in Australia since his day. He reminded his audience that they had a White Australia policy, which meant that they were determined to keep the land as a heritage for the British race. Referring to the recently signed contract to build a bridge over Sydney harbour he said that they in Australia had made up their minds that no foreigner need apply (the contract had just been awarded to a Teesside firm, Dorman Long). 'We are striving', he said, 'to build up a strong, virile, educated people, who will be a great outpost for the Empire.'[1]

Another event to celebrate Cook's bicentenary was the publication of a short book on Cook and the Empire by an Australian politician, Sir Joseph Carruthers, whose obsession with this topic must have often made him a real bore to many that crossed his path, as he himself more or less implies in this extract from the book:

> I meet hundreds of Englishmen in official positions in Crown Colonies in the Pacific, and in the Dominions, as well as scores of them travelling in palatial liners in the Pacific. The best of them, when I remind them of Cook's fine work as the man who 'blazed the track' for them, warm up and enthuse and take one to their hearts for reminding them of what we owe to him and to the crews of his little ships of 300 or 400

tons. But another set of men seem bored to be reminded of such a man, and possibly most of them have never troubled to read or learn what he did for King and Country.[2]

Carruthers had no doubt that Cook's greatest achievement was the discovery of Australia. He brushed aside awkward questions about others having been there first, or about Cook choosing never to return to Australia after his first voyage. He also ignored the fact that Cook was dead by the time the British government decided to turn Botany Bay into a penal colony. Carruthers identified personally with his hero. He himself was a self-made man, having left school at the age of ten, and pulled himself up by his own bootstraps to become first a successful lawyer and then, having entered politics, to achieve a four-year term as prime minister of New South Wales. He therefore saw Cook, with his background of rural poverty, as the blueprint for the ideal Australian citizen. After his retirement from politics he spent enormous time and energy trying to pressurize whomever he could into creating memorials to Cook, both in London and throughout the Pacific, including Australia. He was moderately successful and it may have been largely due to his efforts that just before the outbreak of war in 1914 the first London statue of Cook was put up at Admiralty Arch. The openly racist version of Empire peddled by Carruthers reads rather quaintly today, though it might be not so much the underlying sentiments as the phraseology that is out of fashion:

> To Cook and England we owe Australia, New Zealand, a multitude of fertile islands in the South Seas, and thereby a securer hold upon our other possessions north of those seas. Nearly ten millions of people of English, Irish, Scottish, and Welsh blood hold these southern dominions and colonies of our Empire now. In another century's time, please God, and if we keep our trust, we shall have eighty to one hundred million people, mainly of the fine old Anglo-Saxon breed, in these lands. Mind you, the United States of America in the last one hundred years have similarly increased their population which is, however, only about 52 per cent of Anglo-Saxon origin.[3]

The myth of Cook's founding role has been supremely important for Australia, and also for New Zealand, during the twentieth century, in the establishment of a point of origin for the two nations, a crucial factor in the creation of a national and cultural identity. As Chris Healy puts it, the moment of Cook's first landing 'serves to mark the end of empty time and the beginning of continuous historical time' for settlers in Australia.[4] In Canada, too, Cook was invoked as a local historical icon. In the first two decades of that century the authorities in British Colombia, on which coast Cook had landed in March 1778, included copies of the journals of Cook and his companions in the collection of documents they accumulated as part of their nation building project. One of the leaders in this research, the historian E. O. S. Scholefield, was quite frank as to the object of the exercise:

> It is such a great thing, such a fascinating thing, this founding and building up of a [archives] department devoted to the gathering together and preservation of historical records. It is also a work that must tell in the future. Humble as our beginnings were, we laid, broad and deep, a foundation for a structure which will be the splendid, crowning glory of this great Dominion of ours.[5]

But how far would it be true to say that men like Carruthers, Fuller and Scholefield, with their imperialist obsessions, were hijacking Cook's memory for their own purposes? Surely Cook was a man of science, a man of peace, even to an extent an international figure. In September 1775 he wrote to a young French naval officer who was anxious to become an explorer – or at least someone who understood French wrote for him – 'Il ne me suffit donc point d'avoir les applaudissements de ma nation seule, parce que ce n'est pas pour elle que j'ai travaille en particulier, mais pour toute l'Europe.'[6] (For me it is not enough to receive merely the commendations of my own nation, because I have not worked for her especially, but for all Europe.) This, too, is why the governments of other powers told their navies not to molest him on the high seas. After 1777, France, Spain and America were all at war with Britain, yet such was Cook's fame that all three gave instructions he was not to be seen as an enemy. The French told their commanders to treat him as they would treat any neutral or friendly shipping. On behalf of America Benjamin Franklin declared that he was to be shown every respect and permitted to pass freely 'on account of the benefits he has conferred on mankind through his important discoveries'.[7] And even the Spanish, although very sensitive to any incursions into the Pacific, ordered their viceroys abroad not to injure him – unless, that is, he attempted to land on Spanish territory, in which case he was to be arrested. Perhaps no other explorer in history has been given such international protection by his country's opponents in time of war.

So much for Cook as an international figure. Nevertheless, it has to be recognised that he was also a British naval officer, and that he operated at a time of European rivalry and powerful nationalism. Linda Colley has pointed out that the Act of Union between England and Scotland in 1707 created what was in effect a brand new nation – Britain. This invented nation, like any new nation, needed to be sustained and strengthened by the conscious patriotism of its citizens, and British patriotism did indeed increase during the eighteenth century, partly due to a series of successful wars with France and Spain, and also to the prestige and profits of a vast overseas commercial empire. A potent symbol of growing patriotism was the popularity of Thomas Arne's *Rule Britannia*, composed in 1740, with its references to Britain's divine origin, and her right to rule the waves.[8] The Seven Years War, arguably the most successful war in British history, had finished a few years before Cook first set out. In the post-war period Britain's goal was to build on the dominant world position given her by the Treaty of Paris of 1763, which ended the war, whereas France's goal on the other hand was to try and tip the commercial balance of power back in her own favour. For both nations the empty spaces on the map of the world, some of which Cook would soon fill in, were potential areas for rivalry. The Lords of the Admiralty did not need to suppose that the possibilities of future commerce in the Pacific were certain, or even that large, undiscovered islands or continents actually existed. They only had to make sure that neither the French nor any other power would be able to claim such places first, if in fact they did exist.

There is thus little doubt that nationalism, and in particular commercial rivalry with our main competitor, France, was a strong motive for the voyages. Cook's instructions bear this out. His initial set of instructions from the Admiralty for the voyage of the *Endeavour* describe the voyage's purpose as being to survey the Transit of Venus from Tahiti. In other words, as mentioned in Chapter 8, the voyage had a scientific objective. However, Cook also received additional instructions which spelt out the more nationalist goals of the expedition – to find new lands, preferably a whole new continent, and claim them for Britain:

> Whereas the making Discoverys of Countries hitherto unknown . . . will redound greatly to the Honour of this nation as a Maritime Power, as well as to the Dignity of the Crown of Great Britain, and may tend greatly to the advancement of the Trade and Navigation thereof.[9]

These latter instructions were supposed to be secret, although in fact the press of the day openly speculated about them. But that they were ever described as secret perhaps shows the Admiralty's awareness that, for the sake of public relations, the claims of science should be stressed rather than any overt national self-interest.

Cook's journals also reveal this ambiguity of purpose as between the neutral values of science, and national self-interest. As he wrote to the young Frenchman, he was not working for his own nation alone, but for all of Europe. Undoubtedly he saw himself as one of a brotherhood of explorers from many nations – Spanish, French, Russian. He made full use of the journals of those who preceded him, and no doubt expected future explorers of any nation to do the same with his. As explained earlier, the actual term, 'scientist', may not have been current in Cook's time, but he certainly would have concurred with the values we ascribe to the term – internationalism, impartiality, an absence of prejudice of any kind.[10] On the other hand, he was also a servant of the British flag, and as such, for instance, was expected to survey the defences of European-owned ports at which he docked, in case of future hostilities, and also to assess newly discovered territories as to their future usefulness to Britain. On the first voyage he made a close study of the Portuguese guns protecting Rio de Janeiro Bay, concluding that, if there was ever an attempt by the British to enter the bay forcibly, 'it would require five or Six sail of the line to insure success'.[11] As to future colonies, he thought New Zealand had potential ('it doth not appear to me to be atall difficult for Strangers to form a settlement in this Country'),[12] and that the best places to choose would be either the Bay of Islands or the River Thames. However, New South Wales was unpromising, because 'the Country it self so far as we know doth not produce any one thing that can become an Article in trade to invite Europeans to fix a settlement upon it'.[13] It was the same with Tahiti, although the island, with its fertile soil and balmy climate, might be useful as a stop-over for shipping.[14]

Cook's instructions included that he was 'with the Consent of the Natives to take possession of Convenient Situations in the Country in the name of the King of Great Britain; or, if you find the Country uninhabited take Possession for his Majesty'.[15] The 'Country' mentioned here was the legendary Southern Continent which turned out not to exist except as an ice-bound wilderness, but the instructions also stated that Cook was to 'take possession for His Majesty' of any islands he might discover in the course of his explorations. This 'taking possession' was based on the contemporary legal doctrine of *terra nullius* ('land of no man') which had been developed by various authorities, in particular John Locke, in his *Second Treatise on Government* (1690), where he explains that originally mankind lived in a 'state of nature' in which everything, including land, was held in common. However:

God, when he gave the World in common to all Mankind, commanded Man also to labour, and the penury of his Condition required it of him.

God and his Reason commanded him to subdue the earth, i.e. improve it for the benefit of Life, and therein lay out something upon it that was his own, his labour. He that in Obedience to this Command of God, subdued, tilled and sowed any part of it, thereby annexed to it something that was his Property, which another had no Title to, nor could without injury take from him.[16]

If, therefore, the inhabitants of a certain country had advanced beyond the state of nature by enclosing and cultivating their land, and also by creating a civil society with customs, laws and government, then any European power interested in acquiring that country must either purchase it, or otherwise somehow persuade the people to accept their rule. However, if a group had not yet developed their land in such ways, then Europeans were entitled to consider it as *terra nullius*, in other words, as technically uninhabited, and in such a case they could gain a permanent title to it merely by discovery followed by settlement. Alan Frost explains the procedures involved:

Europeans signified first discovery of a *terra nullius* by leaving proof of their presence (for example, cairns, inscriptions on trees and poles, gifts to inhabitants). They established a *preliminary* right to possess it if, carrying a commission from their sovereign authorising them to do so, they claimed it formally on his behalf, and accompanied their proclamation with symbolic acts of sovereignty, such as the raising of their flag and the firing of salutes. To render a preliminary right *real*, a state had to occupy the region effectively within a reasonable time. This it did when it either transferred a portion of its population, together with its customs and laws, to the region in an extensive colonization, or when, as a minimum, it settled one spot in the region, and sent representatives on regular patrols about the whole.[17]

These claiming ceremonies, which in Cook's case involved a military ritual, with the marines drawn up on shore, and firing their muskets, to be answered by corresponding volleys from the ship, were carried out by him at suitable intervals on all his voyages. Not all Cook's colleagues saw the point of such rituals. George Forster, on the second voyage, dubbed them 'idle ceremonies', and William Anderson, surgeon on the *Resolution* on the third voyage, described one of them as 'not only unjust but truly ridiculous, and perhaps fitter to excite laughter than indignation'.[18] Admittedly, Anderson was writing here about the ceremony of taking possession of Kerguelen Land, where there were no natives at all to witness the ceremony, only penguins.

Having traversed the east coast of Australia, Cook reports that 'we never saw one Inch of Cultivated land in the whole Country, and that the inhabitants 'seem to have no fix'd habitation but move about from place to place like wild beasts'.[19] Moreover, their numbers were small, they lived in scattered groups, and did not seem to possess any social or political units larger than the extended family. Cook therefore concludes: 'We are to Consider that we see this Country in the pure state of nature, the Industry of Man has had nothing to do with any part of it.'[20] Furthermore, during his progress down that coast he found no evidence (no cairns, or inscriptions on trees or poles) of any previous European presence. As a consequence, he was perhaps justified by his own lights in claiming the country for Britain, which he did at regular intervals as he sailed up the coast.[21]

In the case of New Zealand, however, matters were different. The inhabitants were clearly numerous, and in some areas were organized into larger-scale communities, living in well-fortified villages. Nevertheless, Cook went through the usual claiming ceremonies, nor was there any attempt to persuade the inhabitants to place themselves under British rule. At Queen Charlotte Sound some communication with the locals did take place, but it was rather economical with the truth. Cook informed an old man 'that we were come to set up a mark upon the island (Motu-ouru) in order to show to any ship that might put into the place that we had been here before'. But the ceremony that followed was actually to 'take formal possession of it [the island] and the adjacent lands in the name and for the use of his Majesty, we then drank Her Majesty's hilth in a Bottle of wine and gave the empty bottle to the old man [who had followed them up the hill] with which he was highly pleased'.[22] Judging from further entries in Cook's journal, his rationale for claiming land in New Zealand might have been, firstly, that the inhabitants were a highly warlike people, and hence still living in that primitive 'state of nature' before the development of rational society. He writes:

> Whatever place we put in at or whatever people we spoke with upon the Coast they generally told us that those that were at a little distance from them were their enemies, from which it appear'd to me that they were very much divided into parties which make war with one another.[23]

According to Locke, God intended the land 'to the use of the industrious and rational', and not to 'the quarrelsome and contentious'. It is not suggested here that Cook had actually read Locke, but this was also probably an opinion shared by those whom Cook consulted before or during the voyage, and therefore the aggressive lifestyle of the Maori might, in Cook's eyes, have invalidated any claim to permanent ownership of land that these people might have had.[24] In addition to this, the land never appeared to be owned by particular individuals, the conclusion being that they were not sufficiently advanced as to entertain the concept of property. As is explained in the next chapter, Cook, like Locke himself, could hardly conceive of collectively owned land, or collective labour, in a rational society, and so here again the inhabitants were perceived as not being 'rational'.[25] Evidently, this judgement was based on a total misapprehension of Maori culture, which was tribal rather than individualistic. What the individual possessed was what the tribe possessed, and the Maori 'self' was defined in terms of kinship affiliations rather than on the concepts of individual life and property which were at the heart of European legal systems.[26] Nevertheless, such arguments may well have seemed convincing to Cook. However, an additional point, made by Nicholas Thomas, is that, although Cook's claiming ceremonies seem to show he felt entitled to override indigenous claims to the land, yet his use of Maori names for the north and south islands of New Zealand on his own maps seems an implicit acknowledgement that these were Maori lands.[27]

On the second and third voyages Cook continued to claim many of the lands he visited for the first time, irrespective of their degree of cultivation or the attitude of their inhabitants. For instance, in June 1774 at Niue, which Cook christened 'Savage Island', there was hostility and even stone-throwing, reciprocated by musket fire, yet he felt justified in raising the Union Jack and ceremoniously taking possession of the island.[28] A few weeks later he waxed lyrical about the native irrigation of the coastal plains of New Caledonia, and the plantations 'which I observed were laid out with great judgement and cultivated by much labour'. But a few pages later in his journal he reports 'I went a shore and by Vertue of our being the first discoverers of this Country took posession of it in his Majesty's name.'[29]

Cook's policy of staking claims for his country on all newly discovered lands seems to have been pursued even more zealously than his instructions warranted. For instance, he was specifically ordered to explore the coast of New Zealand, but there is no mention in his instructions of his being expected to claim that territory for Britain.[30] As was his wont, he was carrying out these instructions to the letter, and even exceeding them in the perceived interests of his country. The policy may sometimes have been legally dubious, even by contemporary standards, and it certainly was to create much work for the lawyers of the future. Yet Cook was carrying out his duty as he saw it. He may have been a man of science who added enormously to the sum total of world knowledge, but he was in the first place a servant of his nation. Paradoxically, and in spite of what Sir Joseph Carruthers may have thought, the results of the voyages probably turned out to be far more useful for the progress of science generally than for Britain. But perhaps in any case this distinction between science and nationalism was a false one in the contemporary context. Scientific achievements, such as the recording of the Transit of Venus, or Cook's successful efforts to prevent scurvy, very much redounded to the prestige of Britain. Like Wolfe before him and Nelson after him, Cook died the death of a national hero, but unlike them he was also a figure of international prestige, whose achievements were at the service of humanity. After his death, his heroic stature was open to exploitation by various interests for their own ends, and over the years there were many Cooks, Sir Joseph Carruthers' Cook being one of them.

Chapter 16

Trade and Improvement

Between the ages of eight and sixteen James Cook helped his father on the land. The Cook family lived and worked at Aireyholme, a large farm on the edge of the North York Moors owned by Thomas Skottowe. But not much more than half a century earlier this farm had not existed. Instead, its fields had formed part of the unenclosed common land of the village, owned by no one individual, and where the villagers of Great Ayton had the right to collect brushwood and graze their cattle. At that time there had also been three large open fields belonging to the village, which were ploughed and harvested by communal methods inherited from the distant past. The whole system was under the control of a manorial court, presided over by the steward of the lord of the manor, which had powers to fine those who transgressed its numerous regulations. However, by Cook's day, all this, no doubt inefficient and wasteful, yet relatively democratic, system had vanished without trace, to be replaced by private enterprise. Now, every acre of land was in private hands, and instead of the mainly subsistence agriculture of the open fields, enterprising farmers were able to produce goods for the market, and extend their holdings, while the less efficient suffered, and those without any land at all were faced with the options of working for others, or leaving the village.

Enclosures, of course, took place not just in North Yorkshire, but nationally, both in Cook's day and also during the previous two centuries.[1] They were part of an agricultural revolution which reached its climax in the latter half of the eighteenth century, and which included new technology and new crops, the scientific breeding of domestic animals, and better transport by road and by water. Subsistence societies of any kind would thus have seemed backward to Cook's contemporaries, in comparison with modes of farming which could produce surpluses for the market. The new methods were all about the rationalization of production, but they also necessarily involved increasing the gap between rich and poor. It must have been difficult for the young Cook, growing up in his Yorkshire village, to even imagine the old system, or picture a time when the fields were worked communally, and when the farm he knew so well did not exist, but was part of a common without hedges and fences. There may have been elderly folk in the village who could recall how things were done in the old days, over half a century earlier, but to Cook any alternative to the private ownership of land and of the means of production might well have seemed ludicrous, and even contrary to human nature. Or so we can infer from several entries in the journals, such as this one from the second voyage, which concerned Tonga:

> It would be absurd to suppose everything to be in Common in a Country so well cultivated as this. Interest is the great Spring which animates the hand of industry, few would toil themselves in cultivating and planting the land if he did not expect to injoy the fruits of his labour, if every thing was in common the Industrious man would be upon a worse footing than the Idle Sluggard.[2]

On his second voyage Cook had to hand Bougainville's account of his earlier visit to Tahiti, and he sternly corrects Bougainville for believing that the Tahitians had communal property. He writes: 'I much doubt if there is a fruit tree on the whole island that is not the property of some individual on it', and he goes on to echo his judgement on Tonga: 'Indeed it is highly absurd to suppose every thing in Common in a Country where almost every article is raised by cultivation'.[3]

As well as the inevitability of private enterprise and the sanctity of private property, there was another principle which Cook held dear, and that was the need for progress, or 'improvement', to use the eighteenth-century term. Actually, the word had two, overlapping meanings at this time. There was the modern meaning of 'generally making better', and the narrower, capitalist meaning, 'to make a profit from', which was used especially of land-enclosure.[4] 'Improvement' went with private property because a man could improve the land he owned by farming it efficiently, and in doing so he rendered it more profitable, and incidentally also, by so doing, reinforced his title of ownership. But if, like the Australian aborigines, he failed to improve his land, and left it in a state of nature, then he could hardly claim to own it at all (see the previous chapter). Cook did not particularly admire untamed – i.e. unimproved – nature. The day of Wordsworth and Coleridge had not yet dawned, and wild, romantic vistas did not appeal, especially to a practical man like Cook. About the country near the Straits of Magellan he writes:

this is the most desolate coast I ever saw, it seems to be intirely composed of Rocky Mountains without the least appearance of Vegetation, these Mountains terminate in horroable precipices whose craggy summits spire up to a vast height, so that hardly any thing in nature can appear with a more barren and savage aspect than the whole of the coast.[5]

One can imagine that modern tourists on a cruise might have got out their cameras, and used quite different language, but Cook did not have the tourist gaze. What he did admire, and even find romantic, was a countryside that had been worked and modified by the hand of man. Here he is describing his first encounter with New Caledonia:

The plains along the coast on the side we lay appeared from the hills to great advantage, the winding Streams which ran through them which had their direction from Nature, the lesser Streames conveyed by art through the different plantations, the little stragling Villages, the Variaty in the Woods, the shoals on the coast, so variegated the scene that the whole might afford a Picture for romance.[6]

If Cook was hardly a tourist it was not only because the concept had not yet been invented, or the term coined, but also because he was a professional explorer under the employment of his national government. His mission was to size up the lands he discovered, and estimate their future use for Britain, if they were ever to be brought into the world-wide commercial network. The coast of New South Wales, for instance, might at first sight seem almost as barren and unimproved as the Magellan Straits, but Cook could see its potential:

we are to consider that we see this Country in the pure state of nature, the Industry of Man has had nothing to do with any part of it . . . in this Extensive Country it can never be doubted but what most sorts of grain, Fruits, Roots etc of every kind would flourish were they once brought hither, planted and cultivated by the hand of Industry, and here are Provender for more Cattle at all seasons of the year than can ever be brought into the country.[7]

In the short time available to him Cook himself did his best to improve some of the lands he visited. On his ships he carried a range of domestic animals – cows, sheep, goats, pigs and hens. Sometimes these were handed out to islanders with instructions as to their upkeep; sometimes they were left in remote places, in the hope that they would survive and multiply in the wild. He also took vegetable seeds, and occasionally, as in Tahiti on the first voyage, even planted them with his own hands, seemingly an odd thing to do and a sign of his personal enthusiasm since the *Endeavour* carried two professional botanists, Banks and Solander.[8] On the third voyage there was an especially large menagerie of domestic animals to accommodate on the *Resolution* because George III had given 'a Bull, 2 Cows with their Calves & some sheep to carry to Otaheite',[9] in addition to the animals provided by the Admiralty. As Nicholas Thomas points out, this enlarged maritime farmyard must have affected the quality of life aboard the *Resolution*: 'Think of the sheer volume of shit, the mess of damp and rotting feed, the inadequacy of ventilation below leaky decks, the already cramped accomodation.'[10] On the previous voyage, J.R. Forster, who complained bitterly when awarded a cabin adjacent to where the cattle were stalled, would certainly have agreed with this verdict.

All this benevolence was not strictly in the line of duty, but it was nevertheless quite common practice for naval captains on distant stations, and it was clearly something he felt strongly about. The rationale was no doubt to improve the quality of life of the natives, but also an expectation of providing future supplies for visiting ships, and hence of enhancing the effective range of the British navy. Captains such as Cook, although they might not have heard of vitamins, were well aware that supplements of fresh meat and vegetables to a sailor's diet helped prevent disease, especially scurvy. One could therefore hazard that Cook's motives were a combination of medical, imperialist and altruistic. According to Obeyesekere, there was also a profound significance in the symbolism of these gifts of animals and seeds, the practical results perhaps being of less significance than what the acts of giving represented. 'Cook', he argues, 'is the civiliser, bringing a new vision of the world to the savage lands of the South Seas . . . When Cook lands in a new land, he not only takes it over on behalf of the Crown in a series of ceremonial acts but wherever he goes he plants English gardens. The act is primarily symbolic, supplanting the disorderly way of savage peoples with ordered landscapes on the English model.'[11]

A modern ecologist might not entirely approve of Cook's efforts to introduce hitherto unknown plants and animals into Pacific environments, but his contemporaries were full of admiration. Anna Seward made it one of the themes of her elegy composed on the death of Cook:

To these the Hero leads his living store,
And pours new wonders on th'uncultur'd shore;
The silky fleece, fair fruit, and golden grain;
And future herds and harvests bless the plain.

O'er the green soil his Kids exulting play,
And sounds his clarion loud the Bird of day;
The downy Goose her ruffled bosom laves,
Trims her white wing, and wantons in the waves;
Stern moves the Bull along th'affrighted shores,
And countless nations tremble as he roars.[12]

By the third voyage Cook had become pessimistic about the results of his schemes of improvement. Concerning New Zealand he wrote: 'Thus the reader will see how every method I have taken to stock the Country with Sheep and Goats have proved ineffectual.'[13] Pigs left in the wild, however, might have survived. A New Zealander recently told Tony Horwitz that their descendants, nicknamed 'Captain Cookers', were still roaming the woods.[14] In the case of Tahiti, where Cook had left not only cattle, sheep and ducks, but also geese, turkeys and peacocks, Bligh reported in 1788 that all had been destroyed in the course of a civil war between two tribes.[15] On a few Pacific islands some of Cook's seeds might have survived and become naturalised, but on the whole his attempts at improvement failed. It is ironic that one animal that did transport itself successfully with Cook's help was the European black rat which apparently landed in New Zealand from the *Endeavour* and soon started to eliminate its indigenous rival.[16]

The principal way in which it was envisaged that 'improvement' might take place was through trade. Trade was vital for Britain as well as for Cook, and, he believed, also for the various peoples of the Pacific, if they were to make any progress. For Cook himself there was no other way – if one wanted water, wood and fresh food at each new landfall on a long journey, one had to trade with the inhabitants. Markets had to be established as quickly as possible on every suitable occasion, whether at the side of the ship with the visiting canoes, or on the beaches.

For the British government also, trade was a priority. Worldwide commerce provided wealth and prestige to the nation and tax revenue to the government, and its claims were supported by all classes. As Linda Colley explains, the cult of commerce cut across social barriers and political divisions, and its pursuit, or at least its support, had become an increasingly important part of what it meant to be British.[17] From the middle of the century onward the perceived demand for new trading routes had led to repeated calls for exploration, and especially for the systematic exploration of the Pacific, that jealously guarded but under-exploited 'Spanish lake'. John Campbell, the author of an important compilation of voyages, published in 1744, made an impassioned plea for action in this direction:

I call the Arts of Commerce noble and generous, because they extend to all mankind . . . Why not prosecute new Discoveries, at least, why not enlarge our Commerce by the Invention of new Branches? The common Answer is, because the Thing is impossible. Idle, ridiculous, and impious Assertion! Have we not Wool; have we not Cloth; are there not naked nations enough in the World, who would gladly be covered; and was there ever a Nation yet found, that wanted Cloaths, and at the same Time wanted a wherewithal to pay for them.[18]

A few years later, in 1769, Alexander Dalrymple produced another collection of voyages which was to have an important influence on leading decision-makers within government such as Lord Shelburne.[19] Dalrymple, too, justified the need for Pacific exploration on the grounds that it would further British commercial interests, but his approach was slightly different to Campbell's. By this date Britain's richest colony, America, had already embarked on the process which was to lead to revolt and eventual independence, and it was becoming clear to many people in Britain that colonies in the end might be more of a nuisance than an asset. Dalrymple used this insight as an additional reason for seeking new trade routes in other parts of the world:

It must be obvious that if colonies are aiming at independence, and endeavouring to break off all connection with the Mother Country, the only means of preventing these intentions, and of securing the power and prosperity of the Mother Country, must be by extending its commerce to distant nations who can have no connection with those discontented colonies.[20]

Dalrymple stressed the difference between colonization, which, as in the case of America, could have deleterious effects on the mother country, and discoveries, which might lead to 'an amicable intercourse for mutual benefit'.[21] Cook was to take Dalrymple's book with him on his second voyage, and he mentions it more than once in his journal. Building on Dalrymple's thesis, the historian Daniel Baugh has argued that the period after 1763 saw a policy pursued by the British government of what he describes as 'protective maritime imperialism'. This involved the prosecution of voyages of discovery, but only as an insurance policy, in case there did actually turn out to be rich commercial pickings in the Pacific, and France obtained access to them first. Baugh points out that the Admiralty did not actually need to suppose that the possibilities of commerce in this unknown area were of any real importance. Moreover, this policy was relatively cheap: 'The cost of all the British exploratory voyages of the 1760s was probably less than the cost of one ship of the line fully fitted – a reasonable insurance premium.'[22]

After the Seven Years War Britain found herself the owner of a trading empire, a commercial network extending all over the known world. This kind of empire was seen by contemporaries as very different from the older empires, such as those of the Spanish or Portuguese, which had been acquired and maintained by brute force, the conquest and subjugation of other peoples' lands. Cook's contemporaries held that trade represented an entirely different, and distinctively modern way of organizing relationships between the imperial power and any native societies whom it might encounter. Hence, as well as being of material benefit, trade was also ideological. It was an ideology given its classical expression in Adam Smith's *Inquiry into the Nature and Causes of the Wealth of Nations*, published the year that Cook set sail on his second voyage. Smith's message was that a nation's wealth and progress depended not on its reserves of bullion but on its ability to create new trade routes and new markets for its products. Cook has been described as 'Adam Smith's first and perhaps greatest global agent',[23] because he opened up a third of the world to free enterprise. There were many like Cook who lacked conventional religious beliefs, or at least kept them to themselves, but whose profound belief in the virtues of commerce – not just in goods, though this was important, but also in ideas – may have helped fill the ideological vacuum. As the historian and philosopher, J. G. A. Pocock, puts it: 'The concept of commerce took on such an importance that it was in many ways fetishized; certainly, we cannot understand the European perception of history in the age of encounter without constantly placing it at the very center and climax.'[24] This writer goes on to make the very interesting suggestion that there is a clear link between the commercial spirit and the spirit of tolerance displayed by eighteenth-century explorers towards the new cultures and religions they came across. Those who had rejected the religious certainties of their ancestors, and had virtually abandoned the idea that God intervenes in the material world, were prepared to look with indifference on the religious certainties of others. Pocock sums up the link as follows:

> These two strategies – let us label them the commercial and the deist – came together at the point where it was suggested that the inhabitants of commercial societies were peculiarly fitted to recognize that they had only opinions, and never knowledge, of the structure of either god-head or universe, and could do no better than arrange their opinions in tentative and experimental bodies of doctrine, tolerant and respectful of one another.[25]

To learn from other societies, and take what they had to offer – that was the way to advance, and Cook judged the peoples he met largely by their ability to do this. He respected those such as the Hawaiians who were shrewd bargainers, seemed to know the rules of trade, and did not try to bend these rules:

> It is also remarkable that they have never once attempted to cheat us in exchanges or once to commit a theft. They understand trading as well as most people and seem to have discovered what we are plying upon the coast for, for tho they bring off things in great plenty, particularly pigs, yet they keep up their price and rather than despose of them for less than they demand will take them a shore again.[26]

On the other hand, there were many Pacific islanders who seemed unwilling to abide by the conventions of trade, and even worse, who refused to learn about these conventions, or profit from their contacts with Europeans. It was on the third voyage, following his disillusionment with Omai, that he confided to his journal his views about the impossibility of teaching new skills to the Society Islanders.[27]

On his first voyage Cook had admired the Australian aborigines because they were self-sufficient and seemed not to need or want anything the Europeans could offer them. This was a sample of that primitivist admiration of the 'noble savage' which possibly Cook borrowed originally from Banks, but by the third voyage he seems to have abandoned any such opinions. For instance, in Alaska he notes that the natives used valuable sea otter skins to clothe themselves, but did not bother to acquire a surplus of the skins for trade. He therefore suggests that

> a trade with Foreigners would increase their wants by introducing new luxuries amongst them, in order to purchas which they would be the more assiduous in procuring skins, for I think it is pretty evident they are not a scarce article in the country.[28]

In other words, the Alaskans should be brought into the world trading nexus by the artificial creation of consumer demand. Incidentally, a trade in sea otter skins did ensue after Cook, conducted by British, and especially American, merchants, and was in fact the only commercial outcome of his third voyage.[29]

The best way to arrange a smooth trade was obviously to make friends with the chiefs, and Cook was adept at this. By the third voyage it is also clear that he enjoyed the company of chiefs for its own sake. 'It was', he writes, 'my interest as well as inclination to pay my court to all these great men.'[30] The leader of one hierarchical society – those on board *Resolution* and *Discovery* – was charmed to be invited to socialize with other hierarchical leaders. Commentators have sometimes wondered why Cook spent several weeks in the Summer of 1777 sailing round the Friendly Islands, or Tonga group, before heading north towards Alaska, as he was instructed, and this may be part of the answer. The language he uses to describe his meetings with the chiefs of Tonga show his pleasure in their company, and his admiration for their way of doing things (see the description of his relationship with Paulaho in Chapter 12).

As already mentioned, Cook, by the third voyage, had become disillusioned by the failure of many islanders to profit from the European example, or even to comply with the rules of fair trade. To understand and obey these rules required a particular kind of sophistication which had developed in Europe over centuries, and it was not, as Cook tended to assume, inherent in human nature. If one of Cook's officers held out an old shirt in exchange for some fish from a canoe, he was in effect proposing the setting up of an unspoken contract between himself and another individual. Such a contract depended on the other person possessing a certain internal sense of his own individuality – an inner-self, which could then be mediated through various public roles such as the trading role, with its own rules. However, members of a community-based society might not necessarily possess this inner sense of identity. Their view of self might be entirely bound up with their group. So when the native seized the shirt and tried to paddle away without giving up the fish, he might well not have experienced the same sense of guilt and responsibility that a European would have felt on breaking such a contract. Here, for instance, is Stephen Turner describing this communal notion of self in so far as it applied to Maori society:

> The Maori 'self' is understood in terms of kinship affiliations, rather than individual property. Individual status is derived from the tribal group and is inconceivable outside this community. What the individual possesses is what the tribe possesses in the individual. This, ultimately, is the self-understanding of the tribe – its history, traditions, and practices. Correct action involves re-creating the history of the tribe. The British notion of right, depending on the attributes of the individual prior to the formation of civil society, could have no basis in traditional Maori society.[31]

Just as the law of property was not necessarily inscribed within the heart of a Pacific islander, so neither was the law of fair trade. And in the end the improvement on offer from Cook was an illusion for the natives he encountered, even for those who understood, and were prepared to enter into, commercial relationships with the Europeans. Trade between nations of widely differing technological capacity can hardly be equal, or lead to equal advantages. Even if they did their best to participate in the trade offered – which on the whole the Maoris did – they were eventually going to lose out. Such, at least, is the view of the distinguished historian, Bernard Smith. According to his pessimistic judgement:

> ... what Adam Smith's free-market economy offered the South Seas was not really the difference between civilization and savagery but the difference between exploitation and extermination. Those peoples who were sufficiently advanced to grasp the potential advantages of a market economy survived to become the colonial servants of their European masters; those who could not, because of the primitive nature of their societies, like the natives of Tierra del Fuego and Van Diemen's Land, in the fulness of the time of Adam Smith's invisible god, were exterminated.[32]

Chapter 17

Science and Navigation

Cook the mariner is central to Cook the man. As seaman he is the supreme epitome of professional competence, resourcefulness, and a willingness to learn and experiment with new methods. The entire time he was at sea he was handling and navigating his ship, and for much of that time was engaged in surveying and charting unknown coasts. In addition, his journals show him continuously speculating and forming hypotheses on problems of geography, natural history, ethnography and much else.

Cook was lucky that he made his voyages when he did because it was a time of rapid progress in astronomical navigation and also in the making of navigational instruments. But all this progress depended on the seamen, who might or might not grasp the new ideas and try out the instruments. Sailors generally, including captains, were conservative and hostile to change. It needed someone like Cook who had the determination and persistence to absorb the latest innovations and master the techniques. Much of Cook's self-education was achieved when he was an adult, the most obvious example being in Canada in 1758, shortly after he was appointed master of the *Pembroke*, a 64-gun ship commanded by Captain John Simcoe. There was apparently a chance encounter between Cook and a military engineer, Major Samuel Holland. Years later Holland related the incident in a letter to Simcoe's son, then Lieutenant-Governor of Upper Canada:

> The Day after the Surrender of Louisbourg; being at Kensington Cove Surveying and making a Plan of the Place, with its attack & Encampments: I observed Capt. Cook (then Master of Capt. Simcoes ship the *Pembrook* man of war) particularly attentive to my operations; and as he expressed an ardent Desire to be instructed in the use of the Plane Table; (the Instrument I was then using) I appointed the next Day in order to make him acquainted with the whole process.[1]

Under Holland's tuition, and with the enthusiastic support of Capt. Simcoe, who set aside the *Pembroke*'s great cabin for surveying lessons, Cook soon acquired expertise in geometrical surveying methods. Many years later he explained to Holland how these sessions had help launch him on a new career as a hydrographic surveyor:

> Mʳ Cook frequently expressed to me the obligations he was under to Capᵗ. Simcoe; and on my meeting him in London in the year 1776 after his Several Discoveries, he confessed most candidly that the Improvements and Instructions he had received on Board the *Pembrook* had been the Sole Foundation of the Services he had been enabled to perform.[2]

In the summers following his meeting with Holland, Cook was engaged in survey work in Newfoundland, and no doubt in the course of this work he frequently went ashore and carried out triangulations using a plane table. However, on his voyages of discovery he seldom had time or opportunity to make this kind of detailed survey. Instead, his work in the Pacific usually consisted of running surveys conducted from the deck of the *Endeavour* or the *Resolution*. The ship would proceed along the coast making regular 'ship stations' from which bearings were taken of prominent objects on the land, probably with a sextant rather than a compass. The distances between the stations were carefully measured, and regular soundings taken. The angles and bearings noted were later plotted and the position of the various features obtained. Rough sketches were also made of the passing coastline. Weather permitting, the ship's longitude and latitude would be taken each day at noon.

Using such methods Cook on his first voyage surveyed the entire coastline of New Zealand over six months between October 1769 and April 1770, covering an average of 20 miles a day. Some of the difficulties and dangers of such a survey are described by Alan Villiers in his biography of Cook. Villiers was himself a master mariner who had sailed a full-rigged ship round the world in Cook's tracks.

> So he began that extraordinary circumnavigation of both islands of New Zealand which, even in his spectacular seafaring career, was an outstanding achievement. He had to sail over 2,500 miles in difficult water off a dangerous and unknown coast, much of it exposed to the Roaring Forties, extending to within a few degrees of the latitude of Cape Horn. He had to make as good a survey as he could. He had to do all this with a single ship and no means of communication . . .

A sailing-ship Master compelled to coast with the wind blowing onshore, had to keep off or risk wreck; yet if Cook did not sail close in, no one would learn much. Submerged rocks licking their ship-tearing edges just below the surface were difficult to see: ledges of them could be anywhere. To sail into what looked like harbours, even after the Master had done some sounding from a boat, meant some element of risk, and doing things which the prudent seaman most dislikes having to do. Cook was above all else a prudent seaman. He had to be audacious too: if he did not investigate harbours he would never find a base or haven to gather wild celery and other essential anti-scorbutics, or for rest for the people (Maoris permitting) and the chance to cut wood and collect water. These he had to have.[3]

Approximately 2,000 miles of Australia's east coast was given the same treatment over another four months which included 54 days at anchorage in Botany Bay and the Endeavour River. This meant an average of 30 miles per day. Considering that during all this time Cook was in totally unknown waters, and was acting simultaneously as explorer and surveyor, these two surveys must rank amongst his greatest achievements. Many experts, then and since, have commented on the accuracy of the charts derived from them. For example, the contemporary French navigator, Julien-Marie Crozet, who sailed to New Zealand in 1772–3 under Marion du Fresne, wrote:

> As soon as I obtained information of the voyage of the Englishman, I carefully compared the chart I had prepared of that part of the coast of New Zealand along which we had coasted with that prepared by Captain Cook and his officers. I found it of an exactitude and of a thoroughness of detail which astonished me beyond all powers of expression, and I doubt much whether the charts of our own French coasts are laid down with greater precision. I think therefore that I cannot do better than to lay down our track off New Zealand on the chart prepared by this celebrated navigator.[4]

Cook himself was well aware of the quality of his own work, and in a long passage of his journal he expresses satisfaction with his Australian survey, while giving especial praise to the astronomer, Charles Green, for his assistance.[5] Nevertheless, he realized that running surveys could never be as detailed and accurate as the large scale surveys he had made in Newfoundland. On his second voyage, concerning his survey of Vanuatu in the New Hebrides, he comments:

The word Survey, is not to be understood here, in its literal sence. Surveying a place, according to my Idea, is takeing a Geometrical Plan of it, in which every place is to have its true situation, which cannot be done in a work of this kind.[6]

In making these running surveys one great advantage possessed by Cook and not by his predecessors was the ability to fix his position accurately. The theory that any point on the earth's surface could be accurately pin-pointed by naming its coordinates of latitude and longitude had been known for many centuries, but it was not until Cook's time that techniques and instruments were developed that allowed the coordinate system to become a practical reality. Until then, latitude could easily be reckoned but longitude was more elusive. During Cook's first voyage he was able to find longitude by the recently developed system of lunar distances. This method had been first suggested in the early sixteenth century. It was based on the fact that the moon in its movements round the earth can be used as a clock. The idea was to measure from on board ship the angular distance between the moon and the sun, or if at night, between the moon and a prominent star. If it was also known at what time this particular angular distance could have been recorded at Greenwich, then the difference between the ship's local time and Greenwich time could be established, and hence the ship's longitude.

Theory, however, was one thing and practice another. Effective use of the method had to wait until two revolutionary inventions of the mid-eighteenth century. The first was Hadley's quadrant with its two mirrors, which made precise angular measurements of heavenly bodies possible even from the heaving deck of a ship. This had been invented in 1731, and an improved model, the sextant, which incorporated a telescope was developed in 1757. The second innovation was the publication, by Nevil Maskelyn, Astronomer Royal, of annual tables giving various lunar distances every three hours as seen from Greenwich. The first year for which these tables were available was 1767, and Cook had them on the *Endeavour* for 1768 and 1769. Even so, the lunar method required, it was said, about four hours of laborious calculation after the initial measurements had been made, and by this date few naval officers yet understood the process. For instance, Capt. Samuel Wallis, who returned to England from his Pacific voyage in 1768, having discovered Tahiti, reported in his journal that his purser, evidently a mathematician, had fixed the position of that island using the new method. Wallis, however, wrote, 'thro whose means we took the Longitude by taking the Distance of the Sun from the Moon and Working it according to Dr Masculines Method which we did not understand'.[7] Cook himself does not seem to have used the new system in Newfoundland, but he had clearly mastered it before setting out on his first voyage.

Apart from all the fallible and complicated calculations involved, another major disadvantage of the method was that for 15 days in each lunar month the moon was either too near or too far from the sun to permit the measurement of its angular distance. However, an even more revolutionary development, which promised to bypass some of the disadvantages of the lunar method, occurred in time for Cook to use it during his second and third voyages. This was a novel kind of clock which could be set to record Greenwich time and would remain accurate throughout all the vicissitudes of a long voyage. The new method required merely the calculating of local time, usually by taking observations of the sun to establish its noonday zenith. A comparison of local and Greenwich time then gave the ship's longitude.

John Harrison had produced a series of such clocks, or 'chronometers', as they were christened by Alexander Dalrymple. By 1764 the fourth of these (H4) had been successfully tested on a voyage to the West Indies. As is well known, Harrison became embroiled in a controversy with the Board of Longitude as to whether he was entitled to the £20,000 prize offered by act of Parliament for whoever should first solve the longitude problem.[8] The Board, which was dominated by astronomers, led by Nevil Maskelyn, swore by the lunar method, and delayed awarding Harrison his prize. Nevertheless, H4 (or rather K1, an exact copy of it by Larcum Kendal, since Maskelyn refused to allow H4 to leave Greenwich) was sent off with Cook in order to receive further trials. Three other chronometers by another watch maker, John Arnold, went too.

It may well be that for much of the second voyage Cook was not entirely convinced about the new method. This, after all, would only have been natural since he, like other astronomers, had invested much time and energy in mastering lunar distances. As late as September 1774, in a discussion of the lunar method, he describes the chronometers in somewhat lukewarm terms:

> The most expensive article, and what is in some measure necessary in order to come at the utmost accuracy, is a good watch; but for common use and where the utmost accuracy is not required, one may do without.[9]

The context here makes it clear he was referring to K1. However, there is no doubt his admiration for 'the Watch' grew, until on his return to England he reported to the Secretary of the Admiralty:

> Mr Kendal's Watch has exceeded the expectations of its most Zealous advocate and by being now and then corrected by Lunar observations has been our faithfull guide through all the vicissitudes of climates.[10]

K1 was taken to Greenwich on Cook's return and found to be gaining a mere 13 seconds per day. This, after a voyage lasting over three years in which it had been subject to extremes of heat and cold, was an impressive achievement. Arnold's three watches had not performed nearly so well but even so it was clear that the day of the chronometer had dawned. Especially during the three ice-edge cruises towards and into the Arctic circle had K1 proved invaluable. Under the often overcast skies of high southern latitudes there were many days when lunar observations were out of the question but when it was still possible to make out the shape of the sun, even behind hazy cloud, so that local time could be established and hence the chronometer method used to obtain longitude. It is true that Cook and his colleagues also made calculations of longitude using the lunar method whenever they could so that the two methods could be compared, and it is also true that it would be a long time before captains abandoned their 'lunars'. Nevertheless, Cook's experience with K1 on his second voyage was a crucial episode in the history of navigation, and decisively proved the importance of the chronometer.

Cook also took Kendal's watch with him on his final voyage when it again proved totally reliable – for the majority of the voyage. The story goes that it stopped ticking at approximately the same time as Cook was murdered on Kealakehua beach![11] Finally, not only did John Harrison get his £20,000, but also watches like his began to be manufactured in industrial quantities and increasingly cheaply, so that within a few years every ship in the British navy was furnished with at least one.

It was known to the authorities that Cook was a competent astronomer as early as 1767 when observations of a solar eclipse which he made when on survey work in Newfoundland were reported to the Royal Society.[12] His reputation as a man of science was established after his first voyage, and enhanced after his second, when he was elected a Fellow of the Royal Society, and awarded the Society's Copley Medal for the paper he presented on methods of preserving the health of seamen on long voyages. He had become a member of the nation's scientific elite, one of those whom today we might call professional scientists. Even before the second voyage he seems to have been accepted as a colleague and an equal by other men of science. This at any rate is implied by a remark made in a letter written in 1775 by one Fellow of the Royal Society to another. Daniel Wray wrote to the Earl of Hardwicke, 'Cook is returned, and has resumed his seat at the Mitre. He is a right-headed unaffected man; and I have a great authority for calling him our best navigator.'[13] The Mitre was the tavern where the Royal Society dined, and the implication here is that Cook, although not yet a Fellow, was already dining there before his departure on the *Resolution* in 1772.

Indeed, Cook's pursuit of knowledge was methodical and cautious, his hypotheses always backed up by evidence. He took pride in never putting anything onto his maps and charts which he had not verified himself. He was scornful of earlier navigators who failed to produce accurate coordinates for the places they had allegedly discovered, and also of the publishers of charts who endangered the lives of seamen by adding coastal outlines which had not actually been surveyed.

> Neither can I clear Seamen of this fault. Among the few I have known who are capable of drawing a Chart or sketch of a Sea Coast, I have generally, nay almost always observed them run into this error; I have known them lay down the line of a Coast they never have seen and put down soundings where they never have sounded, and after all are so fond of their performances as to pass'd the whole thing off as sterling under the Title of a Survey Plan etc.[14]

In view of this cautious approach it is all the more surprising that on his third voyage Cook allowed himself to be misled by certain inaccurate maps of the northern Pacific, especially one by Jacob von Stählin, Secretary of the St. Petersburg Academy of Sciences, which depicted a number of fictitious islands, and showed Alaska as separated from the rest of America by a wide strait. For Cook this was uncharacteristic behaviour, which may have been due partly to the haste with which this expedition to search for a north west passage was conceived and planned.[15]

Cook was essentially a practical scientist, and he had a distrust, which he shared with other leaders of expeditions, for armchair experts – those who speculated in the comfort of their studies, for instance about the existence of a Southern Continent, or a passage through from the Pacific to the Atlantic. He thought that people should stick to what they could prove, and avoid unnecessary flights of imaginative speculation. On numerous occasions in the journals he starts out on a new subject and then stops himself, on the grounds that he is not qualified to speak further. For example, he wonders whether volcanoes are more active during wet weather, but then adds, 'Here seems to be a field open for some Philosophical reasoning on these extra-ordinary Phenomenon's of nature, but as I have no tallant that way I must content my self with stateing facts as I found, and leave the causes to men of more abilities.'[16] On the subject of the complex and variable tides which swirled round Cape Horn he writes: 'I confess my self unprovided with materials for such a task & believe that the less I say on this subject the fewer Misstakes I shall make.'[17] His disclaimer on not writing a general description of the port of

Batavia epitomises his modest view of his own role: 'This task I shall leave to some abler hand and only take notice of such things as seems to me necessary for seamen to know.'[18] Nevertheless, when the subject was one on which he believed himself qualified to speak, he was prepared to commit himself in his journals to passages of deductive reasoning or speculation which are often lengthy. Examples are his disquisitions on cannibalism in New Zealand, on the migrations of Pacific islanders, and on the nature and origin of ice in the Antarctic.[19] On this last topic, for instance, there is a carefully argued account of the formation of tabular icebergs in which he disproves the theory that they were necessarily formed at the mouth of rivers. He also discusses the prevailing contemporary assumption that sea water could under no circumstances freeze. As Beaglehole says Cook 'struggled with this dogma' but did not go quite so far as to contradict it. Instead, he put forward a compromise theory that Antarctic seas might appear frozen over to all intents and purposes, as the salt water had been overlaid by successive layers of snow that had turned to ice.[20]

George Forster, in the introduction to his own Journal, claimed that Cook, while an accomplished collector of facts, was not good at synthesizing them in order to form 'general views', but these examples and others seem to prove Forster wrong.[21] What is true, however, is that Cook's thoughts on particular topics tend to be scattered throughout his journals, and he often returns to a subject several times, which seems to leave him at a disadvantage when compared, for instance, with the *Observations* of the elder Forster, George's father, in which the author had time to organize and collate his thoughts on a range of scientific topics.[22]

More central to Cook's status as a man of science than these somewhat random speculations are of course the results of his navigations and surveys as set out in his charts and also his journals. Exploration has been called the most empirical of all forms of enquiry and the most destructive of purely *a priori* reasoning.[23] Throughout his voyages Cook was engaged in verifying, and often dismissing, the claims of others, and in this sense he was a true 'man of science', a major player in an age that was coming increasingly to value experience over authority.[24]

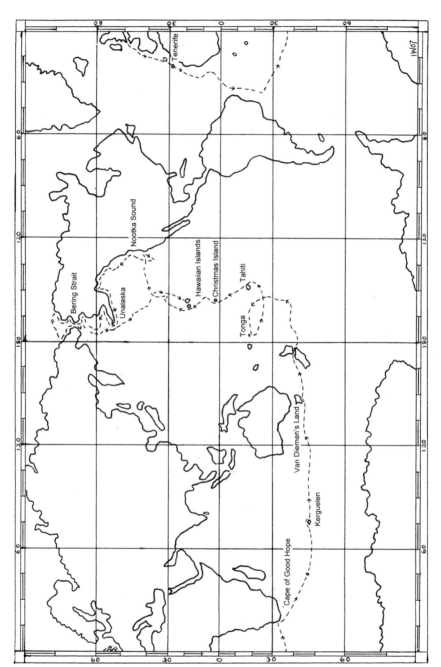

Map 3 James Cook's third voyage with the Resolution and the Discovery (1776–9)

Timeline of the Third Voyage

The Voyage of the *Resolution* and *Discovery*, 1776–80

1697 William Dampier, 'A New Voyage round the World'

I know there have been divers attempts made about a North West Passage, and all unsuccessful: yet I am of opinion, that such a passage may be found. All our Countrymen that have gone to discover the N.W. Passage, have endeavoured to pass to the Westward, beginning their search along Davis's or Hudson's Bay. But if I was to go on this Discovery, I would go first into the South Seas, bend my course from thence along by California, and that way seek a Passage back into the West Seas.

February 1776 Andrew Kippis, 'The Life of Captain James Cook', 1788

His advice was particularly requested with regard to the properest person for conducting the voyage. To determine this point, the captain, Sir Hugh Palliser, and Mr Stephens were invited to Lord Sandwich's to dinner. Here, besides taking into consideration what officer should be recommended to his majesty for accomplishing the purposes in view, many things were said concerning the nature of the design. Its grandeur and dignity, the conse-quences of it to navigation and science, and the completion it would give to the whole system of discoveries were enlarged upon in the course of the conversation. Captain Cook was so fired with the contemplation and repre-sentation of the object, that he started up, and declared that he himself would undertake the direction of the enterprise.

14 February 1776 Cook to John Walker

Dear Sir/ I should have Answered your last favour sooner, but waited to know whether I should go to Greenwich Hospital, or the South Sea. The latter is now fixed upon; I expect to be ready to sail about the latter end of Ap[l] with my old Ship the Resolution and the Discovery, the ship lately purchased of M[r] Herbert. I know not what your opinion may be on this step I have taken. It is certain I have quited an easy retirement, for an Active, and perhaps Dangerous Voyage. My present disposition is more favourable to the latter than the former, and I imbark on as fair a prospect as I can wish. If I am fortunate enough to get safe home, theres no doubt but it will be greatly to my advantage.

24 June 1776 Journal

At 6 o'clock in the Morning I set out from London in company with Omai . . . His behavour on this occasion seemed truly Natural; he was fully sencible of the good treatment he had met with in England and entertained the highest ideas of the Country and people but the prospect he now had of returning home to his native isle loaded with what they esteem riches, got the better of every other consideration and he seemed quite happy when on board the ship.

12 July 1776 Journal

At 8 PM Wieghed and stood out of the Sound [Plymouth Sound] with a gentle breeze at NWbW.

22 October 1776 David Samwell, surgeon's mate on the Resolution, from Cape Town, to Matthew Gregson

We arrived here all hearty the 19th ins[t] after a pleasant Passage of something better than three months. We called in our way and staid 3 Days at the Island of Teneriffe taking in Wine and other Refreshments – the Cape is a very plentiful Country & we live upon the Fat of the Land during our stay which will be about a Month, then we shall set off for Otaheite where we expect to be about the time you will receive this Letter which I imagine will be some time in Feb[y] or March. I do not suppose we shall stay long at Otaheite as we must embrace the summer season to try for the North west passage; if we find it we shall be in England next Winter. We have various Opinions about it some think we shall & others that we shall not find it.

26 November 1776 Cook to Banks

Dear Sir/ Your very obliging favour I received by Captain Clerke who arrived here on the 18th Inst. Something more than three weeks after me and nearly the same time as I sailed from Plymouth before him. [Charles Clerke, captain of the *Discovery*, had been delayed in London owing to an action for debt] We are now ready to proceed on our Voyage, and nothing is wanting but a few females of our own species to make the Resolution a compleate ark for I have added considerably to the Number of Animals I took onboard in England. Omai consented with raptures to give up his Cabbin to make room for four Horses.

24 January 1777 Journal

At 3 AM we made the Coast of Van Diemen land [Tasmania].

12 February 1777 Journal

Anchored at our old station in Queen Charlottes Sound [in New Zealand; 'old station' because they had stayed there several times on the two previous voyages].

25 February 1777 Journal

On Tuesday the 25th at 10 AM a light breeze springing up at NWbN we weighed, stood out of the Sound and made sail through the Strait with the Discovery in company.

[By the end of March, having struggled north-eastwards against the prevailing winds, they encountered an unknown group of islands, now called the Cook Islands. However, the islanders seemed hostile, and little fodder was available for the cattle on board, so they sailed on]

6 April 1777 Cook to Clerke, at sea

Whereas the contrary winds we have met with of late, and which still continue, have render'd it impossible for us to touch at Otaheite and the Society Isles and have afterwards time enough to endeavour to find a Passage into the Western Ocean by the North Pole, during the Summer of the present year, and whereas both the Sloops are in want of Water, and the Cattle I have on board are in great want of Food also; it is absolutely necessary to repair to some place where these wants can be supplied; and as I know of no place so convenient as the Islands of Rotterdam, Amsterdam or Middleburgh [in the Tonga group], to one of these places therefore I intend to proceed forthwith.

10 June 1777 Journal

At length about 2 PM we arrived at our intended Station, being a very snug place formed by the shore of Tongatabu [known also as Amsterdam] on the SE and two small islands on the East and NE: here we anchored in 10 fathom Water over a bottom of owsey [oozy] sand, distant from the shore one third of a mile. Soon after we had Anchored, I landed accompanied by Omai and some of the Officers, we found the King [Fatafehi Paulaho] waiting for us on the beach, ready to conduct us to a small neat house, situated a little within the skirts of the woods with a fine large area before it; this house the Chief told me was at my service during my stay and a better situation we could not wish for.

17 July 1777 Journal

We took leave of the Friendly Islands [the Tonga group] and their inhabitants after a stay of between two and three Months, during which time we lived together in the most cordial friendship, some accidental differences its true now and then happened owing to their great propensity to thieving, but too often incouraged by the negligence of our own people. But these differences were never attended with any fatal consequences, to prevent which all my measures were directed. Also during this time we expended very little of our Sea Provisions but lived upon the produce of the islands.

[They now proceeded to the Society Islands, where they left Omai on the island of Huaheine before sailing northwards into unknown waters]

2 November 1777 Journal

Omai went ashore, after taking a very affectionate farewell of all the Officers; he sustained himself with a manly resolution till he came to me then his utmost efforts to conceal his tears failed, and Mr King, who went in the boat, told me he wept all the time in going ashore. Whatever faults this Indian had they were more than over ballanced by his great good Nature and docile disposition, during the whole time he was with me I very seldom had reason to find fault with his conduct.

19 January 1778 Journal

At this time we were in some doubt whether or no the land before us [Oahu, one of the western islands of the Hawaiian group] was inhabited, this doubt was soon cleared up, by seeing some Canoes coming off from the shore towards the Ships, I immediately brought to to give them time to come up, there were three and four men in each and we were agreeably surprised to find them of the same Nation as the people of Otahiete and the other islands we had lately visited . . . As soon as we made sail the Canoes left us, but others came off from the shore and brought with them roasting pigs and some very fine Potatoes, which they exchanged, as the others had done, for what-ever was offered them; several small pigs were got for a sixpenny nail or two apiece, so that we again found our selves in the land of plenty.

6 March 1778 Journal

On the 6th at Noon being in the latitude of 44° 10, longit. 234½, we saw two Seals and several whales, and at day break the next Morning, the long looked for Coast of new Albion [the modern state of Oregon] was seen extending from NE to SE distant 10 or 12 leagues.

4 May 1778 Samwell's Journal

Today we saw the high Mountain called by Bering Mount St Elias, it is the highest Mountain we have seen on the [American] Coast and is covered with Snow, it rises in the form of a Piramid with its base in a ridge of Mountains and may be seen at sea at the distance of 60 or perhaps 70 Leagues . . . As we sail along the Coast we find it trending to the Southward & Westward according to Muller's Chart of Bering's Discoveries, which reduces our Hopes of finding a Northwest passage to a low ebb. Today Cap[n] Cook accompanied by the Surgeon [William Anderson] went ashore on an Island off which Bering came to anchor, he mentions it as lying not far from Mount S[t] Elias & we found its situation agree pretty well with his Acc[t]. Capt[n] Cook went up the Hill above the Beach and left a Bottle there containing a paper on which was wrote an acc[t] of our two Ships touching here etc.

3 August 1778 *Journal*

M[r] Anderson my Surgeon who had been lingering under a consumption for more than twelve Months, expired between 3 and 4 this after noon. He was a Sensible Young Man, an agreeable companion, well skilld in his profession, and had acquired much knowlidge in other Sciences, that had it pleased God to have spar'd his life might have been usefull in the Course of the Voyage. Soon after land was Seen to the Westward, 12 leagues distant, it was supposed to be an Island and to perpetuate the Memory of the dieseased for whom I had a very great regard, I named it Andersons Island [today called St Lawrence Island].

10 August 1778 *Samwell's Journal*

Captain Cook having now run along the western Coast of America till he fell in with the Coast of Asia in Lat. 65°34′ & Long. 189°26′E, He has proved that there is no passage through the Continent of America; for tho' we did not keep the Land in Sight all the way, yet the shoal water we had all along affords a sufficient Proof of the Continuation of the Coast, & precludes the possibility of any considerable opening in that short Space of it which we did not see which lies between. We are now in Bering's Straits which divide Asia from America as high as these two Continents are known, & our only Hopes of a Passage now is round the Northern Extremity of America.

29 August 1778 *Journal*

The 29th in the Morning we saw the Main ice to the Northward . . . The season was now so very far advanced and the time when the frost is expected to set in so near at hand, that I did not think it consistant with prudence to make any farther attempts to find a passage this year in any direction so little was the prospect of succeeding. My attention was now directed towards finding out some place where we could Wood and Water, and in the considering how I should spend the Winter, so as to make some improvement to Geography and navigation and at the same time be in a condition to return to the North in further search of a Passage the ensuing summer.

14 October 1778 *Journal*

In the evening, as Mr Webber and I was at an Indian Village a little way from Samgoonoodha [on the Aleutian island of Unalaska], a Russian landed there who I found was the principal person amongst the Russians in this and the neighbouring islands. His name was Erasim Gregorioff Sin Ismyloff, he came in a Canoe carrying three people . . . Both Mr Ismyloff and the others affirmed that they knew nothing of the Continent of America to the Northward . . . From what we could gather from Mr Ismyloff and the others, the Russians have made several attempts to get a footing upon that part of the Continent which lies adjacent to the islands, but have always been repulsed by the Natives, whom they describe as a very treacherous people; they mentioned too or three Captains or chief men, that had been Murdered by them and some of the Russians here shewed us wounds which they said they received there.

30 November 1778 *Journal*

In the after noon of the 30th being off the NE end of the island, several Canoes came off to the Ships, the most of them belonged to a Chief named Terryaboo [the king of the Hawaiian Islands] who came in one; he made me a present of two or three small pigs . . . In the evening we discovered another island to windward which the Natives call O'why'he the name of the one we had been off we now learnt was Mow'ee [Maui]

17 January 1779 *Journal*

In the Evening Mr Bligh returned and reported that he had found a bay [Kealakekua Bay] in which was good anchorage and fresh water tolerable easy to come at, into this bay I resolved to go to refit the Ships and take in water.

[This is the last day for which Cook made a journal entry. He was killed at Kealakekua on 14 February 1779. His officers continued the voyage, finally returning home in October 1780]

Chapter 18

The Death of Cook

Cook's death, along with that of four marines, on a beach in Hawaii on 14 February 1779 was a muddled affair, the culmination of a series of accidents and misjudgements, and there are conflicting versions of events in the various surviving journals. The only account from a participant in the actual fracas on the beach was by Molesworth Phillips, Lieutenant of Marines, whose written report has been lost, although Charles Clerke reproduced part of it in his journal. Lieutenant James King was responsible for the official narrative of the events leading up to Cook's death, as published by the Admiralty, but there is a suspicion that King may have shaped his version so as to remove any possible blame from Cook himself. Anne Salmond also suggests the possibility that Clerke destroyed the missing last three weeks of Cook's journal, just as he is known to have destroyed Phillip's written complaint against Williamson.[1] The account which is given here follows Gavin Kennedy who has made a painstaking analysis of the various reports concerning Cook's final hours.[2]

In mid-January the *Resolution* and *Discovery* anchored in Kealakehua Bay, Hawaii, and for the next fortnight Cook and his men received generous hospitality from the islanders, a welcome which was probably due to the fact they imagined Cook to be an incarnation of one of their gods, Lono. On 4 February Cook took his ships out of the bay, intending to continue the search for a northwest passage, but a week later they were forced to return to their anchorage as the *Resolution's* foremast had been badly sprung in a gale. This time their reception was not nearly so friendly, an outcome subsequently explained by the timing of this second appearance which conflicted with established myths concerning Lono and his place in the Hawaiians' religious calendar. Incidents involving pilfering and the harassment of working parties on shore included a humiliating episode on the 13 February when a party from the *Discovery* led by the Master, Thomas Edgar, was attacked on the beach while trying to recover items stolen from the ship. Even worse, that same night the

Discovery's large cutter was stolen from its mooring. When this was made known to Cook early the following morning he reacted by devising a plan to seize canoes in the bay and hold them against the return of the cutter. He therefore ordered boats from both the *Resolution* and the *Discovery* to take up positions in a line across the entrance of the bay with orders to fire on any canoes attempting to escape. While the boats were taking up their positions a large canoe under sail was spotted making for the open sea and Cook ordered his master, William Bligh, in the *Resolution's* cutter, to pursue it. Bligh's men fired on the canoe and forced it back to land, and at about the same time the larger guns from the ships were fired at two other canoes.

It was only after these events that Cook must have decided on a change of plan. It had become clear that the noise of the guns would have alerted all those in the vicinity of the bay, and that unless something were done quickly, the leading Hawaiians, and especially their king, the elderly Kalaniopuu, would flee, leaving no one in authority with whom to negotiate the return of the cutter. He therefore decided on a second plan, to persuade Kalaniopuu to board the *Resolution*, and there to hold him hostage until the cutter was returned. Speed was of the essence, so immediately, without having time to inform Clerke on the *Discovery*, or some of the other officers strung out across the bay maintaining the blockade, Cook took ashore a small party of nine marines in order to find the King in his house in the village of Kowrowa near the southern point of the bay. To support them he had a pinnace with armed sailors under the command of a master's mate, Henry Roberts, and as he proceeded towards the land he was also able to call across to Lieutenant Williamson in the *Resolution's* launch to quit the blockade and join him.

At about 7.30 am Cook landed at Kowrowa with his marines, and marched round the village looking for the King's house which they eventually found, but only after a crowd had assembled, no doubt wondering what this show of force betokened. Cook sent Phillips into the house to bring out Kalaniopuu who surprisingly was still asleep and seemed somewhat bemused, but agreed to go with them to the beach. Accompanied by the crowd, now numbering two or three thousand, they reached some rocks on the shoreline, off which the boats were waiting for further orders. At this juncture two crucial events occurred which would jeopardize Cook's hostage-taking scheme, though their sequence and exact timing is uncertain. One of Kalaniopuu's wives accompanied by two other chiefs appeared and started warning him not to go on board, arguing that Cook intended to have him killed. Secondly, news reached the beach that one of the boats stationed at the entrance to the bay had fired on a canoe and killed an important chief. The crowd now became noisier and more emotional, and some brandished spears and wooden knives. Meanwhile the old

King sat dejectedly on a rock being harangued by Cook on one side and his wife and companions on the other. Phillips, the marine lieutenant, advised an immediate withdrawal to the boats, but was overruled, so instead he asked, and was granted, permission to draw up the marines, who were surrounded by jostling Hawaiians and had no room to present their muskets, in a line close to the water's edge.

An incident then took place which precipitated the final assault. The accounts differ but it seems likely that someone threw either a stone or a breadfruit that struck Cook in the face, and he reacted vigorously to the insult. He may have lashed out with the butt of his musket, or he may have first fired small shot at his assailant, his musket being loaded with shot in one barrel and the more lethal ball in the other. In either event he then fired with ball and killed a Hawaiian, although it is uncertain whether it was the stone-thrower or the man standing next to him. This enraged the crowd and there was a shower of stones while many rushed forward with raised weapons. The marines opened fire with a single volley but before they could reload their line was overwhelmed and they then showed their indiscipline and lack of training by throwing down their muskets and turning tail. Those who could swim made for the nearby pinnace and those who could not remained to be stabbed or beaten to death by the mob. Phillips was next to Cook but could not see what happened to him as he was himself knocked down by a stone and stabbed before managing to scramble to the boat. However Samwell, although not an eyewitness, pieced together a dramatic account of Cook's last moments:

Captain Cook was now the only man on the Rock, he was seen walking down towards the Pinnace, holding his left hand against the back of his head to guard it from the Stones & carrying his Musket under the other Arm. An Indian came running behind him, stopping once or twice as he advanced, as if he was afraid that he should turn round, then taking him unaware he sprung to him, knocked him on the back of his head with a large Club taken out of a fence, & instantly fled with the greatest precipitation; the blow made Captain Cook stagger two or three paces, he then fell on his hand & one knee & dropped his Musket, as he was rising another Indian came running to him & before he could recover himself from the Fall drew out an iron Dagger he concealed under his feathered Cloak & stuck it with all his force into the back of his Neck, which made Capt. Cook tumble into the water in a kind of a bite by the side of the rock where the water is about knee deep; here he was followed by a croud of people who endeavoured to keep him under water, but struggling very strong with them he got his head up

& looking towards the Pinnace which was not above a boat hook's Length from him waved his hands to them for Assistance, which it seems it was not in their power to give. The Indians got him under water again but he disengaged himself & got his head up once more & not being able to swim he endeavoured to scramble on the Rock, when a fellow gave him a blow on the head with a large Club and he was seen alive no more.[3]

How far was Cook responsible for his own death, and what do these traumatic events tell us of his state of mind and powers of judgement at the time? One can perhaps dismiss the charge subsequently made against him by evangelical critics that by agreeing to play the role of a Hawaiian god he committed the sin of hubris, and therefore that his death was divine retribution for such blasphemy. There has recently sprung up a furious academic argument over whether in fact it was true that Cook was seen by the Hawaiians as an incarnation of their god Lono, and this debate has widened into a broader one about the politics of cultural interpretation. How far is it possible to describe cultures very different from one's own without inevitably imposing one's own assumptions and agendas on the other? According to the Sri Lankan anthropologist, Gananath Obeyesekere, the Hawaiians were not so stupid, not so devoid of the universal faculty of 'practical rationality', as to fail to distinguish between their god and an English sea captain. To allege that they identified Cook with Lono is to impose a typically demeaning and patronising imperialist myth. However, another celebrated anthropologist, Marshall Sahlins, argues that Western assumptions about rationality do not necessarily apply world-wide. To say that the Hawaiians would have had too much common sense than to deify Cook is entirely to misunderstand their native culture and the concept of divinity that pervaded it. Hence, according to Sahlins, it is Obeyesekere who is guilty of patronising the Hawaiians, and of observing the world through blinkered Western eyes.[4]

This debate, fascinating as it is no doubt, is not entirely relevant to a consideration of Cook himself who may or may not have suspected that the Hawaiians were according him unusual veneration – unfortunately his extant journal ceases on his arrival in Hawaii so we cannot be sure. In any case, he can hardly be blamed for taking advantage of this favourable treatment, and he could not have been expected to begin to grasp the intricacies of the Hawaiian pantheon on first contact. Nor was he to blame for the damage caused to the *Resolution's* foremast during the night of 7 February, and the consequent decision to return to Kealakekua on a date which Hawaiians perceived as outside the period of Lono's influence. Nevertheless, it does seem that he might be charged with certain errors of judgement during the fatal morning of 14 February. For example:

1. Two different, and incompatible, plans. The blockade of the bay took up considerable resources in the shape of boatloads of armed sailors and would inevitably involve gunfire which would forego any element of surprise. The second plan, to take Kalaniopuu hostage, required either a peaceful invitation without the threat of arms, or to be accompanied by overwhelming force, if once the Hawaiians had been alerted by the noise of gunfire.
2. Inadequate preparations for hostage-taking. Cook took with him only nine marines, which was less than a third of the 31 available on the two ships, and furthermore he did not give himself time to alert his colleagues about his new plan, which meant that when the crucial moment came most of his officers were scattered across the bay and unable to help.
3. Failure to quit the beach in time. It may have been Cook's reluctance to lose face by abandoning his plan to seize the King which led to him ignoring Phillip's advice to board the pinnace while this was still possible.
4. The shooting dead of a stone-thrower. This action, while understandable in the circumstances, led directly to the final assault. It seems that Cook firmly believed what he is reported to have said about the Hawaiians on a previous occasion: 'I am sure they will not stand the fire of a musket'.[5]

With hindsight, these actions taken by Cook on the morning of 14 February might all be classed as fatal errors, but in fact they were not so different from similar decisions he had taken in the past. On several occasions, at Tahiti, Raiatea and Tongatapu, he had successfully taken a chief hostage, and he had also fired into a hostile crowd with intent to kill, as at Erromanga in August 1774. He may well, as Beaglehole says, have been psychologically exhausted after the strains of the voyage, but this is not to say that he suddenly snapped, or acted totally out of character.[6] It may be, as Nicholas Thomas suggests, that the crucial factor that distinguished the Hawaiian situation from other tight corners that Cook had been in was the god-like status they accorded their kings.[7] Without knowing it, Cook, as Lono, was pitting himself against another Hawaiian god, Ku, with whom Kalaniopuu was identified in the eyes of his people. In other words he died not so much from his own misjudgements as because 'he had gotten tangled up with a myth'.[8]

According to James King, just before Cook was cut down:

Some of the Indians had been observd coming behind the Marines, & going to strike them with their iron daggers, upon which some of the

men in the boats fyrd without orders. Be it as it may, the Captⁿ calld to
them to cease fyring & to come in with the boats, intending to embark
as fast as Possible, this humanity perhaps provd fatal to him.[9]

It seems unlikely that Cook would have called for a ceasefire in such a desperate
situation, though he might well have been urging the boats to come in.
Nevertheless, the statement was repeated by King in the officially published
narrative of the voyage, and it was taken up by John Webber in his famous
picture, *The Death of Captain Cook*, in which Cook is about to be stabbed by
a tall savage just behind him, yet is holding up his right hand in a clear signal
to the boat crews to cease firing. Webber's composition, with its accompanying caption which included the phrase, 'a victim to his own humanity', was
reproduced in dozens of later editions of Cook's story, and also sold widely
as a separate print. Through such means the public learnt of the myth of the
martyred humanist who preferred to give up his own life rather than take
the lives of some unruly islanders. This was a version of Cook's death which
conveniently ignored the attempt to take hostage the sacred person of the king
which had provoked the riot, and also ignored the uncounted, but probably
numerous, Hawaiians killed during the fight on the beach, to say nothing of
those killed in revenge over the next few days.[10]

In a typically British fashion this humanist myth could readily be combined
with nationalism in popular productions such as the pantomime *Omai, or, a
Trip round the World*, staged at Covent Garden in 1785 and 1788, which ended
by the descent onto the stage of a huge painted backdrop by de Loutherbourg,
in which Cook was shown ascending to heaven, crowned by Britannia and
Fame.[11] In paintings, poetry and theatrical presentations Cook was eulogised
as tragic hero and as the humane personification of the Enlightenment. Such
representations, combined with the frequent comparisons of his selfless
behaviour with that of more rapacious earlier explorers, helped bolster a
favourable self-image for the British, especially regarding their overseas role.
Cook's sterling qualities seemed to secure, at the very moment of first contact,
the innocence of appropriating other peoples' lands, and the worth of the
entire imperialist project. The official narrative of Cook's life culminating in his
martyrdom served as an early example of something with which today we are
all too familiar, the exercise of power and violence against weaker nations in the
name, and employing the vocabulary, of peace and liberal values.

Cook's apotheosis suited the times. It was taken up by the anti-slavery
movement, then just underway, but it appealed also across the political spec-
trum. For instance, two of the earliest poems celebrating Cook's achievements
were written by the Tory, Anna Seward, and by Helen Maria Williams, soon to

be a fervent supporter of the French Revolution. The narrative of his life and death appealed to a Britain dominant in world markets and with an undiminished appetite for expansion, and yet somewhat ambivalent about the issue of colonialism during and after the fiasco of the American war. The lavishly produced three-volume edition of the third voyage, heavily subsidised by the government, was priced at four and a half guineas, but still sold out within three days.

Conclusion

Since Cook's death there have been many Cooks. Over the years his story has been exploited by various special interests with their own axes to grind, among them missionaries, nationalists and imperialists, so that, as Rod Edmond puts it, his name has become a floating signifier.[1] Some of these 'Cooks' have been referred to in earlier chapters, for example, the Cook who died because he had blasphemed, and the Cook who founded Australia.[2] Another Cook altogether figures in the social memory of Australian Aborigines, to whom the phrase, 'Captain Cook' refers to far more than events in the lifetime of one individual explorer, as in this extract from an oral account by Hobbes Danaiyairi of the Northern Territory:

> Captain Cook getting ready for the country, going to try to take it away . . . Three weeks' time and pack up his gear and put it in the sailing boat and keep going right round, follow the sea. Every pocket him go in and have a look around on another people. Same thing. Shooting right round . . . When him got to Darwin, that's the biggest place . . . And Captain Cook come up, see that old fellow sit down makembad [make] spear there, hunting fish . . . 'By Christ, that's good land here. Your country, it's a big one? Many people round here?' 'Oh, lotta people round here. We big mob here', he said . . . 'This we country. We never look whitefellow come through here . . . We can be ready for you. Got a big mob spear. We don't want whitefellow . . . 'Get ready for this, old fellow. We might start here'. [He] start to put the bullet in the magazine, start to shoot people, same like Sydney . . . 'Really beautiful country', Captain Cook reckoned. 'That's why I'm cleaning up the people, take it away'.[3]

Cook never went anywhere near Darwin, but clearly his name functions here as a metaphor for the general shape of colonial relations between settlers and natives over centuries.

Today there are several, overlapping Cooks. There is the post-Beaglehole Cook of academic scholarship, and also the Cook of enthusiasts worldwide, as represented by the popular Captain Cook Society. In addition, Cook has been adopted by the world's most successful and fastest growing industry – tourism. The modern cultural tourist has been defined, somewhat unkindly, as someone engaged in a constant but fruitless search for authentic experience. Museum curators and others who service the industry do their best to provide such experiences which, in the case of Cook, might include, for instance, a display of ethnic dancing by Pacific islanders, or a glimpse of a tea set once the property of Cook's widow. History has been simplified and sanitised for popular consumption, and tourist settings throughout the world attempt to exhibit, or mimic, slices of historical 'reality'. Such cultural mirages operate in much the same way as did once those medieval cathedrals which lured the faithful with a display of holy relics. One consequence is that the price of so-called historical artefacts has gone through the roof. In 2003 a walking stick supposed to have been made from the wood of the spear that killed Cook went for £135,000 at auction.

To go back to the beginning, the first 'Cook' of all was of course the one he himself crafted in his journals. Those who write about themselves inevitably process and present their own experiences, recording them in that form for others to read, including future historians. Meaning does not inhere automatically in events but it may be put there by participants, as well as by retrospective interpreters. Cook himself, together with his editors and biographers up to the present day, is complicit in this process. But who, then, was the real Cook? This is a valid question which, however, cannot be answered since Cook is no longer with us, and all we have to go on is a series of primary and secondary texts purporting to represent 'Cook'. All we can do is to examine these representations as closely as we can, given our own limitations, assumptions and prejudices. To quote the Canadian historian and Cook scholar, Daniel Clayton:

> However assiduous our scholarship on Cook might be, we cannot avoid the issue that Cook the man, the actor, and the messenger is, in good measure, a construction. He has been constructed in various ways from the 1770s to the present. There is no original or definitive Cook. From Douglas and Beaglehole, to Howay and Sage, to Fisher, and, most recently, to Obeyesekere and Sahlins, the explorer has been used to

ignite issues of historical development, colonial and postcolonial identity, and the appreciation of cultural difference.[4]

Nevertheless, it would be inappropriate to end a book entitled *In Search of Captain Cook* without some effort to summarize one's findings, and here I should like to refer to the fascinating thesis proposed by John Tosh and Michèle Cohen concerning public images of masculinity in the eighteenth century.[5] Apparently there may have taken place a shift in cultural values in England during the second half of the century towards a new definition of successful manliness, and if so, Cook's public persona seems to exemplify this shift rather neatly. One aspect of the change was the novel idea that one's occupation might form a crucial part of one's perceived identity. Hitherto, according to Tosh and Cohen, most work had been regarded as a necessary burden, including, as it often did, a servile dependence on patronage. Now, partly under the influence of the new evangelical morality, and partly owing to changes in the structure of the economy, work – for the 'middling' sort at least – was starting to take on its modern definition as an occupation, even a 'calling'.[6] In Cook we see a man who by all accounts defined himself by his professional role, a man whose personal life appears attenuated and subsumed under concepts of duty and ambition, for the successful pursuit of which he possessed every necessary qualification. Cook may still have needed patronage to get where he did, but there is no doubt that he lived for his work, which was certainly for him a vocation and not a burden. From causes perhaps connected with his own origins he had attitudes to life and work which were new to the sea service at the time and which went a long way to make his achievements possible.

Cook also exemplified a second aspect of the new masculinity, again perhaps influenced by the religiosity which was starting to permeate society – a certain repression of the self. It was now held that a man who would have authority over others must first master himself, his appetites and passions, and a charge of effeminacy might be laid against those who relaxed all restraint or surrendered to their every desire.[7] Cook's readiness to adapt his diet to whatever was available, his abstemiousness in regard to alcohol, his extreme reticence regarding his own illnesses, and above all his sexual self-control are all apposite here. Although he had discovered in Tahiti an Arcadia as alluring as Circe's enchanted island was to Ulysses' companions, he alone of all his company, we are told, resisted her seductions, thus justifying his position as commander-in-chief.

A third aspect of these changes in public attitudes and expectations towards successful men concerned social language and demeanour. As mentioned earlier, Cook's language and personality were described approvingly by many commentators as 'manly'.[8] James King, who 'loved and honoured Captain Cook, and never spoke of him but with respect', nevertheless admitted to Edmund Burke that he 'lamented the Roughness of his manners and the violence of his Temper'.[9] Yet after he had become relatively famous Cook was enthusiastically received by polite society, including Boswell, Johnson and the Burney household. Very likely this would not have been the case earlier in the century. Previously, social graces and especially the art of conversation had been seen as essential for a gentleman, whatever his achievements in more distant fields. Now, these attributes were no longer thought 'manly', and instead they were often associated negatively with over-indulgence in female company, and perhaps also with undesirable French influence. Successive wars against France had helped to instill a sense of British patriotism of which the flip side was a rejection of French cultural hegemony – of everything considered as frivolous, effeminate and French. A true Englishman was now almost expected to be taciturn and even brusque in company, and such qualities not seen as blemishes but rather as indications of self-discipline and strength.[10] Again here, Cook fits the bill.

Was Cook a hero? Possibly not, if it is true that 'As befits our age, there are no more heroes.'[11] In this book I have attempted to present my 'Cook', a man inevitably of certain limitations, but clearly also of enormous and varied talents, who succeeded, both in his own eyes and in those of his contemporaries, in everything he set out to accomplish, and more. The reader may well feel that justice has hardly been done to some of these accomplishments. Perhaps not enough has been said, for instance, of the numerous islands throughout the Pacific which Cook was the first European to visit, of his expert charting of unknown waters and coastlines, or his navigational and astronomical skills. All this is true; in defence I can only say that I was concerned here not so much with Cook's achievements, which have been repeatedly chronicled and celebrated over the years, as with an attempt, however inadequate, to discuss him as a man. Such an attempt was always bound to end in partial failure owing to the nature of the sources, yet I feel it was worth doing, if only to release poor Captain Cook from the sterile pantheon of British heroes and place him where he belongs, among fallible humanity like the rest of us.

Abbreviations used in References

Banks   J. C. Beaglehole (ed.), *The* Endeavour *Journal of Joseph Banks 1768–1771*, 2 vols. (Sydney, 1962)

Beaglehole   J. C. Beaglehole, *The Life of Captain James Cook* (Stanford, California, 1974)

Douglas   John Douglas (ed.), *A Voyage to the Pacific Ocean. Undertaken by the Command of his Majesty, for Making Discoveries in the Northern Hemisphere*, 3 vols. (London, 1784)

G. Forster   George Forster, *A Voyage round the World in his Britannic Majesty's Sloop Resolution*, 2 vols. (London, 1777)

J. R. Forster Michael E. Hoare (ed.), *The Resolution Journal of Johann Reinhold Forster, 1772–1775*, 4 vols. (London, Hakluyt Society, 1982)

Hawkesworth   John Hawkesworth, *An Account of the Voyages Undertaken by the Order of His Present Majesty for Making Discoveries in the Southern Hemisphere*, 3 vols. (London, 1773).

Journals I   J. C. Beaglehole (ed.), *The Journals of Captain James Cook: The Voyage of the Endeavour, 1768–1771* (Cambridge, 1955, reprinted 1968)

Journals II   J. C. Beaglehole (ed.), *The Journals of Captain James Cook: The Voyage of the Resolution and Adventure, 1772–1775* (Cambridge, 1961, reprinted 1969)

Journals III   J. C. Beaglehole (ed.), *The Journals of Captain James Cook: The Voyage of the Resolution and Discovery, 1776–1780*, 2 vols. (Cambridge, 1967)

Kippis   Andrew Kippis, *The Life of Captain James Cook* (London, 1788)

References

Introduction

1 Besant, Walter, *Captain Cook* (London, 1894), p.89: Besant, however, was probably using the versions of Cook's second and third journals as 'improved' by his editor, John Douglas.
2 Beaglehole, J.C., 'On the Character of Captain James Cook', in *The Geographical Journal*, vol. cxxii, part 4 (Dec 1956), p.418.
3 Innes, Hammond, *The Last Voyage; Captain Cook's Lost Diary* (London, 1996), p.vii.
4 Beaglehole, p.417.

1 Cook the Unknown

1 *Forster J. R.* I, p.72.
2 Samwell, David, surgeon's mate on the *Resolution*, quoted in *Kippis*, pp.488–9.
3 Cordingly, David, 'The Discovery of a Lost Portrait of Captain Cook', in Cordingly, David (ed.), *Capt. James Cook: Navigator* (Greenwich, 1988).
4 Beaglehole, J.C., 'On the Character of Captain James Cook', in *The Geographical Journal* (Dec 1956), p.418.
5 *Journals* II, p.425; Horwitz, Tony, *Into the Blue* (London, 2002), p.89.
6 Williams, Glyndwr, 'The *Endeavour* Voyage: A Coincidence of Motives', in Lincoln, Margarette, (ed.), *Science and Exploration in the Pacific* (London, 1998), p.17.
7 Williams, p.31.
8 *Journals* I, p.85, fn.3.
9 unless one counts George Jackson, assistant secretary to the Lords of the Admiralty, who had links with Great Ayton, and after whom Port Jackson, the future site of Sydney, was named.
10 quoted in *Kippis*, p.490. The memorial is at Chalfont St. Giles.
11 Hoare, M.E., 'Cook the discoverer: an essay by George Forster, 1787', in *Records of the Australian Academy of Science*, vol. I, no.4 (Nov 1969); *J.R. Forster, passim*.
12 Penrose, C.V., *A Memoir of James Trevenen*, Navy Records Society Publications vol. 101 (1959), quoted in *Journals* III, cliii; Sparrman, Anders, *A Voyage Round the World*, (London, 1953), p.51.
13 *Journals* II, p.643.
14 admittedly he had been ill for some time.

15 Beaglehole, p.423.

16 Cook to Latouche-Tréville, 6 Sept 1775, quoted in *Journals* II, p.695.

17 Kippis, p.483; *Journals* III, p.427.

18 Forster, J.R., III, p.444.

19 Forster, G., I, Preface.

20 *Journals* II, p.960.

21 *Journals* I, p.380.

22 *Journals* II, p.322.

23 Thomas, Nicholas *Discoveries: The Voyages of Captain Cook*, (London, 2003), pp.218–9.

24 *Journals* II, p.124 fn 3.

25 *Journals* III, pp.410–11.

26 *Journals* III, p.xxxi. For the dinner party, see also p. 215.

27 Watt, Sir James, 'The Effect of Health on Cook and his Crew', in Cordingly, David, (ed.), *Captain James Cook, Navigator* (London, 1988), p.104; for Cook's illness, see Chapter 9.

28 Obeyesekere, Ganath, *The Apotheosis of Captain Cook: European Mythmaking in the Pacific* (Princeton, New Jersey, 1992), pp.133 & 28; Salmond, Anne, *The Trial of the Cannibal Dog: Captain Cook in the South Seas* (London, 2003), especially pp.319 & 431; Smith, Bernard, *Imagining the Pacific: In the Wake of the Cook Voyages* (Melbourne, 1992), p.207.

29 Quoted in Obeyesekere, p.15.

30 Thomas, pp.332, 396, 442.

2 Entertaining the Reader

1 Thomas, Nicholas, *Discoveries: The Voyages of Captain Cook* (London, 2003), p.8.

2 *Journals* II, p.2.

3 *A Voyage towards the South Pole, and Round the World, Performed in His Majesty's Ships the Resolution and Adventure, In the Years 1772, 1773, 1774, and 1775 . . .*, 2 vols (London, 1777), p.xxxvi.

4 *The Critical Review: or, Annals of Literature*, 43 (1777), pp.371–2.

5 *The Gentleman's Magazine*, xlvii (1777), p.491.

6 Lewis, W. S., (ed), *The Yale edition of Horace Walpole's correspondence* (Yale, 1965), vol. 33, p.436, quoted, with other references to Walpole's opinion about Hawkesworth, in Abbott, J. L., *John Hawkesworth Eighteenth century Man of Letters* (London, 1982), p.223.

7 *The Idler*, no.97 (23 Feb 1760).

8 Ryskamp, Charles, and Pottle, Frederick A., (eds), *Boswell: The Ominous Years 1774–76*, (London, 1963), pp.308 & 310.

9 Boswell, James, *Life of Johnson* (London, 1851), vol.8, p.312.

10 Lobo, Jeronimo, and Johnson, Samuel, *A Voyage to Abyssinia* (1st edn 1735), (New York, 1978), p.14.

11 *Monthly Review*, 34 (Jan–June 1766), p.127.

12 *The London Magazine* (June 1777), p.324.

13 *Monthly Review*, New Series, 21 (1796), p.1.

14 quoted in Percy, C.E., 'The Language of Captain Cook', unpub. Oxford PhD thesis (1990), p.144.

15 Swift, Jonathan, *Gulliver's Travels* (1994 edn), pp.6–7, 84.

16 *Forster, G.*, vol.I, p.ix.; a 'palinurus' was a steersman, from the name of Odysseus's steersman.

17 *The London Magazine, loc.cit.*

18 *Hawkesworth* II, pp.vi–vii.

19 Walter, Richard, and Robins, Benjamin, *Voyage Round the World* (2nd edn London, 1748).

20 For the story of Anson's voyage see Williams, Glyndwr, *The Prize of All the Oceans* (London, 1999).

21 Porter, Roy, *Enlightenment; Britain and the Creation of the Modern World* (London, 2000), pp.130–156.

22 Sprat, Thomas, *The History of the Royal Society of London for the Improving of Natural Knowledge* (London, 1734), p.113.

23 von Kotzebue, Otto, *Voyage of Discovery into the South Seas* (London, 1821), quoted in Stafford, Barbara, *Voyage into Substance: Art, Science, Nature, and the Illustrated Travel Account 1760–1840*, (London, 1984), p.50.

24 Lamb, Jonathan, 'Minute Particulars and the Representation of South Pacific Discovery', *Eighteenth-Century Studies* 28 (1995), p.287.

25 Young, Rev. George, *The Life and Voyages of Captain James Cook*, 2 vols. (London, 1836), II, p.861.

26 *Kippis*, pp.482–3; I owe this reference to Harriet Guest.

27 *The Critical Review* (July 1784), p.96.

28 *Journals*, III, p.lxxviii.

29 Cohen, Michèle, 'Manliness, effeminacy and the French: gender and the construction of national character in eighteenth-century England', in Hitchcock, Tim, and Cohen, Michèle, (eds), *English Masculinities 1660–1800* (London, 1999), pp.44–62.

30 Jardine, Captain Alexander, *Letters from Barbary, France, Portugal, etc.*, 2 vols (London, 1788), I, pp.268, 360, quoted by Michèle Cohen, p.56.

31 *Edinburgh Review*, II (1802), pp.33–4.

3 Bookmakers

1 for Hawkesworth see Abbott, J. L., *John Hawkesworth: Eighteenth Century Man of Letters* (Wisconsin, 1982); & Pearson, W. H., 'Hawkesworth's Alterations', in *Journal of Pacific Studies* VII (1972), pp.45–72.

2 quoted in Abbott, p.143.

3 *Hawkesworth* I, 'General Introduction'.

4 *Hawkesworth* I, p.vi; *Journals* II, p.661.

5 Abbott, p.173.

6 *Hawkesworth* II, pp.116–17.

7 Pearson, p.64.

8 John was the second son of the Thomas Skottowe who had employed Cook's father.

9 *Journals* II, 661–62 & fn; Sparrman, Anders, *A Voyage Round the World*, (London, 1944), p.202.

10 Lamb, Jonathan, 'Minute Particulars and the Representation of South Pacific Discovery' in *Eighteenth-Century Studies*, vol.28, no.3 (1995), p.292.

11 Lamb, p.283.

12 for more about the attacks on Hawkesworth, see Chapters 13 and 14.

13 quoted in Abbott, p.154.

14 Boswell, James, *Life of Johnson* (1912 edn.), vol. 6, pp.102–3.

15 Burney, Frances, *Journals and Letters*, (Penguin edn., 2001), p.24.
16 quoted in Wallis, Helen, 'Publication of Cook's Journals: some new sources and assessments' in *Pacific Studies* I, no. 2 (Spring 1978), p.172.
17 *Journals* I, p.652.
18 see Chapter 13.
19 Percy, Carol, 'Eighteenth-Century Normative Grammar in Practice; The Case of Captain Cook', in Britton, Derek, (ed.), *English Historical Linguistics* (Amsterdam/ Philadelphia, 1994), p.358.
20 for Douglas see the *Oxford Dictionary of National Biography*, and his obituary in *The Gentleman's Magazine* (6 May 1807).
21 Boswell, vol.2, p.214.
22 Douglas's autobiographical notes : BL Egerton MS 2181, ff.48–49.
23 BL Egerton MS 2180 f.234, quoted in Wallis, p.173.
24 Cook to Commodore Wilson (22 June 1776): *Journals* II, p.cxliii.
25 *Journals* II, p.175; Thomas, Nicholas, *Discoveries: The Voyages of Captain Cook*, (London, 2003), p.xxviii.
26 *Journals* III, pp.cci–ccii.
27 *Journals* III, p.7 & fn.
28 *Douglas* II, p.97.
29 *Journals* III, p.300; Douglas II, p.276.
30 *Journals* III, p.308; Douglas II, pp.286–87.
31 *Morning Chronicle* (18 Jan 1783), quoted in Wallis, p.187.

4 Journals as History

1 *Journals* I, p.v.
2 *Journals* I, pp.cxciv–ccxviii.
3 see Gott, Ron, *Henry Bolckow, Founder of Teesside* (Middlesbrough, 1968).
4 BL Add MSS 27886 & 27888; *Journals* II, pp.cxv–cxxiii.
5 BL Egerton MS 2177 A; *Journals* III, pp.clxxi–clxxvi. On the missing month, see also Chapter 18.
6 see, for example, Thomas, Nicholas, *Discoveries: The Voyages of Captain Cook*, (London, 2003), p.xxxvi.
7 *Journals* I, p.ccii; *Beaglehole*, p.251.
8 *Beaglehole*, p.108.
9 for Forster see Chapter 8. For the rehabilitation see Andrew Cook's introduction to the reissue of Dalrymple's *An Account of the Discoveries made in the South Pacific Ocean* (Sydney, 1996); also, Hoare, Michael E., *The Tactless Philosopher: Johann Reinhold Forster [1729–98]* (Wellington NZ, 1979).
10 *Journals* I, p.cclviii.
11 this point is made by Obeyesekere, Gananath, *The Apotheosis of Captain Cook* (Princeton, 1992), p.261. The journals were subsequently printed in full in: Holmes Christine, (ed.), *Captain Cook's Final Voyage: The Journal of Midshipman George Gilbert*, (Horsham, Sussex, 1982) & Zug, James, (ed.), *The Last Voyage of Captain Cook; The Collected Writings of John Ledyard* (Washington, 2005).
12 *Journals* II, pp.cxxxv, cxxxix.
13 Nat. Archives: Adm 52/1263 p.113.
14 *Journals* II, p.906.
15 Beaglehole, pp.283–4.

16 Latham, Robert, (ed.), *The Shorter Pepys*, (London, 1985), p.xxxiv.

17 *Journals* I, p.ccxxviii.

18 *Journals* II, p.651, fn.3.

19 *Journals* I, pp.cciv–ccx.

20 *Journals* I, pp.169–70.

21 Beaglehole J.C., (ed.), *The Endeavour Journal of Joseph Banks*, (London, 1963), quoted in *Journals* I, p.170, fn.1.

22 *Journals* I, p.323; for Magra (who later changed his name to Matra) see Frost, Alan, *The Precarious Life of James Maria Matra: Voyager with Cook, American Loyalist, Servant of Empire* (Melbourne, 1995).

23 *Journals* I, pp.440–41.

24 Salmond, Anne, *The Trial of the Cannibal Dog*, (London, 2003), pp.433–42.

5 Journals as Narrative

1 *Journals* II, pp.313–14.

2 *Journals* II, p.309.

3 *Journals* II, pp.289–90; I borrow this example of hindsight from Edwards, Philip, *The Journals of Captain Cook*, (Penguin edn, 1999), p.xii.

4 *Journals* II, p.cxli.

5 *Journals* II, p.293.

6 *Journals* II, p.819.

7 unless that task belonged to Richard Pickersgill, master's mate.

8 Lysaght, A.M., (ed.), *The Journal of Joseph Banks in the Endeavour*, facsimile edn. (London, 1980), p.17.

9 Edwards, Philip, *The Story of the Voyage: Sea Narratives in Eighteenth-Century England* (Cambridge, 1994) p.92.

10 Foulke, Robert, *The Sea Voyage Narrative* (London, 1997); part of this passage is quoted above, p.22.

11 *Journals* I, p.127.

12 *Journals* III, p.978.

13 *Journals* I, p.78.

14 *Journals* III, p.219.

15 *Journals* II, p.403; *Hawkesworth* III, p.650; Percy, Carol, *Cook's Log*, vol. 18, no. 4 (1995).

16 *Journals* II, pp.225–6.

17 It should be pointed out, however, that some of these variations, such as musquet and ax, were quite common at this time.

18 Percy, Carol, 'Eighteenth-Century Normative Grammar in Practice: The Case of Captain Cook', in Britton, Derek, (ed.), *English Historical Linguistics* (Amsterdam/ Philadelphia, 1994), pp.339–362.

19 *Journals* II, pp.clxv–clxvii.

20 *Journals* I, p.286.

21 *Journals* III, pp.322–23.

22 Thomas, Nicholas, *Discoveries: The Voyages of Captain Cook* (London, 2003), p.203.

6 The Ships' Companies: Officers

1 Carter, Harold, *Sir Joseph Banks 1743–1820* (London, 1988), p.86.
2 *Journals* I, p.437.
3 *The Gentleman's Magazine*, Jan–June 1807, p.424.
4 *Journals* I, p.cxxx.
5 *A Journal of a Voyage round the World*, (London, 1771) p.101; Beaglehole presents the evidence that Magra was the author: *Journals* I, pp.cclvi–cclxiv.
6 *Journals* I, pp.272–3.
7 *Forster G.* I, p.540.
8 *Journals* II, p.315, fn.3.
9 for more on Wedgeborough see the next chapter.
10 *Journals* III, pp.352–3.
11 *Journals* II, p.651.
12 Lambert, Andrew, 'Retracing the Captain', in Williams, Glyndwr, (ed.), *Captain Cook: Explorations and Reassessments* (London, 2004), p.250.
13 *Journals* II, p.328.
14 he was in command of a launch stationed off the beach, and was accused by some of not doing sufficient to save his colleagues.
15 *Journals* III, pp.1342–3.
16 *Journals* III, pp.lxxix–lxxxi (Beaglehole), pp.136–7 & 267 (Cook), pp.1347–9 (Williamson).
17 *Journals* II, p.xxxvii.
18 *ibid.*
19 *Journals* I, p.cxxii.
20 *Journals* III, p.lxxxvii.
21 *Journals* I, p.323. For Magra see p. 59.
22 Holmes, Christine, (ed.), *Captain Cook's Second Voyage: The Journals of Lieutenants Elliott and Pickersgill* (London, 1984), p.43.
23 Williams, Glyndwr, '"As befits our age, there are no more heroes" reassessing Captain Cook', in Williams (ed.), *Explorations and Reassessments*, p.234.
24 *Journals* III, p.303 fn.2.
25 *Journals* III, p.551, fn.1.

7 The Ships' Companies: Men

1 quoted in Thomas, Nicholas, *Discoveries: The Voyages of Captain Cook*, (London, 2003), p.15.
2 Dening, Greg, *Islands and Beaches*, (Hawaii, 1980), p.159.
3 *Journals* I, p.346.
4 Hegarty, Neil, 'Unruly Subjects', in Lincoln, Margarette, (ed.), *Science and Exploration in the Pacific*, (London, 1998), pp.183–5.
5 *Forster, G.*, p.536.
6 *Journals* III, p.260.
7 which was doubtful; (see Chapter 9.)
8 *Journals* I, p.74.
9 *Journals* II, p.187.
10 *Journals* I, p.366.
11 *Journals* I, p.445.

12 *Journals* III, p.479.

13 *ibid*, fn.4.

14 *Forster, G.*, p.535.

15 *Journals* II, p.66.

16 *Journals* I, p.159 (Readon) & p.448 (Ravenhill).

17 *Journals* I, p.217, fn.1.

18 *Journals* II, p.255.

19 Thomas, p.207.

20 Dening, Greg, *Mr Bligh's Bad Language* (London, 1992), p.63.

21 *Forster, G.*, p.31.

22 See pp.93 & 119.

23 *Journals* II, pp.403–4; see also Cook's strict attitude to desertion on the third voyage: *Journals* III, p.cxiii.

24 quoted in *Journals* II, p.574, fn.2. For an example of Cook's 'primitivism' see p. 140.

25 *Journals* II, pp.361; 476 fn.1; 499 fn.1; 595.

26 *Journals* II, p.499 fn.1.

27 Rodger, N. A. M., *The Command of the Ocean* (London, 2005), pp.452–3.

28 Salmond, Anne, *The Trial of the Cannibal Dog* (London, 2003), p.415.

29 Salmond, pp.172 & 466.

8 Men of Science

1 Conrad, Joseph, 'Geography and Some Explorers', in *Last Essays* (London, 1926), p.10, quoted by Baugh, Daniel A., 'Seapower and Science', in Howse, Derek, (ed.), *Background to Discovery: Pacific Exploration from Dampier to Cook* (London, 1990), p.3.

2 for more detail see Chapter 17.

3 Williams, Glyndwr, 'The *Endeavour* Voyage: A Coincidence of Motives', in Lincoln Margarette, (ed.), *Science and Exploration in the Pacific: European Voyages to the Southern Oceans in the Eighteenth Century* (1998), pp.7–9.

4 *Journals* III, p.lxxxiv.

5 Bitterli, Urs, *Cultures in Conflict* (London, 1989), p.162; public sponsorship of science through exploration started somewhat earlier in France: Baugh, p.37.

6 Marshall P. J., and Williams, Glyndwr, *The Great Map of Mankind: British Perceptions of the New World in the Age of Enlightenment* (London, 1982), p.259.

7 Withey, Lynne, *Voyages of Discovery: Captain Cook and the Exploration of the Pacific* (London, 1987), p.19.

8 Bitterli, p.162.

9 Cook, James, and King, James, *A Voyage to the Pacific Ocean . . . for Making Discoveries in the Northern* Hemisphere, 3 vols (London, 1784), Introduction (Douglas).

10 Hoare, M.E., 'Cook the Discoverer: an essay by Georg Forster, 1787', in *Records of the Australian Academy of Science*, vol. 1, no. 4 (Nov. 1969), pp.14–15.

11 quoted by Williams, Glyndwr, '"To make discoveries of countries hitherto unknown": the Admiralty and Pacific exploration in the eighteenth century', in *The Mariner's Mirror*, vol. 82, no. 1 (1996), p.22.

12 Agnew, V. H., 'Red Feathers, White Paper, Blueprint: Exchange and Informal Empire in George Forster's *Voyage Round the World*', unpublished PhD thesis (Cardiff, University of Wales, 1998), p.12.

13 Villiers, Alan, *Captain Cook, the Seamen's Seaman* (London, 1967), pp.82–3.

14 Ellis, John to Linnaeus, 19 Aug. 1768, quoted in *Beaglehole*, p.146; Beaglehole comments that the figure of £10,000 was certainly exaggerated.

15 *Banks*, p.76.

16 On the other hand might he have resented all the adulation Banks received on their return?

17 for Solander see Duyker, Edward, *Nature's Argonaut: Daniel Solander 1733–1782* (Melbourne, 1998), especially pp.275–6.

18 *Beaglehole*, p.295.

19 *Journals* II, p.688.

20 (Tewsley, U., trans), *Zimmermann's Account of the third voyage of Captain Cook, 1776–1780* (Wellington, NZ, 1926), p.48; *Beaglehole*, p.502; *Journals* II, p.xlvi.

21 This James Lind is not to be confused with the author of a treatise on scurvy, of the same name.

22 *Beaglehole*, p.302.

23 Hoare, Michael E., *The Tactless Philosopher: Johann Reinhold Forster (1729–98)*, (Melbourne, 1976).

24 *Forster, J. R.*, II, pp.550–1.

25 *Forster, J. R.*, II, p.365.

26 *Forster, J. R.*, II p.438.

27 Forster, J. R., *Observations Made during a Voyage round the World*, (Honolulu, 1996); first edn. 1778.

28 *Voyages II*, pp.333–4.

29 Spate, O. H. K., 'Seamen and Scientists: The Literature of the Pacific, 1697–1798', in MacLeod, Roy and Rehbock, Philip F., (ed), *Nature in its Greatest Extent. Western Science in the Pacific* (Honolulu, 1985), p.21.

30 see p.15.

31 *Journals* I, p.392.

32 *Journals* I, p.448.

33 *Journals* II, p.580.

34 Vancouver made the same decision on his great survey of 1791.

35 *Forster, J. R.*, II, pp.438–9.

9 Health Among Seamen

1 *Kippis*, pp.484–5.

2 *Journals* III, p.419 & fn.3.

3 *Journals* II, p.247.

4 *Journals* II, p.129.

5 *Forster J. R.*, I, p.181.

6 *Journals* II, p.333.

7 *Forster J. R.*, III, pp.547–48.

8 Thrower, W.R., 'Contributions to Medicine of Captain James Cook, F.R.S., R.N.' in *The Lancet*, ccxli, II (1951); Watt, Sir James, 'Medical Aspects and Consequences of Cook's Voyages', in Fisher Robin, and Johnston Hugh, (eds), *Captain James Cook and His Times* (London, 1979), pp.154–57.

9 [Marra, John,], *Journal of the Resolution's Voyage in 1772, 1773, 1774 and 1775* (London, 1775), pp.21–2.

10 *Journals* II, pp.954–5.

11 Rodger, N.A.M., *The Command of the Ocean* (London, 2005), p.308.

12 This might have been true of both Charles Green and Tupaia on the first voyage: see Lamb, Jonathan, 'Captain Cook and the Scourge of Scurvy', on www.bbc.co.uk/history/.

13 Cuppage, Francis E., *James Cook and the Conquest of Scurvy* (Westport, Connecticut, 1994), p.31; Rodger, p.308.

14 Bartholemew, Michael, 'James Lind and Scurvy: a Revaluation', in *Journal for Maritime Research* (Greenwich, Jan 2002).

15 Wallis Helen, (ed.), *Carteret's Voyage round the world, 1766–69*, Hakluyt Society series II, CXXV (1883), 2 vols., II, p. 378.

16 Yet some authors continue to accept Cook's evaluation. For example, Dava Sobel writes, 'By adding generous portions of the German staple [i.e. sauerkraut] to the diet of his English crew the great circumnavigator kicked scurvy overboard': *Longitude* (paperback edn, London, 1998), p.138.

17 *Journals* I, p.74.

18 Stubbs, Brett J., 'Captain Cook's beer: the antiscorbutic use of malt and beer in late 18th century voyages', in *Asia Pacific Journal of Clinical Nutrition* vol. 12 part 2 (2003), p.135.

19 Pringle, J. 'A Discourse upon Some Late Improvements of the Means for Preserving the Health of Mariners', in *Six Discourses* (London, 1783), quoted in Cuppage (1994), p.70.

20 *Banks* I, pp.250–1.

21 Trohler, U., 'James Lind and scurvy: 1747 to 1795', *The James Lind Library*, on www.jameslindlibrary.org

22 Listed in Cuppage Francis E., *et al*, 'James Cook's Eighteenth-Century Prevention of Scurvy by the Use of Indigenous Plants as Dietary Supplements', in *Terrae Incognitae*, no. 26 (1994), pp.40–43.

23 *Journals* III, p.1456.

24 *Journals*, III, p.lxxxix.

25 Stubbs, p.133.

26 *Journals* III, p.479; the beer which the crew refused in Hawaii was made from sugar cane, but may not have contained other vegetable matter: for this confrontation see also Chapter 7.

27 Lamb, p.4.

10 How to Study Natives

1 The term 'native' should be read throughout this and the following chapters as if in quotation marks. It stands in this context as shorthand for 'indigenous Pacific persons'.

2 *Journals* I, p.93.

3 *ibid.*

4 Salmond, Anne, *The Trial of the Cannibal Dog* (London, 2003), p.75.

5 Thomas, Nicholas, *Discoveries: The Voyages of Captain* Cook (London, 2003), p.68.

6 Bulwer, John, *Chirologia: or the Naturall Language of the Hand* (London, 1644), quoted in Paxman, David '"Distance Getting Close": Gesture, Language, and Space in the Pacific', in *Eighteenth-Century Life*, vol. 26 no. 3 (2002) p.86.

7 *Journals* II, p.485.

8 Salmond, p.270.

9 *Journals* II, p.484.

10 *Journals* II, p.484,fn.4.

11 *Journals* I, p.cclxxxiii & II, p.clxviii.

12 *Journals* III, p.1110.

13 *Journals* I, p.134.

14 *Journals* III, p.166.

15 quoted in *Journals* II, p.234 fn.5.

16 *Forster G.*, II, pp.456–7, quoted in *Journals* II, p.576, fn.5.

17 Pinker, Steven, *The Language Instinct* (London, 1994), p.153.

18 Salmond, p.269.

19 *Journals* II, pp.354–5; Salmond, p.215.

20 Thomas, p.225.

21 *Journals* III, pp.412–3.

22 *Journals* III, p.166.

23 *Journals* III, p.839.

24 *Journals* III, p.151, fn.1.

25 *Journals* III, p.460 & fn.1.

26 *Journals* III, p.131.

27 *Journals* III, p.110.

28 *Journals* I, p.145.

29 *Journals* II, p.600 fn.2. The tribe encountered on the first voyage were the Haush, and on the second, the Yaghans.

30 *Journals* II, pp.466–7 & fn.1.

31 *Journals* I, p.399.

32 *Journals* II, p.207.

33 *Journals* II, p.293 & fn.2; Thomas thinks that on this occasion the New Zealanders may have exaggerated their cannibalism to impress the Europeans: Thomas, p.211.

34 *Journals* II, p.294.

35 Locke, John, *Second Treatise of Government* (London, 1776), chap. v, section 49.

36 The contemporary 'four stages theory' (hunting, pasturage, agriculture, and commerce) is discussed by Meek, Ronald: *Social Science and the ignoble savage* (London, 1976).

37 *Journals* II, p.493 fn.3.

38 *Journals* III, p.54 fn.2.

39 *Banks* I, p.353.

40 *Journals* I, p.136.

41 Herder, Johann Gottfried von, *Reflections on the Philosophy of the History of Mankind*, (Chicago, 1968), p.78.

42 But see Michael Hoare's, Introduction to *The Resolution Journal of Johann Reinhold Forster* (London, 1982), especially p.113.

43 Malinowski, Bronislaw, *Argonauts of the Western Pacific*, (London, 1922); Tylor, E. B. *Primitive Culture*, (London, 1871).

44 It was Lieutenant James King who, in a long, introspective passage in his journal, best sums up the explorers' predicament: 'We come here more unprepar'd & have not that test within ourselves whereby to judge of the workings of the human mind in its rude state': *Journals* III, p.1406.

11 How to Treat Natives

1   Williams, Helen Maria, 'The Morai: An Ode', in *Poems* (London, 1786).

2   More, Hannah, *Slavery. A Poem* (London, 1788).

3   Seward, Anna, *Poems* (London, 1780) where the line reads 'It was Benevolence', and also as an appendix in *Kippis*.

4   *Kippis*, p.503.

5   Edmond, Rod, 'Killing the god; the afterlife of Cook's death' in *Representing the South Pacific: Colonial Discourse from Cook to Gauguin* (London, 1997), p.38.

6   *Journals* I, p.514.

7   *ibid.*

8   Colley, Linda, *Britons: Forging the Nation 1707–1837* (London, 2003), p.350. This Collingwood was the brother of Nelson's famous colleague. Turner's painting, *The Slaveship*, is about the event.

9   Lysaght A. M., (ed.), *Joseph Banks in Newfoundland and Labrador, 1765* (London, 1971), p.211.

10   on the massacre, see also Chapter 12.

11   *Forster G.*, II, p.458.

12   *Kippis*, p.493.

13   *Journals* III, p.1044.

14   *Journals* II, p.493.

15   quoted in Chapter 3; *Journals* II, p.175.

16   *Journals* I, p.399.

17   *Journals* I, p.507.

18   *Journals* II, p.272–3.

19   *Journals* II, p.479.

20   *Journals* II, p.499. For Wedgeborough, see Chapter 7.

21   Sparrman, Anders, *A Voyage Round the World with Captain James Cook in H.M.S. Resolution*, (1953 edn), p.151.

22   *Journals* I, 514.

23   *Journals* II, 417.

24   Salmond, Anne, *The Trial of the Cannibal Dog* (London, 2003), p.330.

25   *Journals* I, p.124.

26   *Journals* III, p.483.

27   Tewsley, U. (trans.), *Zimmerman's account of the third voyage of Captain Cook, 1776–1780* (Wellington NZ, 1926), p.41.

28   *Journals* III, p.265.

29   Salmond, pp.186 & 218.

30   quoted in Obeyesekere, Gananath, *The Apotheosis of Captain Cook* (1997 edn, Princeton), pp.30–1.

31   *Journals* III, p.142.

32   *Journals* III, p.229.

33   *Journals* II, p.378.

34   *Journals* I, p.171.

35   *Journals* I, p.ccxi.

36   *Journals* I, p.169; II, p.487; III, p.142.

37   *Journals* I, p.196.

12 Natives Cook Knew

1 Most of what follows on Tupaia is taken from Williams, Glyndwr, 'Tupaia: Polynesian Warrior, Navigator, High Priest – and Artist', in Felicity A. Nussbaum (ed.), *The Global Eighteenth Century* (Baltimore & London, 2003), pp.19–52.

2 *Banks* I, pp.312–13.

3 Williams, p.39 & refs.

4 Carter, Harold B., 'Note on the Drawings by an Unknown Artist from the Voyage of HMS *Endeavour*', in Lincoln Margarette, (ed.), *Science and Exploration in the Pacific: European Voyages to the Southern Oceans in the Eighteenth Century* (London, 1998), pp.133–44.

5 Williams, p.49.

6 *Journals* I, p.240.

7 *Journals* I, p.291.

8 *Journals* II, p.172

9 [Marra, John], *Journal of the Resolution's Voyage* (London, 1775), p.182.

10 *Journals* I, p.442.

11 Williams, p.50.

12 Turnbull, David, 'Cook and Tupaia, a Tale of Cartographical *Méconnaissance?*' in Lincoln, p.129.

13 Burney's report quoted in Salmond, Anne, *The Trial of the Cannibal Dog* (London, 2003), p.2.

14 Charles, Clerke, may have been an exception to this: *Journals* III, p.69 fn. 2.

15 Quoted in Salmond, p.4.

16 *Journals* III, p.68.

17 *Journals* III, pp.68–9.

18 *Journals* III, p.69.

19 Salmond, pp.3 & 315–6.

20 His name was in fact Mai, the prefix 'O' meaning 'it is', or 'he is', as in 'Otahiti', but he is Omai or Omiah in the journals.

21 *Journals* II, p.428 fn. 2.

22 *Journals* III, p.1514.

23 Quoted in McCormick, Eric, *Omai, Pacific Envoy* (Auckland, NZ, 1977), p.169.

24 McCormick, p.170.

25 *Journals* III, p.229; see also Chapter 11.

26 *Journals* III, p.241.

27 *Journals* III, pp.240–41.

28 *Journals* III, p.880.

29 *Journals* III, p.115 (Cook) & p.1306 (Clerke).

30 *Journals* III, pp.1031–2.

31 Thomas, Nicholas, *Discoveries: The Voyages of Captain Cook* (London, 2003), p.318.

32 *Journals* III, p.117.

33 *Journals* III, p.175.

34 *Journals* III, p.1310.

35 Nicholas, Thomas, describes this as 'a romance of adoptive kinship with indigenous aristocrats': Thomas, p.256.

13 Sex in the South Seas

1   Robertson, Jillian, *The Captain Cook Myth* (Sydney, 1981), p.48; Tewsley U., (trans.), *Zimmerman's account of the third voyage of Captain Cook, 1776–1780* (Wellington NZ, 1926), p.41.

2   Carter, Harold, *Sir Joseph Banks 1743–1820* (London, 1988), p.82; Solander's remarks were recounted by Charles Blagden.

3   *Journals* II, p.546; III, p.468.

4   Fornander, Abraham, *An Account of the Polynesian Race* (London, 1880), pp.162–3, quoted in *Journals* III, p.266, fn.1.

5   Sahlins, Marshall, *Islands of History* (London, 1987), p.3, fn.4.

6   *Journals* II, p.207, fn.1.

7   *Journals* I, p.85.

8   *Journals* II, p.444.

9   *Beaglehole*, p.713.

10 Wallace, Lee, *Sexual Encounters, Pacific Texts, Modern Sexualities* (London, 2003), pp.9–13.

11 Orr, Bridget, '"Southern passions mix with northern art": Miscegenation and the *Endeavour* Voyage', in *Eighteenth Century Life*, no.18 (3) (1994), p.225.

12 for Forster's comment, see above, p. 12; for a discussion of Cook as a 'man's man', see Lee, Wallace, in Lamb, Jonathan, 'The South Pacific in the Eighteenth Century: Narratives and Myths', in *Eighteenth Century Life*, no.18 (3) (1994), pp.237–240.

13 Morris, Robert J., 'The Cook Expedition; Journal References to Aikane', in *Journal of Homosexuality*, vol. 19, no. 4 (1990), p.33; for the theft of the cutter, see Chapter 18.

14 *Journals* III, pp.1171–2.

15 *Journals* III, p.519.

16 *Journals* III, p.lxxviii; Wallace, *Sexual Encounters*, pp.47–49.

17 *Journals* III, p.61.

18 Parkinson, Sydney, *A Journal of a Voyage to the South Seas in his Majesty's Ship* The Endeavour (London, 1784 edn.), p.32; Anon [Magra?], *A Journal of a Voyage round the World* (London, 1771), p.57.

19 *A Poetical Epistle* (London, 1775), quoted in Dening, Greg, *Performances* (Melbourne, 1996), p.154.

20 *Journals* I, p.76.

21 Gonorrhoea was probably the disease that concerned Cook. Syphilis may also have been transmitted to native populations by the visitors but this is more difficult to be certain about since yaws, with symptoms closely related to syphilis, was already endemic in Polynesia.

22 *Journals* I, p.99.

23 *Journals* I, pp.138–9.

24 *Journals* I, p.128.

25 *Journals* I, p.126.

26 *Hawkesworth* II, p.142; *Journals* I, pp.93–4; Thomas, Nicholas, *Discoveries: The Voyages of Captain Cook* (London, 2003), pp.157–9; for Wesley's comment, *Journals* I , p.ccli; for Voltaire, *Correspondence* (Geneva, Banbury and Oxford, 1968–77), vol. XLI, p.17, cited & translated by Rennie, Neil, 'The Point Venus Scene', in Lincoln, Margarette, (ed.), *Science and Exploration in the Pacific* (London, 1998), p.143. See also Balme, Christopher B., 'Sexual Spectacles', in *The Drama Review*, vol. 44, no. 4 (2000).

27 *Journals* I, p.94.

28 *Journals* I, p.128.

29 *Journals* I, p.123. See also Porter, Roy, 'The Exotic as Erotic', in Rousseau G.S., and Porter, Roy, (eds.), *Exoticism in the Enlightenment* (London, 1990), pp.117–144.

30 *London Evening Post*, 23 July 1771; *General Evening Post*, 29 July 1771; both quoted in *Journals* I, pp.644, 647.

31 *The Modern Tourist*, nd., quoted in Smith, Bernard, *European Visions and the South Pacific* (Yale, 1985), p.47.

32 *Banks*, p.47.

33 *An Epistle from Mr Banks* (London, 1773), quoted in Dening, p.155.

34 *Journals* II, p.574, fn.1.

35 *Journals* II, p.238.

36 *Journals* II, p.235.

37 *Journals* III, p.73.

38 *Journals* III, p.70.

39 *Journals* II, p.236.

40 *Journals* II, p.cxlvi.

41 Smith, Bernard, *Imagining the Pacific in the Wake of the Cook Voyages* (Melbourne, 1992), p.198.

42 *Journals* III, p.253.

43 *Forster, J. R.*, p.508.

44 *Journals* III, p.1154.

45 Sahlins, Marshall, *Islands of History* (Chicago, 1985), p.24.

46 *Journals* III, pp.265–6; for the wording of Cook's regulations on arrival in Hawaii, see *Journals* III, pp.1534–5.

47 quoted in Thomas, p.331.

48 *Journals* III, p.474.

49 *Journals* III, p.1075.

14 Cook and Divine Providence

1 Lysaght A.M., (ed.), *The Journal of Joseph Banks in the Endeavour*, facsimile edn. (London, 1980), 2 vols., II, pp.287–88.

2 *Hawkesworth*, I, pp.xxii–xxiv.

3 These issues are also aired in fictional form in Denis Diderot's *Jacques the Fatalist*, written shortly before 1778.

4 For a discussion about 'Providence', and also the various categories of contemporary deists, see 2 essays in *Studies in Voltaire and the Eighteenth Century*: Gusdorf, Georges, 'Declin de la Providence', vol. CLIII (1976) and May, Henry F., 'The Decline of Providence', vol. CLIV (1976).

5 Boswell, James, *Journal of a Tour to the Hebrides* (London, 1930 edn.), p.349.

6 *Forster, G.*, pp.4 & 45.

7 Tewsley U., (trans.), *Zimmermann's Account of the Third Voyage of Captain Cook 1776–1780* (Wellington NZ, 1926), p.41.

8 *Journals* I, p.113.

9 *Journals* I, p.84. This statement, however, may well have been taken from Banks, who writes, 'Religion has been in ages, is still in all Countreys Cloak'd in mysteries unexplicable to human understanding.': *Banks*, I, p.379.

10 *Journals* II, p.236.

11   He also named Providential Channel, through the Great Barrier Reef, and Providence Bay in Unalaska: *Journals* I, p.381 & III, p.389.
12   *Journals* II, p.556.
13   *Journals* I, p.ccxiii.
14   Colley, Linda, *Britons: Forging the Nation 1707–1837* (London, 2003 edn), especially chap1.
15   Graves, Rev. John, *The History of Cleveland* (Carlisle, 1808), pp.226–27.
16   *Journals* II, p.689.
17   Allen, Richard C., '"Remember me to my good friend Captain Walker": James Cook and the North Yorkshire Quakers', in Williams, Glyndwr, (ed.), *Captain Cook: Explorations and Reassessments* (London, 2004), pp.21–36.
18   Rae, Julia, *Captain James Cook Endeavours* (London, 1997), pp.25–28.
19   Dunn, Oliver, & Kelley Jr., James E., (trans.), *The* Diario *of Christopher Columbus's First Voyage to America 1492–1493*, (Oklahoma, 1988), p.141.
20   See page 140.
21   quoted by Jonathan, Lamb, in 'Minute Particulars and the Representation of South Pacific Discovery', in *Eighteenth Century Studies*, vol. 28, (3) (1995), p.285.
22   *The Quarterly Review*, vol. II (Aug–Nov 1809), p.45.
23   quoted in Obeyesekere, Gananath, *The Apotheosis of Captain Cook* (Princeton, 1992), p.126.
24   Obeyesekere, pp.161–62.
25   *Douglas*, I, p.lxxvii.
26   *Kippis*, p.504.
27   Young, George, *The Life and Voyages of Captain James Cook* (London, 1836), p.47.
28   Young, George, *A History of Whitby*, 2 vols (Whitby, 1817), II, pp.861–2.
29   quoted in Sivasundaram, Sujit, 'Redeeming memory', in *Captain Cook: Explorations and Reassessments*, p.205.

15 Nation and Empire

1   *North Eastern Gazette*, Middlesbrough, 10 Sept 1928.
2   Carruthers, Joseph, *Captain Cook R. N. One Hundred and Fifty Years After* (London, 1930), pp.194–5.
3   Carruthers, pp.195–6.
4   Healy, Chris, *From the Ruins of Colonialism: History as Social Memory* (Cambridge, 1997), p.30.
5   Scholefield to Howay, F. W., 5 October 1911, quoted by Clayton, Daniel W., *Islands of Truth: The Imperial Fashioning of Vancouver Island* (Vancouver and Toronto, 2000), p.58.
6   *Journals* II, p.695.
7   *Journals* III, p.135.
8   and to Britons never becoming slaves, conveniently forgetting the approximately 9,000 African slaves in the country at the time: Colley, Linda, *Britons: Forging the Nation 1707–1837* (London, 2003 edn.), p.352.
9   *Journals* I, p.cclxxxii. These instructions do not prove that the British Government at this time had a long-term, coherent imperialist policy: see Baugh, Daniel, 'Seapower and Science', in Howse Derek, (ed.), *Background to Discovery: Pacific Exploration from Dampier to Cook* (Berkeley, California, 1990).
10   See Chapter 8.

11 *Journals* I, p.31.

12 *Journals* I, p.278.

13 *Journals* I, p.397.

14 *Journals* I, p.136.

15 *Journals* I, p.cclxxxiii.

16 Locke, John, *Second Treatise on Government* (London, 1690), chap. v, sect. 31.

17 Frost, Alan, 'New South Wales as terra nullius', in Janson, Susan, and MacIntyre, Stuart, (eds.), *Through White Eyes*, (Sydney, 1990), p.67.

18 *Journals* II, p.436 fn.1, & III, p.769.

19 *Journals* I, p.396.

20 *Journals* I, p.397

21 It was not until 1992 that the judgement of the Australian High Court in the *Mabo* case started to erode the *terra nullius* doctrine.

22 *Journals* I, p.242.

23 *Journals* I, p.281.

24 Locke, *Second Treatise*, chap. v, sect. 33.

25 *Journals* II, p.270.

26 Turner, Stephen, 'Captain Cook in the State of nature', in *Voyages and beaches: Pacific Encounters, 1769–1840* (Auckland NZ, 1993), pp.89–99.

27 Thomas, Nicholas, *Discoveries: The Voyages of Captain Cook* (London, 2003), p.109.

28 *Journals* II, pp.433–5 & 436, fn.1.

29 *Journals* II, pp.534 & 539.

30 *Journals* I, p.cclxxxiii.

16 Trade and Improvement

1 Great Ayton was enclosed in 1658, in an agreement between the better-off landowners. The majority of 'open field' villages in England were enclosed by act of Parliament during the following century.

2 *Journals* II, p.270.

3 *Journals* II, p.235.

4 Williams, Raymond, *Keywords* (London, 1976), p.161.

5 *Journals* II, p.590.

6 *Journals* II, p.534.

7 *Journals* I, p.397.

8 Rigby, Nigel, 'The Politics and Pragmatics of Seaborne Plant Transportation, 1769–1805', in Lincoln, Margarette, (ed.), *Science and Exploration in the Pacific* (London, 1998), p.81.

9 *Journals* III, p.4.

10 Thomas, Nicholas, *Discoveries: The Voyages of Captain Cook* (London, 2003), p.275.

11 Obeyesekere, Gananath, *The Apotheosis of Captain Cook* (1997 edn., Princeton), p.12.

12 quoted in *Kippis*, p.509.

13 *Journals* II, p.297.

14 Horwitz, Tony, *Into the Blue: Boldly going where Captain Cook has gone before* (London, 2002), p.127.

15 *Journals* III, p.194.

16 Sparrmann, Anders, *A Voyage round the World* (1783) (London, 1953 edn.), p.42.

17 Colley, Linda, *Britons: Forging the Nation 1707–1837* (London, 2003), p.56.

18 Campbell, John, *Navigantium atque Itinerantium Bibliotheca, or, a Complete Collection of Voyages and Travels*, 2 vols (London, 1744), I, pp.xv–xvi.

19 Wallis, Helen, Introduction to *Carteret's Voyage Round the World 1766–1769*, vol I, (Hakluyt Society, 1965), p.9.

20 Dalrymple, Alexander, *A Historical Collection of the Several Voyages and Discoveries in the South Pacific Ocean*, 2 vols (London, 1769) (Amsterdam and New York, 1967 edn.), p.xxi.

21 ibid. p.xxviii.

22 Baugh, Daniel A., 'Seapower and Science: the Motives for Pacific exploration', in Howse Derek, (ed.), *Background to Discovery: Pacific Exploration from Dampier to Cook*, (Berkeley, California, 1990).

23 Smith, Bernard, *Imagining the Pacific in the Wake of the Cook Voyages* (London, 1992), p.208.

24 Pocock, J.G.A., 'European Perceptions of World History in the Age of Encounter', in Alex Calder *et al* (eds), *Voyages and Beaches: Pacific Encounters 1769–1840*, (Univ. of Hawaii, 1999), pp.27–8.

25 Pocock, *loc.sit.*

26 *Journals*, III, p.483.

27 *Journals*, III, p.241; for Omai see Chapter 12.

28 *Journals* III, p.372.

29 On this highly profitable trade see Gibson, James R., 'Russian Tenure in the North Pacific', in *Pacific Studies*, vol. 1, no. 2, (Spring 1978), pp.119–46; also Brian M. Fagan, *Clash of Cultures* (California, 1998), pp.237–244.

30 *Journals* III, p.115.

31 Turner, Stephen, 'Captain Cook in the state of nature', in *Voyages and Beaches*, p.94.

32 Smith, p.209.

17 Science and Navigation

1 Holland to Simcoe, J.G., 11 Jan 1792, quoted in David, Andrew, (ed.), *The Charts and Coastal Views of Captain Cook's Voyages*, vol. I, *The Voyage of the Endeavour 1768–1771* (Hakluyt Society, 1988), p.xix.

2 *ibid.*

3 Villiers, Alan, *Captain Cook, the Seamen's Seaman* (Penguin edn, 1969), p.160.

4 David, p.xxxiv.

5 *Journals* I, pp.391–2.

6 *Journals* II, p.509, fn. 4.

7 quoted by Beaglehole, J.C., 'Cook the Navigator', in *Proceedings of the Royal Society*, A 314, (1969), p.32.

8 for this controversy see Sobel, Dava, *Longitude* (London, 1996).

9 *Journals* II, p.525.

10 *Journals* II, p.692.

11 Sobel, p.151.

12 see Chapter 1.

13 quoted by Beaglehole, *op. cit.*, p.27.

14 *Journals* I, p.413.

15 Williams, Glyndwr, 'Explorers and geographers: an uneasy alliance in the eighteenth-century exploration of the Pacific', in Merwick, Donna, (ed.), *Dangerous Liasons: Essays in Honour of Greg Dening*, (Melbourne, 1994), pp.102–105.

16 *Journals* II, p.498.
17 *Journals* II, p.611.
18 *Journals* I, p.442.
19 cannibalism and migrations are discussed in Chapter 10.
20 *Journals* II, pp.643–46.
21 *Forster G.*, I, pp.viii–xii.
22 Forster, Johann Reinhold, *Observations made during a voyage round the world* (1778) (University of Hawaii Press, 1996).
23 Parry, J.H., quoted by Rennie, Neil, *Far-fetched Facts: the Literature of Travel and the Idea of the South Seas* (Oxford, 1995), p.30.
24 On these generalisations see Richardson, Brian W. *Longitude and Empire: How Captain Cook's Voyages Changed the World* (University of British Columbia, 2005), pp.21–45.

18 The Death of Cook

1 Salmond, Anne, *The Trial of the Cannibal Dog* (London, 2003), p.420.
2 Kennedy, Gavin, *The Death of Captain Cook* (London, 1978).
3 *Journals* III, p.1198; the assassin with the feathered cloak was probably a chief named Nuha, and the dagger he wielded made at Matthew Boulton's Soho factory in Birmingham: Marshall Sahlins, *How "natives" think: about Captain Cook*, for example (Chicago, 1995), pp.130–1.
4 See Obeyesekere, Gananath, *The Apotheosis of Captain Cook* (Princeton, New Jersey, 1992), and Sahlins.
5 Kennedy, quoting an anonymous diary kept by an officer from the *Resolution*, p.52. Clerke agreed that it was Cook's action that precipitated the crowd's attack: *Journals* III, pp.538–9.
6 *Journals* III, p.cliv.
7 Thomas, Nicholas, *Discoveries; The Voyages of Captain Cook* (London, 2003), p.397.
8 Rose, Deborah Bird, 'Worshipping Captain Cook', in *Social Analysis*, no 43 (Adelaide, Dec 1993), p.43.
9 *Journals* III, p.556.
10 Edmond calculates that 17 Hawaiians were killed on the beach on the morning of February 14: Edmond, Rod, *Representing the South Pacific: Colonial Discourse from Cook to Gauguin* (Cambridge, 1997), p.56. Nicholas Thomas thinks about 30 may have been killed in revenge: Thomas, p.401.
11 Joppien, Rüdiger, 'Philippe Jacques de Loutherbourg's Pantomime 'Omai, or, a Trip round the World' and the Artists of Captain Cook's Voyages', in Mitchell T.C., (ed), *Captain Cook and the South Pacific* (London, 1979), p.89.

Conclusion

1 Edmond, Rod, *Representing the South Pacific: Colonial Discourse from Cook to Gauguin* (Cambridge, 1997), p.51.
2 see Chapters 14 and 15.
3 Rose, Deborah Bird, 'The saga of Captain Cook: Morality in Aboriginal and European Law', in *Australian Aboriginal Studies*, 2 (1984), quoted in Healy, Chris, *From the Ruins of Colonialism: History as Social Memory* (Cambridge, 1997), p.60.

4   Clayton, Daniel W., *Islands of Truth* (Vancouver, 2000), p.63; Howay, Sage and Fisher were principally historians of Canada.

5   Tosh, John, 'The old Adam and the new man: emerging themes in the history of English masculinities', and Cohen, Michèle, 'Manliness, Effeminancy and the French: gender and the construction of national character in eighteenth century England', both in Hitchcock, Tim, & Cohen, Michèle, (eds.), *English Masculinities 1660–1800* (London, 1999).

6   Tosh, p.234.

7   Tosh, p.232.

8   see pp.33–4.

9   Clayton, p.249.

10 Cohen, pp.52–61.

11 quoted by Glyndwr, Williams, in Williams, Glyndwr, (ed.), *Captain Cook: Explorations and Reassessments*, (London, 2004), p.230.

Suggested Reading

Most of the books and articles I have used are mentioned in the footnotes to each chapter. This is merely a brief and personal list of a dozen books I have enjoyed and found valuable.

Beaglehole, J. C., *The Life of Captain James Cook*. Stanford University Press, Stanford, (California, 1974), (pbk.) 0804720096.
Easily the most comprehensive and definitive biography of Cook which, however, somewhat idealizes its subject.

Dening, Greg, *Mr Bligh's Bad Language: Passion, Power and Theatre on the Bounty*, (Cambridge University Press, 1992) (pbk.) 0521467187.
Not just about Bligh but full of insights into maritime exploration, contact with native peoples, and much else.

Edwards, Philip, (ed.), *The Journals of Captain Cook*, (Penguin Books, 1999) (pbk.) 0140436472.
Excellent abridged version of Cook's three journals for those without the inclination to buy the Hakluyt volumes.

Moorehead, Alan. *The Fatal impact: an Account of the Invasion of the South Pacific, 1767–1840*. (Penguin Books, 1974) (pbk.) 0140027730
Although written a long time ago, and clearly one-sided, this is still a useful corrective to smug assumptions of Western moral superiority.

Obeyesekere, Gananath. *The Apotheosis of Captain Cook: European mythmaking in the Pacific*, (Princeton University Press, Princeton, New Jersey, 1997) (pbk.) 0691057524.
A powerful, often provocative attack on certain assumptions and prejudices connected with Cook, and especially his death.

O'Brian, Patrick, *Joseph Banks, A Life*, (The Harvill Press, London, 1989) (pbk.) 1860464068.
The most readable life of Banks, with copious quotes from his lively *Endeavour* journal.

Robson, John. *The Captain Cook Encyclopaedia* (Chatham Publishing, London, 2004). 1861762259.
An essential reference for all matters connected with Cook.

Rodger, N. A. M., *The Wooden World: An Anatomy of the Georgian Navy*, Fontana Press, (London, 1988) (pbk.). 0006861520.
A rewarding and anecdotal tour round the eighteenth-century British navy.

Salmond, Anne, *The Trial of the Cannibal Dog: Captain Cook in the South Seas*. Allen Lane, (London, 2003). 0713996617.
Another detailed yet accessible account of Cook's voyages by an eminent New Zealand anthropologist.

Thomas, Nicholas, *Discoveries: the Voyages of Captain Cook*. Allen Lane, (London, 2003). 0713995572.
The most important narrative of the voyages since Beaglehole. Essential reading for all students of Cook.

Withey, Lynne, *Voyages of discovery: Captain Cook and the exploration of the Pacific*. Hutchinson, (London, 1987). 0091736021.
A scholarly and balanced, yet easy to read, account of British eighteenth-century discovery.

Finally, I want to mention two useful websites: http://pages.quicksilver.net.nz/jcr/~cooky.html which contains John Robson's invaluable Cook biography, and www.captaincooksociety.com the website of the Captain Cook Society.

Index